iPod.pedia

The Ultimate iPod and iTunes Resource

Michael Miller

800 East 96th Street
Indianapolis, Indiana 46240

iPodpedia The Ultimate iPod and iTunes Resource

Copyright © 2007 by Pearson Education, Inc.

ISBN-10: 0-7897-3674-8

ISBN-13: 978-0-7897-3674-1

Printed in the United States of America

First Printing: April 2007

10   09   08   07   4   3   2

Trademarks

Warning and Disclaimer

Associate Publisher
Greg Wiegand

Acquisitions Editor
Stephanie J. McComb

Development Editor
Rick Kughen

Managing Editor
Patrick Kanouse

Project Editor
Mandie Frank

Copy Editor
Indexer
Keith Cline

Proofreader
Leslie Joseph

Technical Editor
Marc Charney

Publishing Coordinator
Cindy Teeters

Designer
Anne Jones

Page Layout
Mark Shirar

Bulk Sales

Que Publishing offers excellent discounts on this book when ordered in quantity for bulk purchases or special sales. For more information, please contact

U.S. Corporate and Government Sales

1-800-382-3419

corpsales@pearsontechgroup.com

For sales outside of the U.S., please contact

International Sales

international@pearsoned.com

Library of Congress Cataloging-in-Publication Data

Miller, Michael, 1958-

iPodpedia / Michael Miller.

p. cm.

Includes index.

ISBN 0-7897-3674-8

1. iPod (Digital music player) I. Title.

ML74.4.I48M55 2007

006.5--dc22

2007009617

This Book Is Safari Enabled

 The Safari® Enabled icon on the cover of your favorite technology book means the book is available through Safari Bookshelf. When you buy this book, you get free access to the online edition for 45 days.

Safari Bookshelf is an electronic reference library that lets you easily search thousands of technical books, find code samples, download chapters, and access technical information whenever and wherever you need it.

To gain 45-day Safari Enabled access to this book:

- Go to http://www.quepublishing.com/safarienabled
- Complete the brief registration form
- Enter the coupon code 4ARS-UTDQ-XWKB-BMQE-R4W1

If you have difficulty registering on Safari Bookshelf or accessing the online edition, please e-mail customer-service@safaribooksonline.com.

Contents at a Glance

Table of Contents

About the Author

Michael Miller has written more than 75 nonfiction how-to books in the past two decades, including Que's *Googlepedia: The Ultimate Google Resource, YouTube 4U, Absolute Beginner's Guide to Computer Basics, Absolute Beginner's Guide to eBay,* and *How Microsoft Windows Vista Works.* He also writes about digital lifestyle topics for a variety of websites.

Mr. Miller has established a reputation for clearly explaining technical topics to nontechnical readers, and for offering useful real-world advice about complicated topics. More information can be found at the author's website, located at www.molehillgroup.com.

Dedication

To Sherry—you're number one on my playlist.

Acknowledgments

Thanks to the usual suspects at Que Publishing, including but not limited to Greg Wiegand, Stephanie McComb, Rick Kughen, Mandie Frank, Keith Cline, and Marc Charney.

We Want to Hear from You!

As the reader of this book, *you* are our most important critic and commentator. We value your opinion and want to know what we're doing right, what we could do better, what areas you'd like to see us publish in, and any other words of wisdom you're willing to pass our way.

As an associate publisher for Que Publishing, I welcome your comments. You can email or write me directly to let me know what you did or didn't like about this book—as well as what we can do to make our books better.

Please note that I cannot help you with technical problems related to the topic of this book. We do have a User Services group, however, where I will forward specific technical questions related to the book.

When you write, please be sure to include this book's title and author as well as your name, email address, and phone number. I will carefully review your comments and share them with the author and editors who worked on the book.

Email: feedback@quepublishing.com

Mail: Greg Wiegand
         Associate Publisher
         Que Publishing
         800 East 96th Street
         Indianapolis, IN 46240 USA

Reader Services

Visit our website and register this book at www.quepublishing.com/register for convenient access to any updates, downloads, or errata that might be available for this book.

Introduction

I love music.

I was a musician back in the day, and today I spend several hours each day listening to or playing music. I have a CD collection that's somewhere north of 1,200 discs (and still growing), and I can't take even a short drive without turning up the tunes in my car.

For me, the iPod is a necessity.

I'm now on my fourth iPod. I started with a second-generation unit, moved on to a bright green iPod mini, and now have both an 80GB 5.5-generation video iPod and a 2G iPod shuffle. I take the big iPod with me when I travel to visit my girlfriend, which I do every few weeks, to provide music in my hotel room. I have the shuffle sitting next to my drumset in my home recording studio, and I use it to play along with my favorite tunes.

Of course, I'm not alone in my reliance on my iPods. There are more than 30 million iPod users out there—people like you and me who like to listen to music no matter where we might be. The iPod lets us do just that, and much more.

It's the much more that inspired me to write this book. *iPodpedia: The Ultimate iPod and iTunes Resource* is for the iPod user who wants to get as much as possible out of the iPod experience. It's not just about listening to songs; it's about downloading songs, ripping and burning them to and from CDs, creating interesting playlists, editing track data and artwork, and making your iPod sound as good as possible. And it doesn't stop with music; iPods can be used to play videos, podcasts, audiobooks, even games. You can use your iPod as a scheduler and a workout trainer. You can also use it to store and view digital photographs and to transfer data files from one computer to another.

And that's what this book is about—learning to do more stuff with your iPod. Much more stuff.

Not an Apple Lovefest

I should note that although I know a lot about what the iPod does and how it works, I'm not an Apple insider. I don't work for Apple and had no official contact with Apple while writing this book. That means I don't always take the company line. I tell you, as honestly as possible, when Apple gets it right and when it doesn't. After all, just because Apple is a benevolent dictatorship doesn't mean that it always acts in our best interests. I'm not obligated to put on a positive face, which means you get the straight poop, good or bad.

I also try to remove myself, as much as possible, from Steve Jobs' legendary "reality distortion field." (I've experienced the field firsthand; during Jobs' late 1980s sabbatical from Apple, I was present at his introduction of the NeXT computer—and was so mesmerized I almost bought one on the spot.) I don't buy into everything Apple does just because it's Apple; style is fine, but real-world use is more about practicality than it is about Apple cool.

And here's something else. Like the vast majority of iPod users, I use a Windows PC. I don't use a Mac, and I never have, which means I approach the iPod from a purely Windows perspective. If that annoys a few Mac diehards, I apologize, but the reality is that the iPod is living in a Windows world, and that's how I deal with it.

So, don't expect an unquestioning Apple lovefest within these pages. Yeah, the iPod is the height of cool, and it does what it does very well, but it isn't perfect. And that's probably why you're buying this book, after all. If the iPod were flawless and totally self-explanatory to use, you wouldn't be looking for more information, would you? And more information is what this book contains.

How This Book Is Organized

iPodpedia contains a lot of information between its front and back covers. It was my job to supply the information; it's your job to find the information you want.

To make your job easier, this book is organized into six main parts, as follows:

- **Part I, "Background,"** provides an introduction to everything iPod—the history, the various models released over the years, and the new iPhone.

- **Part II, "Operation,"** provides step-by-step instructions for using the iPod, the iTunes software, and the iTunes Store.

- **Part III, "Applications,"** shows how to use your iPod and iTunes for the most popular applications—music, podcasts, audiobooks, photos, videos, and games.

- **Part IV, "Special Uses,"** details some very specific uses for the iPod—in the living room, in the car, as a portable storage device, to record audio and podcasts, for running and exercise, as a calendar/scheduler, and to manage your iTunes purchases.

- **Part V, "Secrets,"** goes inside the iPod and iTunes and presents all manner of fun and useful tips, tricks, and hacks.
- **Part VI, "Support,"** provides a detailed listing of available iPod accessories and software, and offers plentiful advice for troubleshooting iPod problems.

Finally, an appendix offers additional iPod-related resources—websites, blogs, forums, books, and the like.

Although I recommend reading this book in consecutive order, that isn't completely necessary because each facet of iPod operation exists independent of the other facets. Just as it's okay to skip around through the iPod's various modes of operation, it's also okay to skip around through the various chapters in this book. Read it in chapter order if you want (I think it flows fairly well as written) or read just those chapters that interest you. It's okay either way.

Conventions Used in This Book

I hope that this book is easy enough to figure out on its own, without requiring its own instruction manual. As you read through the pages, however, it helps to know precisely how I've presented specific types of information.

Menu Commands

The iTunes software operates via a series of pull-down menus and submenus. The iPod itself operates via a series of clickable menus and submenus. To indicate navigation through both types of menu system, I use the following notation:

Main menu > Submenu

All you have to do is follow the instructions in order, using the Click Wheel to click through the iPod menus or your mouse to click through the iTunes menus. For example, if I tell you to select Music > Playlists on your iPod, you know to click Music on the main menu and then select Playlists on the next menu. It's pretty easy.

Shortcut Key and Button Combinations

Some iTunes operations are best accomplished via the computer keyboard, often by pressing two keys at the same time. For that matter, some iPod operations require pressing two buttons at the same time. These two-key or two-button combinations are shown as the key/button names joined with a plus sign (+).

For example, Menu + Select indicates that you should press the iPod's Menu and Select buttons at the same time. You know how it works.

Given the preponderance of Windows-based iPod users, I lead with the Windows menu and keyboard commands. When Mac commands differ, I place them in parentheses following the Windows command. But know that all the instructions presented in this book can be used by both Windows and Mac users.

Web Pages

Obviously, there are lots of web page addresses in the book, like this one: www.apple.com. When you see one of these addresses (also known as a URL), you can go to that web page by entering the URL into the address box in your web browser. I've made every effort to ensure the accuracy of the web addresses presented here, but given the ever-changing nature of the Web, don't be surprised if you run across an address or two that's changed. I apologize in advance.

Compatibility

Throughout the book I mention a lot of third-party iPod accessories and software. Most of these items can be used by both Windows and Mac users, but I'll make an effort to point out those that are Windows only or Mac only. (This is especially important when it comes to software.)

In addition, most of the instructions in this book apply to all model iPods, from the earliest first-generation unit to today's fifth-generation iPods, nanos, and shuffles. Note, however, that some operations are possible only on newer units; by necessity, this book covers the very latest models and the most recent version of the iTunes software (iTunes 7). Although you can probably translate some instructions for older models and versions, this book unapologetically focuses on the latest and greatest.

Special Elements

As you read through this book, you'll note several special elements, presented in what we in the publishing business call "margin notes." There are different types of margin notes for different types of information, as you see here.

In many chapters, you'll also find some personal commentary, presented in the form of a sidebar. These sections are meant to be read separately, because they exist "outside" the main text. And remember—these sidebars are my opinions only, so feel free to agree or disagree as you like.

note This is a *note* that presents information of interest, even if it isn't wholly relevant to the discussion in the main text.

tip This is a *tip* that might prove useful for whatever it is you're in the process of doing.

caution This is a *caution* that something you might accidentally do might have undesirable results.

AUTHOR'S PICKS This is a *pick*—an iPod accessory or software program that I personally recommend.

Get Ready to iPod!

With all these preliminaries out of the way, it's now time to get started. But first, a few personal notes.

While you're researching iPod resources on the Web, I urge you to visit my personal website, located at www.molehillgroup.com. Here you'll find more information on this book and other books I've written—including an errata page for this book, in the inevitable event that an error or two creeps into this text. (Hey, nobody's perfect!)

You can also visit **iPodpedia: The Blog**, located at ipodpediatheblog.blogspot.com. This is where you'll find updates to the information presented in this book and the latest iPod-related news and developments.

Finally, know that I love to hear from readers of my books. If you want to contact me, feel free to email me at ipod@molehillgroup.com. I can't promise that I'll answer every message, but I do promise that I'll read each one!

Background

The History

The Apple iPod is to the 2000s as the portable CD player was to the 1990s, the Sony Walkman was to the 1980s, and the transistor radio was to the 1960s. The iPod is a portable audio player, of course, a means of playing music while on the go; but it's more than that. It builds on the breakthroughs of the previous technologies, and takes portable music one giant step beyond—both technologically and socially.

Previous portable audio players were revolutionary in their way, but with limitations. The transistor radio freed music from the confines of the power outlet, but it limited listeners to the restricted playlists beamed from AM radio stations. The Walkman let listeners play their own music on the go, but it limited playback to the 90 minutes or so of music that would fit on an audiocassette. Same thing with the portable CD player; you could only play one CD at a time.

The iPod removes all those restrictions. Not only does it offer music on the go, it lets users take with them a seemingly limitless number of songs. Even the smallest iPod, the 1GB iPod shuffle, lets users store 500 songs (compared to 30 or so songs on a 90-minute audiocassette); the big 80GB iPod can hold up to 40,000 songs. The iPod represents total music freedom.

We're now five years into the iPod phenomenon, and it shows no sign of waning.

The iPod Phenomenon

Five years after its launch, Apple's iPod is more than just a product or a technology; it's a true social phenomenon. The iPod so dominates the MP3 player market that the term *iPod* is often used generically to represent any portable audio player, much to the lament of Apple's legal staff.

How big an impact has the iPod had on 21st-century society? No other product has so dominated an emerging marketplace.

Since its initial release, Apple has sold approximately 80 million iPods to more than 30 million users.[1] (That's right, most iPod users tend to buy more than one unit over the years.) As you can see in Figure 1.1, sales really took off in calendar year 2005, when yearly sales surpassed 31 million units. And sales continue to climb; during the fourth quarter of 2006, Apple sold more than 15 million units[2]—that's more than 150,000 iPods sold every day.

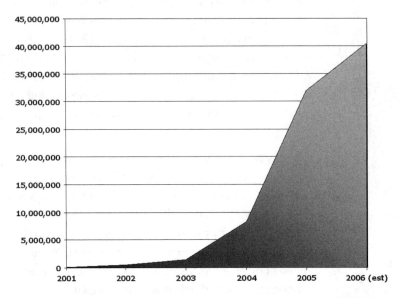

FIGURE 1.1

iPod sales through the years. (Unit sales provided by Apple.)

With these numbers, it's no surprise that the iPod completely dominates the market for portable music players, with a 68% market share.[3] (The number two player, Creative Labs, has just a 6% market share.) The iPod is becoming virtually ubiquitous among music lovers, particularly in the younger age groups; one third of all American teenagers own an iPod—up from just 1% in 2003.[4]

[1] Apple financial reports
[2] NPD Group, Inc.
[3] Solutions Research Group
[4] The Harrison Group

The Apple iPod is so mainstream that many users are now on their second or third units. The average iPod user replaces his or her unit every 1.5 years, and users with multiple iPods (augmenting a larger iPod with an iPod shuffle, for example) are becoming more common.

Accordingly, Apple's iTunes Store is the dominant online music store today, with an 88% share of the legal download market. The iTunes Store has sold more than 2 billion songs, 50 million television episodes, and 1.3 million full-length movies since its launch in 2003.[5] iTunes sales in the first three quarters of 2006 grew a whopping 84% over the prior-year period;[6] iTunes now has close to 21 million users.

What other product has had such an impact in just five years?

The iPod Story: Conception to Birth and Beyond

Just a little over five years ago, the iPod was nothing more than a few scratches on an engineer's drawing board. It took less than a year for the iPod to evolve from initial concept to final product, and another year for the iPod to sell its first half-million units. That's a very fast development time; it's amazing that a product that launched so quickly was so successful in the marketplace.

But how, exactly, was the iPod conceived? Read on to learn the thumbnail history of the iPod, from initial concept to current-generation models.

2000: Apple's Quest

In 2000, Apple was staging a comeback after a somewhat-disappointing period in the late 1990s. The low-priced iMac was a newfound consumer hit, and Apple founder Steve Jobs was thirsting for additional opportunities to tap into the mass market. As part of this effort, his staff began looking at all manner of digital devices that could connect to a computer and drive sales of the company's entire line of Macintosh computers.

One of the opportunities that Apple recognized was that of digital music. Research indicated that people were using their computers to download songs (for free) from Napster and similar file-trading services. They were also using their PCs to listen to this music, and to rip and burn their own mix CDs. Unfortunately, Apple wasn't a big player in this market; although Mac users were avid music lovers, the company didn't have its own music player program for them to use.

[5] Apple press release
[6] comScore

To this end, Apple licensed the SoundJam MP music player program from developer Casady & Greene. Apple also hired the software's head programmer, Jeff Robbin, and directed him to turn SoundJam into a music player that Apple could distribute with all its Macintosh computers. That music player would be called **iTunes**, to go along with Apple's other *i* products.

2001: The Concept Develops

The iTunes music player software was introduced to the public at Macworld Expo on January 9, 2001. Although version 1 of iTunes was designed for Mac-based digital music management and playback (a Windows version would be released in 2003), it also served to pave the way for the introduction of the iPod itself, nine months later. (Figure 1.2 shows iTunes version 1 on Mac OS X.)

FIGURE 1.2

The very first version of the iTunes music player program.

Simultaneous with the launch of the iTunes software, another group within Apple was looking at opportunities revolving around digital devices for the mass market. They examined the digital camera and camcorder markets, but saw no opening for Apple with either type of product; both markets were fairly mature, with well-designed products and established distribution channels.

The next product Apple examined was the MP3 player, which was relatively new yet extremely promising. In contrast to other existing digital devices, MP3 players of that era were either big and bulky or small and fairly useless, lacking in both performance and sexiness. Most of the smaller MP3 players used fairly low-capacity Flash memory chips; with a maximum of 64MB memory, such a device could only hold a few dozen songs. The larger MP3 players, such as the Creative Nomad Jukebox, used a 2.5-inch Fujitsu hard disk drive and could hold thousands of songs, but were bigger and heavier than that era's portable CD players, making them singularly unappealing. Neither type of player was taking the market by storm.

This, then, was the opportunity that Apple was looking for.

Apple's engineers began to strategize how they could improve on the current crop of portable music players. Users wanted to carry an entire library of songs with them, not just a CD's worth of music, so higher capacity was the way to go. This meant focusing on hard drive players. But a smaller size was also desirable, which argued for some sort of compromise between size and capacity—or the use of newer technology.

With this in mind, engineer Jon Rubinstein traveled to Tokyo to talk to Apple's current supplier of hard drives, Toshiba. Executives there showed him a new 1.8-inch drive that could hold 5GB of data—enough storage for about a thousand songs. Rubenstein realized that this new drive could be used to construct a smaller and lighter music player than the competition, which was still using the larger 2.5-inch Fujitsu drive.

Rubinstein also decided to take advantage of other technology advances to improve upon the performance of competing music players. Better displays and longer-lasting batteries were appropriated from the cell phone industry, and a FireWire connection was used to provide faster song transfer than was available with the current USB 1.1 standard.

The basic components in place, Apple hired an outside consultant, Tony Fadell, to put all the pieces together and design the player itself. Fadell was an independent contractor who had helped to develop handheld devices at both Philips and General Magic. He had the idea of building a business around an MP3 player tied into a Napster-like online music service, and was shopping it around to various companies; this business concept dovetailed into Apple's emerging plans.

Fadell was hired by Apple in early 2001 and tasked with putting a player on retail shelves by the fall of that year, not quite nine months away. He was assigned a team of 30 designers, programmers, and hardware engineers, and got quickly to work.

One of the first things Fadell did was to contract with Silicon Valley start-up PortalPlayer, which was already working on reference designs for several different types of digital music players. The reference design that caught Fadell's eye was a player about the size of a pack of cigarettes. "It was fairly ugly," PortalPlayer's Ben Knauss recalled in a *Wired* article;[7] "it looked like an FM radio with a bunch of buttons."

Fadell, however, recognized the design's potential—and the fact that Apple now wouldn't have to create a product totally from scratch. PortalPlayer's design was about 80% complete, which meant that Apple could build on this design and have a product on the market relatively quickly.

However, Apple had to compete with PortalPlayer's other clients; about a dozen other companies were building MP3 players based on PortalPlayer's reference design, IBM and Teac among them. (IBM's design, which never came to market, was for a small, black player using the company's own mini hard drive, featuring a circular screen and wireless Bluetooth headphones.)

When Apple entered the picture, however, PortalPlayer dropped all its other customers. For the next eight months, the company's 280 employees focused exclusively on developing the iPod for Apple's fall launch. They had to incorporate all the features that Apple wanted as part of the initial player—larger playlists, use of the AAC file format, a five-band equalizer, and a new interface.

PortalPlayer worked closely with Fadell and his team, who in turn worked closely with Apple's other in-house departments. As Jon Rubenstein put it, "We need a power supply, we've got a power supply group. We need a display, we've got a display group. We used the architecture team. This was a highly leveraged product from the technologies we already had in place."[8]

The software for the iPod was acquired from Pixio, a privately held software company that developed operating systems for cell phones. Apple's interface design group, led by Tim Wasko, then built the iPod interface on top of the Pixio operating system.

Apple's head of marketing, Phil Schiller, came up with the idea for the iPod's scroll wheel. He also suggested that menus scroll faster the longer the wheel is turned. The scroll wheel and its operation are what distinguishes the iPod from its numerous competitors.

Prototype after prototype were turned out by Apple's design group, headed by Jonathan Ive. In an interview with the *New York Times*,[9] Ives noted that the key to the iPod wasn't sudden flashes of genius, but rather the design process itself. His group worked closely with PortalPlayer and Apple's engineers, constantly tweaking and refining the design.

---

[7] "Inside Look at the Birth of the iPod," Wired, Leander Kahney, July 21, 2004
[8] "Straight Dope on the iPod's Birth," Wired, Leander Kahney, October 17, 2006
[9] "The Guts of a New Machine," New York Times, Rob Walker, November 30, 2003

As the project developed, Apple leader Steve Jobs became more and more personally involved. By the time the first prototypes were built, Jobs was giving his input on a daily basis. He was focused on ease of use—how many button pushes it took to play a song, how fast the menus displayed, and so on. Knauss recalls that Jobs was

note Interestingly, Apple had previously trademarked the name iPod for a never-released Internet kiosk. The iPod team apparently was not aware of this earlier internal usage of the name.

even integral in the sound of the iPod; because Jobs is partially deaf, he "drove the sound up so he could hear it," which is why even today the iPod is louder than most other MP3 players.

Jobs's impact was felt at all levels of the project. He kept the team focused on simplicity of operation. As Ive recalls, "It was about being very focused and not trying to do too much with the device." The iPod was designed to do one thing and do it well; that simplicity was to be key to its success.

Even with all this high-level attention, the iPod almost didn't make it to market. As the product approached its fall launch date, tests showed that the iPod's batteries only lasted about three hours, because of the hard disk drive spinning continuously while songs were playing. That short battery life would have been the kiss of death in the marketplace.

So, with production lines ready to go, Apple's engineers went back to the drawing boards. The solution was to load selected songs into a 32MB memory buffer, which drew much less power than running the disk drive. This extended battery life to 10 hours, which was competitive, and enabled the iPod to make its way to production.

Production ready to go, it was time for marketing to step up to the plate. The primary task was to name the product; that challenge was given to Vinnie Chieco, a freelance copywriter who was part of a team of marketing consultants hired by Apple. Chieco came up with the iPod moniker, thinking of the device as one of several "pods" that connect to the central Macintosh hub. The analogy was that of small spaceships, or pods, returning to a mother ship to refuel. When Chieco saw the white iPod prototype, his thinking was reinforced—"As soon as I saw the white iPod, I thought *2001*. Open the pod bay door, Hal!" The *i* prefix fit in with Apple's other *i* products, including the recently launched iTunes player.

On October 23, 2001, the iPod was introduced to the public at a special event at Apple's Cupertino,California, headquarters. This first-generation iPod incorporated Toshiba's 5GB hard drive and enabled users to put "1,000 songs in your pocket." It was priced at $399; the first iPod shipped two weeks later, on November 10.

That wasn't the last announcement that year, however. On November 2, 2001, Apple released version 2.0 of the iTunes player, with full iPod support.

2002: Expanding the Market

Despite all the hoopla, the iPod launch was overshadowed by the September 11 terrorist attacks. Sales for the 2001 holiday season were a meager 125,000 units—a promising but not earth-shattering start.

On March 20, 2002, Apple announced a second iPod, a 10GB device that could hold 2,000 songs. This new player, still a Mac-only product, could also display business card-like contact information. It sold for $499—a $100 premium over the 1G model.

A more important announcement came on July 17, when Apple unveiled its second-generation iPods. These 2G iPods were fully PC compatible, which opened up the market beyond the limited universe of Macintosh users. The new iPods used a touch-sensitive scroll wheel (sometimes called a "touch wheel") rather than a moving wheel, which proved more durable in the long run. Apple also introduced a new 20GB model, priced at $499; prices of the older 5GB and 10GB units were lowered to $299 and $399, respectively.

At the same time, Apple released version 3.0 of the iTunes program for the Macintosh. Unfortunately, there was not yet a version of iTunes for Windows; to support its non-Macintosh users, Apple provided a version of the competing MusicMatch software. It was a poor compromise.

By fall 2002, Apple had expanded distribution of the iPod from its own stores and websites to mass merchants such as Best Buy and Target. This break from Apple's previously controlled distribution was to prove crucial to the iPod's continuing success.

These moves helped to dramatically increase iPod sales. For the full year, Apple moved 470,000 units.

2003: More Models, More Music

Apple introduced its third-generation iPods on April 28, 2003. These new models (available in 10GB, 15GB, and 30GB

note In December 2002, Apple released its first limited-edition iPods. These 20GB models featured the engraved signatures of Madonna, Beck, No Doubt, or Tony Hawk, for a $49 premium—resulting in a $548 selling price.

versions) used a new dock connector in place of the previous standard FireWire port.

But the bigger news on that day was the launch of Apple's **iTunes Music Store**. At launch, the store offered 200,000 songs at 99 cents each. The songs were licensed from the five largest record labels at the time—BMG, EMI, Sony Music Entertainment, Universal, and Warner Brothers.

note iTunes' major-label offerings were later augmented with music by more than 600 independent artists. The first independent artist added to the store (on July 29, 2003) was Moby.

The iTunes Music Store (iTMS) was an immediate success, selling 275,000 tracks in its first 18 hours and more than a million tracks in its first 5 days. By the end of the year, iMS had sold more than 25 million songs.

On June 23, Apple announced that it had sold its one millionth iPod. The line was refreshed on September 8, with models offering larger storage capacities. These newer 3G iPods included a 20GB model at $399 and a 40GB model at $499.

2004: Introducing the mini

Apple's most important announcement in 2004 was the introduction of a second type of iPod, dubbed the **iPod mini**. Announced on January 6 and shipped on February 17, the mini was smaller than the traditional iPod, using a 1-inch microdrive hard disk with 4GB capacity and a new Click Wheel controller. It sold for $249, and was available in five metallic colors. The mini quickly became the best-selling model in the entire iPod line. (At the same time, Apple replaced the 20GB entry-level iPod with a 15GB model that was soon discounted by most retailers to $249.)

Apple launched the fourth generation of the iPod family on July 17. These new models had thinner bodies and a longer battery life, and used an iPod mini-style Click Wheel. The 4G models included a 20GB model at $299 and a 40GB model at $399.

On August 10, the iTunes Music Store (iTMS) catalog reached one million songs. By September 1, the number of songs downloaded from iTMS hit 125 million; the 150 million level was hit on October 12. By this point in time, iTMS had more than 4 million downloads per week.

note On August 27, 2004, Hewlett-Packard announced the first non-Apple iPod. The "Apple iPod from HP" was actually a repackaged version of the 4G iPod with HP-centric manuals and technical support. This unit began shipping on September 15; sales were discontinued less than a year later, on July 29, 2005.

October 26 saw the launch of the first iPod with a color screen. Dubbed the **iPod Photo**, it was available in 40GB and 60GB version. Apple also launched an **iPod U2 Special Edition**, a $349 unit with black body and engraved signatures from the popular rock band.

2005: The Market Explodes

January's MacWorld Expo saw the introduction of the **iPod shuffle**, a smaller player with Flash memory storage. Two models were launched: a 512MB model at $99 and a 1GB model at $149. The shuffle was (and remains) controversial due to its lack of display screen. This is promoted as a plus by Apple, allowing users to play back their music in totally random order—although critics point out that competing Flash players with screens offer more control over playback at similar or lower prices.

On February 23, Apple discontinued the 40GB iPod Photo, replacing it with a 30GB iPod Photo at $349. At the same time, Apple reduced the price of the 60GB iPod Photo to $449. Also introduced on this date was the second-generation iPod mini, with a brighter-colored case and longer battery life. Two new models were available, a 4GB version at $199 and a 6GB version at $249.

Apple's iPod and iPod Photo lines were merged on June 28. The last of the monochrome iPods were discontinued in favor of lower-priced color iPods with photo capability. These new models included a 20GB unit at $99 and a 60GB unit at $399. Apple also dropped the price of the 1GB iPod shuffle to $129.

Since its launch, the iPod mini had been Apple's most popular iPod model. On September 7, Apple replaced the mini with the smaller **iPod nano**. The nano is a Flash-based player, available in 2GB and 4GB models, priced at $199 and $249, respectively. Also launched on this date was the Motorola **Rokr E1**, an iTunes-compatible cellular phone.

On October 12, Apple launched its fifth-generation iPod models with full video playback capability and larger 2.5-inch screen. The two 5G models included a 30GB unit at $299 and a 60GB unit at $399. Both units are available with either white or black bodies.

To coincide with the new 5G video iPods, Apple added videos for downloading from the iTMS. Episodes from five television shows and 2,000 music videos are available for sale at $1.99 each. Videos are formatted specially for the iPod's 320x240 pixel display. By the end of October, iTMS had sold more than a million videos; by the end of the year, more than three million videos were sold.

The biggest news of 2005, however, was the iPod's exploding sales. For the full calendar year, Apple sold than 31 million units, almost quadrupling the prior year's 8 million units sold. This was the year that the iPod truly became a mass-market product, with 14 million units sold during the holiday season and a year-ending installed base of more than 30 million users.

2006: Business as Usual—and Then Some

Unusually, Apple didn't announce any new iPod models at January's MacWorld Expo, instead using the event to trumpet the prior year's huge sales numbers. Sales were also booming at the iTMS, which sold its one billionth download on February 22.

Apple's first new product announcement of the year was on February 7. On this date, Apple announced a 1GB iPod nano at $149, and dropped the prices of the 512MB and 1GB iPod shuffles to $69 and $99, respectively.

Later that month, on February 28, Apple announced the **iPod Hi-Fi**, a hi-fidelity tabletop speaker system for the iPod. Critics pounced on the announce-ment because the iPod Hi-Fi is considerably higher-priced than competing speaker systems and lacks Apple's usual stylistic flair.

On September 12, Apple added full-length movies to the now-renamed **iTunes Store**, priced from $9.99 to $14.99. (The word *music* was dropped from the title.) Video resolution was upped from 320x240 to a near-DVD quality 640x480, enhancing playback on larger PC monitors. At the same time, Apple added iPod games to the iTunes Store, priced at $4.99 per title.

That date also saw the launch of enhanced 5G iPods with brighter screens and larger capacities; models include a 30GB unit at $249 and an 80GB unit at $349. Also launched was a new second-generation iPod nano with colored aluminum case, in 2GB ($149), 4GB ($199), and 8GB ($249) versions, and a completely revamped 1GB iPod shuffle in a new brushed-metal body, at $70. Apple also announced version 7 of the iTunes software, complete with gapless music playback and a unique CoverFlow display.

2007: Introducing the iPhone

The year 2007 started with a bang when Apple introduced the **iPhone** at January's MacWorld Expo. The iPhone is a unique device that functions as a combination widescreen/touchscreen iPod and Internet-enabled smartphone. Long-anticipated, the

> **note** On October 13, 2006, Apple launched the **PRODUCT (RED)** iPod nano, a special red-cased 4G unit with $10 of every purchase going to AIDS charities in Africa.

iPhone looks to make a big splash in the cellular phone market—and give iPod users another option in their choice of models.

iPods in the Future

If Apple follows tradition, new iPod models will continue to be introduced at the company's MacWorld Expo each January. Additional product announcements are likely throughout the year, as the market (and technology) demands.

What are new iPod models likely to look like? If trends continue, expect larger storage at similar or lower prices, bigger and higher-resolution screens, and smaller and lighter units. Particularly likely are larger-capacity Flash-based nanos and shuffles; a 16GB nano is not out of the question in the near future.

It's also likely that newer iPod models will better embrace emerging technologies, much as current iPods have been tweaked for photo display, video playback, game playback, and the like. Expect the full-face touchscreen display of the iPhone to migrate further into the iPod line, too.

Also possible in future iPods is WiFi capability and the ability to access the Internet, much as the iPhone currently does. Turning the iPod into a portable email and web browser is a natural step for Apple to take.

Whatever comes from Cupertino, expect iPod sales to continue to grow for the foreseeable future. The iPod has a virtual lock on the portable audio player market, despite increased competition from Microsoft, Creative, Sansa, and others. It will take a substantial shift in consumer loyalty or some as-yet-unknown new technology to displace Apple as the undisputed market leader.

The iPod Family

At the heart of the iPod phenomenon is the iPod itself. That said, there is no such thing as *the* iPod. Apple makes a number of different iPod models, with different styles, features, functionality, and capacity. And today's iPods are subtly different from previous iPods, even within the same model line.

Read on, then, to learn a little more about the different iPod models—and to get to know the entire iPod family.

Common Features

Whether you have an 80GB fifth-generation iPod or a shiny metallic iPod shuffle, the basic functionality is similar. All iPods play back digital audio files and multiple-file playlists, in either sequential or random order. The more advanced iPods also display digital photographs and play back digital video files, in addition to offering a variety of nonplayback functions, such as game play, calendar, alarm, and so forth.

Audio and Video Playback

In terms of audio, every iPod released to date can play back files in the following digital audio formats:

- MP3
- AAC (with the M4A file extension)
- Protected AAC (with the M4P file extension)
- AIFF
- WAV
- Apple Lossless
- Audible audiobook

> **note** The iPod does not support the Microsoft Windows Media Audio (WMA) file format. This means that files downloaded from other online music stores, such as Napster and URGE, will not play on the iPod without involved technical manipulation.

The fifth-generation iPod can also play back video files, in the MPEG-4 (MP4) and QuickTime video file formats—and can show photos and other color images

Audio and video files are transferred from a host computer using the iTunes software. Files are synchronized between the two devices whenever the iPod is connected to the host PC.

File Storage

Files are stored on the iPod's microdrive hard disk (for basic iPod models) or in the iPod's Flash memory (for the iPod nano and shuffle). If the iPod is formatted on a Windows computer, it uses the FAT32 file system. If the iPod is formatted on a Macintosh computer, it uses the HFS Plus file system. (The only exception to this is the iPod shuffle, which uses the FAT32 file system exclusively.)

Because the iPod is formatted with one of these standard computer file systems, it can also be used as a standard data storage device; that is, you can use your iPod as a portable disk drive for your computer files. In addition, any iPod formatted with HFS Plus can serve as a boot disk for a Macintosh computer.

Operating System and Memory

The iPod's operating system is stored on the internal hard drive or in the iPod's Flash memory. Each iPod also includes

> **note** Learn more about the iPod's data storage functionality in Chapter 15, "Using Your iPod as a Portable Storage Device."

an additional Flash ROM chip (either 512KB or 1MB) that contains a boot-loader program that tells the iPod to load its operating system from the storage medium.

All iPods also include 32MB of RAM (64MB on the 60GB and 80GB fifth-generation models). A portion of this RAM is used to hold the operating system, after it has booted from the firmware, although the majority is used to cache songs from the main storage medium.

Connections

The original iPods used a FireWire cable to connect to and recharge from the host computer. Starting with the third-generation iPod, the unit used a proprietary dock connector that could connect to a computer using either FireWire or USB. (USB was more common on non-Apple PCs.) The fourth-generation iPod was the first that allowed recharging via USB; FireWire was fully discontinued as of the fifth-generation iPod.

Batteries

The first- and second-generation iPods used lithium polymer batteries. All later models use lithium-ion batteries for longer life.

Controller

The initial iPod revolutionized MP3 player control by using a mechanical scroll wheel to navigate the unit's menus. Users scrolled the wheel clockwise to move down the menus and increase the unit's volume, and counterclockwise to scroll up the menus or decrease volume.

This mechanical controller was replaced by a touch-sensitive wheel controller (by Synaptics) on the second-generation unit, and by the current Click Wheel beginning with the iPod mini (and later on the fourth-generation iPod). The Click Wheel integrates the previously separate selection buttons; now you can make selections by clicking the wheel controller itself.

Comparing iPod Models

Even though the current-generation iPod looks a lot like the original model, there have been significant changes over the years. We'll look at each generation and model separately, but you can use Table 2.1 to perform a basic comparison.

Table 2.1 iPod Model Comparison

Model/ Generation	Capacity	Storage Medium	CPU	Controller	Connection	Changes Introduced	Launch Price	Launch Date
iPod 1G	5GB, 10GB	1.8" Toshiba hard drive	Two 90MHz ARM CPUs	Mechanical scroll wheel	FireWire	Initial model	$399, $499	October 2001
iPod 2G	10GB, 20GB	1.8" Toshiba hard drive	Two 90MHz ARM CPUs	Touch-sensitive scroll wheel	FireWire	Windows compatibility	$399, $499	July 2002
iPod 3G	10GB, 15GB, 20GB (later), 30GB, and 40GB models	1.8" Toshiba hard drive	Two 90MHz ARM 7TDMI CPUs	Touch-sensitive scroll wheel	FireWire, USB (for syncing only—not for recharging)	Central row of touch-sensitive buttons, dock connector	$299, $399, $499	April 2003
iPod 4G	20GB, 30GB, 40GB	1.8" Toshiba hard drive	Two 80MHz ARM 7TDMI CPUs	Click Wheel	FireWire, USB	Buttons integrated to form single Click Wheel	$299, $349, $399	July 2004
iPod Photo	40GB, 60GB	1.8" Toshiba hard drive	Two 80MHz ARM 7TDMI CPUs	Click Wheel	FireWire, USB	Color display and photo viewing	$399, $599	June 2005
iPod 5G	30GB, 60GB	1.8" Toshiba hard drive	Two 80MHz ARM 7TDMI CPUs	Click Wheel	USB	Slimmer case, first black case, larger screen, video playback, no AC adapter or universal dock included	$299, $399	October 2005
iPod 5.5G	30GB, 80GB	1.8" Toshiba hard drive	Two 80MHz ARM 7TDMI CPUs	Click Wheel	USB	Brighter display, longer battery life, music search function	$249, $349	September 2006
iPod mini 1G	4GB	1" Hitachi microdrive	Two 80MHz 7TDMI CPUs	Click Wheel	FireWire, USB	Initial release, five case colors	$249	January 2004
iPod mini 2G	4GB, 6GB	1" Hitachi microdrive	Two 80MHz 7TDMI CPUs	Click Wheel	FireWire, USB	Brighter case colors with matching Click Wheel lettering, longer battery life, no AC adapter	$199, $249	February 2005

Table 2.1   iPod Model Comparison

Model/ Generation	Capacity	Storage Medium	CPU	Controller	Connection	Changes Introduced	Launch Price	Launch Date
iPod nano 1G	1GB, 2GB, 4GB	Flash memory	Two 80MHz 7TDMI CPUs	Click Wheel	USB	Initial release, replaces iPod mini, color screen, white case	$149, $199, $249	September 2005
iPod nano 2G	2GB, 4GB, 8GB	Flash memory	Samsung System-On-Chip	Click Wheel	USB	Anodized aluminum case in six colors, brighter screen, longer battery life	$149, $199, $249	September 2006
iPod shuffle 1G	512MB, 1GB	Flash memory	SigmaTel STMP 3550 chip	5-button control pad	USB	Initial release, first iPod without a screen, white case	$99, $149 (later reduced to $69 and $99)	January 2005
iPod shuffle 2G	1GB	Flash memory	SigmaTel STMP 3550 chip	5-button control pad	USB	Aluminum case, smaller form factor, built-in clip	$79	October 2006

SELLING YOUR IPOD

It seems that almost as soon as you get your music loaded on your new iPod, Apple makes it obsolete by introducing new and improved models. In fact, most iPod users replace their iPods before they wear out, in the quest to possess the latest and greatest player available.

When you replace a working iPod, what do you do with your old model? Many users choose to sell their old iPods, either on eBay or locally. Unfortunately, old iPods don't retain a lot of their original value—that is, you can expect to take a big loss over what you originally paid.

So just how much is a used iPod worth? An ongoing survey of iPod sales on eBay by iLounge (www.ilounge.com) indicates that the value of your iPod is just 83% of its original price three months after purchase. That value falls to 76% after six months, and drops to 62% after a year. A two-year old iPod is worth only 42% of its original price, a three-year old model is worth just 28%, and a four-year old iPod commands just 20% of its original price.

Put into practical terms, if you paid $299 for your iPod a year ago, you can probably sell it for about $185 today. That same iPod purchased two years ago is worth only $125 today. And so on.

For this reason, many iPod users keep their old iPods, using them as auxiliary units in the bedroom or in the car. If you're a music lover, you can never have enough music players!

The iPod

Throughout the generations, Apple's main iPod has remained the flagship of the iPod line. The main iPod holds thousands (if not tens of thousands) of songs, using a Toshiba 1.8-inch hard drive for storage. Later models offer larger color screens to facilitate photo viewing and video playback, in addition to the traditional digital audio playback.

The first-generation iPod, shown in Figure 2.1, was available in 5GB and 10GB versions, priced at $399 and $499, respectively. This initial unit, released in October 2001, used Apple's original mechanical scroll wheel controller and connected to Macintosh-only computers with a FireWire cable.

FIGURE 2.1

The first-generation Apple iPod. (Photo courtesy of Apple.)

The second-generation iPod was the first to be compatible with Windows PCs. Released in July 2002, it was available in 10GB and 20GB models, priced at $399 and $499. As you can see in Figure 2.2, it looked identical to the first-generation unit, although the original mechanical scroll wheel was replaced with a touch-sensitive wheel controller.

The third-generation iPod, shown in Figure 2.3, added a row of touch-sensitive buttons above the scroll wheel. In addition, it added USB connectivity to the original FireWire connectivity. More important, the 3G iPod was much slimmer than previous units, with softer front corners. Originally available with a maximum of 20GB storage, later 3G units offered 30GB and 40GB capacities.

FIGURE 2.2

The second-generation Apple iPod. (Photo courtesy of Apple.)

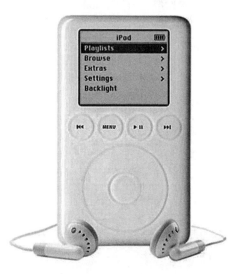

FIGURE 2.3

The third-generation Apple iPod. (Photo courtesy of Apple.)

The fourth-generation iPod, shown in Figure 2.4, changed the controller from the previous "touch wheel" design to an integrated Click Wheel, which included the previously separate button controls as part of the wheel controller. A later 4G model, dubbed the iPod Photo, included Apple's first color display, increased capacity (60GB), and could store and view digital photos. (Figure 2.5 shows the iPod Photo with a photo collage onscreen.)

FIGURE 2.4

The fourth-generation Apple iPod. (Photo courtesy of Apple.)

FIGURE 2.5

The iPod Photo. (Photo courtesy of Apple.)

Shown in Figure 2.6, the fifth-generation iPod (a.k.a. the Video iPod) added video playback to the previous music and photo functionality. It also removed the FireWire connection, making the iPod a USB-only device. Later "5.5"- generation models added a brighter display, longer battery life, and a higher- capacity 80GB unit.

FIGURE 2.6

The fifth-generation Apple iPod, in black. (Photo courtesy of Apple.)

SPECIAL EDITION IPODS

In addition to the standard model iPods discussed in this chapter, Apple has also sold a number of special-edition models. The first special edition iPods were introduced in December 2002; there were signature models for Madonna, Beck, No Doubt, and Tony Hawk, available at a $49 premium over regular models.

In October 2004, Apple introduced a U2 Special Edition iPod, shown in Figure 2.7. This was a basic 4G model with a special black case, red scroll wheel, and engraved signatures of all U2 band members. The U2 iPod was updated with Apple's iPod Photo and 5G models.

Another limited-edition 4G iPod was the Special Edition Harry Potter iPod. This unit was engraved with the Hogwarts crest on the back, and was available only to purchasers of *Harry Potter* audiobooks.

The latest special edition iPod was introduced in October 2006. The (PRODUCT) RED iPod nano is a 2G iPod nano in a special red case, available in 4GB and 8GB versions. There is no premium for this limited-edition model; instead, Apple donates $10 for each model sold to the Global Fund to Fight AIDS, Tuberculosis, and Malaria.

FIGURE 2.7

The U2 Special Edition iPod. (Photo courtesy of Apple.)

The iPod mini

As popular as the iPod was, it didn't appeal to all sectors of the portable audio player market. Some users wanted a smaller, lighter player than the standard iPod, even if it didn't hold quite as many songs.

To meet this market demand, Apple released the iPod mini. The mini used a 4GB 1-inch microdrive hard disk that was both smaller and lighter than the 1.8-inch hard drive used in the regular iPod. The mini also was the first unit to use Apple's innovative Click Wheel, which integrated the previously separate function buttons into the wheel controller itself.

The first-generation iPod mini, shown in Figure 2.8, was released in January 2004. Unlike previous iPods, it didn't embrace Apple's signature white "bar of soap" design; instead, it had a metallic case and was available in five colors. The mini quickly became Apple's best-selling iPod.

In February 2005, Apple refreshed the mini with new 4GB and 6GB models. The biggest change in these 2G minis was almost wholly stylistic; the case colors were brighter, and the lettering on the Click Wheel matched the case color.

FIGURE 2.8

The iPod mini. (Photo courtesy of Apple.)

The iPod nano

Apple is not afraid to eat its young in the chase for market domination. Case in point: the iPod nano, which replaced the best-selling iPod mini in September 2005. The nano bested the mini by using Flash memory in place of the mini's microdrive hard disk, which made for a smaller, lighter player that didn't skip when jostled. The first-generation nano, shown in Figure 2.9, was available in 1GB, 2GB, and 4GB versions, and included a color screen. Unlike the mini, the 1G nano was available in only white or black.

The iPod nano was totally revamped for its second generation, released in September 2006. The 2G nano had twice the capacity (2GB, 4GB, and 8GB) and a mini-inspired anodized aluminum case, available in six bright colors. (See Figure 2.10.)

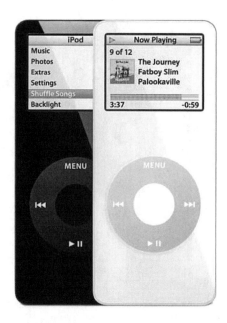

FIGURE 2.9

The first-generation iPod nano, in black and white. (Photo courtesy of Apple.)

FIGURE 2.10

The second-generation iPod nano, in various colors. (Photo courtesy of Apple.)

The iPod shuffle

Finally, we have the iPod shuffle. Like the nano, the shuffle is a Flash-based player, which makes it small, light, and skip resistant. Unlike the nano and all previous iPods, the shuffle doesn't have a screen; this was originally thought to be a drawback, even if Apple promoted this curious omission as a "plus" to potential buyers. (Apple also, quite smartly, marketed the shuffle not as a standalone player but as an accessory for existing iPod owners, an "iPod lite" they could carry with them when a bigger iPod might not be appropriate.)

The first-generation iPod shuffle, shown in Figure 2.11, was available in 512MB and 1GB versions. Priced at $99 and $149, respectively, it was not entirely competitive with lower-priced Flash-based MP3 players. That said, it did carry the iPod cachet and sold well.

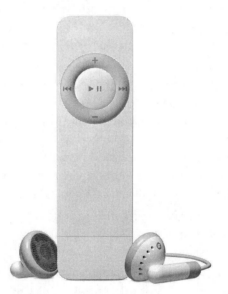

FIGURE 2.11

The first-generation iPod shuffle. (Photo courtesy of Apple.)

The second-generation iPod shuffle, shown in Figure 2.12, is a complete revamp of the original concept. This new shuffle is as small as a matchbook, no bigger than its control pad, and comes with a handy clip that attaches the shuffle to belts, purses, and other articles of clothing. The shuffle has 1GB of Flash memory and is priced at a competitive $79; originally introduced in a single color (silver), Apple now offers it in a variety of shiny colors.

FIGURE 2.12

The second-generation iPod shuffle. (Photo courtesy of Apple.)

TO SHUFFLE OR NOT TO SHUFFLE

The iPod shuffle has invited criticism and controversy since its initial first-generation release. Although ostensibly an extension of the iPod line, it can also be seen as just another Flash-based MP3 player—albeit one lacking key features found on many competing models.

For $79, the second-generation iPod shuffle is an attractive but otherwise unremarkable MP3 player. Unlike competing players, the shuffle doesn't have a display, doesn't offer a built-in FM radio, and won't let you select which songs you hear. Compare the shuffle, for example, to SanDisk Sansa c240, also priced at $79. Like the iPod shuffle, the Sansa offers 1GB of Flash-based memory, but also offers a color display, manual song selection, digital photo viewing, and a built-in FM radio. That's a lot more functionality than the shuffle, for the same price.

Of course, the Sansa isn't an iPod, which means it doesn't have the same cachet among some consumers. But for $79, which player is the best deal? Frankly, I'd choose the Sansa—but then, I'm not a shuffle fan.

My biggest gripe with the shuffle is the lack of control. Because there's no screen, you can't see or choose what's playing. Whereas Apple pushes the shuffle's randomness as a good thing, I disagree. Although I like random playback, I want it within limits—the random shuffle within a playlist or genre, for example. The iPod shuffle doesn't offer that; it's a totally random experience. And, as I said, I want more control than that.

That said, I am an iPod shuffle owner, and I use mine everyday. My particular use (to generate music to practice drums to) doesn't require a display; playing random songs is just what I need. For any other purposes, however, I'd chose a more controllable iPod nano or (my preferred model) the big hard-disk iPod.

The iPhone

On January 9, 2007, at MacWorld San Francisco, Apple introduced its most innovative iPod ever. The iPhone melds the iPod's music and video playback features with the features of a high-end smartphone—and adds a super-large high-resolution display, for good measure. The iPhone is set to revolutionize the mobile phone market, and is a great option for tech-savvy iPod users who want a single device to perform multiple functions.

Introducing the iPhone

Apple's iPhone, shown in Figure 3.1, is more than just a cell phone with iPod capabilities, or an iPod that can make cellular calls. It's a completely new device that combines the functionality of three distinct products:

FIGURE 3.1

Apple's revolutionary iPhone. (Courtesy of Apple.)

- iPod media player with widescreen display and touchscreen controls
- Mobile phone with built-in Bluetooth wireless and smartphone capabilities
- Internet communications device with built-in web browsing, email, maps, and WiFi wireless connectivity

In other words, you can use the iPhone to listen to music, watch videos, make cellular phone calls, and connect to the Internet. No other single device on the market today performs all these functions—certainly not with the same functionality and style as the iPhone.

Size-wise, the iPhone is a little bigger than a standard cell phone, or even most existing smartphones. For example, it's slightly taller and wider than a Palm Treo, although it's much thinner. Unlike current smartphones, there is no keypad; all data is entered via the touchscreen display.

Apple is offering two iPhone models, both using Flash memory storage. The 4GB iPhone sells for $499, and the 8GB model sells for $599. The first models ship in June 2007.

note Due to publishing deadlines, this chapter was written before the iPhone officially shipped. The information in this chapter is based on pre-release information provided publicly by Apple; details are subject to change.

What It Does

First and foremost, the iPhone is a mobile phone. It uses the Global System for Mobile Communications (GSM) quad-band cellular standard and is optimized to work with the Cingular cellular network. (In fact, the iPhone is sold by both Apple and Cingular.) Dialing is accomplished by pressing the touchscreen; the iPhone also offers Bluetooth connectivity and a 2-megapixel camera phone.

> **note** The iPhone is sold in the United States with a two-year subscription to the Cingular service. In Canada, sales will be handled by the Rogers cellular provider, probably starting in late 2007. Sales in Asia and Europe are slated to begin in 2008; details on non-U.S. service will be available then.

Second, the iPhone is an iPod media player—in essence, a video-enabled version of the iPod nano. Like the nano, the iPhone uses Flash memory storage, with either 4GB or 8GB available. The iPhone eschews Apple's traditional Click Wheel navigation in favor of touchscreen controls; just touch an album cover or song title to begin playback.

The iPod capability also includes video playback, which is especially compelling on the 3.5-inch widescreen display. The display takes up most of the face of the iPhone, which makes it much better for watching movies than on a normal iPod. In addition, the iPhone has a built-in motion sensor that knows when you're holding it vertically or horizontally; tilt it on its side, and movies automatically display in widescreen mode.

Finally, the iPhone is an Internet communications device. It comes with a built-in web browser (Safari) and email client (provided by Yahoo! Mail), and wirelessly connects to the Internet via WiFi. It also comes bundled with Google and Yahoo! search applications and a special version of Google Maps. You can also add a variety of "widgets" to perform specific operations, such as downloading news headlines, stock tickers, sports scores, and the like.

How It Does It

The power behind the iPhone operation is a special version of Apple's OS X operating system. OS X enables the iPhone to multitask—which means you can check email while browsing the Web.

Operation depends on efficient use of the touchscreen display. Apple employs what it calls multi-touch technology, with which specific finger gestures initiate specific operations. For example, to scroll through a list of tunes, just flip your finger up the screen; the list scrolls rapidly and then gently slows to a stop, much like a roulette wheel. Or to shrink a picture, pinch your thumb and forefinger together on the screen, as if you were physically resizing the picture. It's very effective.

Also key are iPhone wireless technologies. In addition to the quad-band GSM cellular communications, the iPhone supports Cingular's EDGE high-speed data network, 802.11b/g WiFi, and Bluetooth 2.0 (to work with cordless headsets). The iPhone can use either EDGE or WiFi to connect to the Internet.

In addition, the iPhone uses a built-in accelerometer to detect when the device is rotated from portrait to landscape usage, and then flips the display accordingly. Hold the device vertically, like a normal phone or iPod, and the display shows in portrait mode; hold the device horizontally to watch a movie or view photos, and the display shows in landscape mode.

Finally, the iPhone includes a built-in proximity sensor, which is used to shut off the display when you're talking on the phone. Move the iPhone to your ear and the display shuts off—which both prevents inadvertent screen presses and conserves battery power.

Specifications

Now, for all you spec-hounds, Table 3.1 details how the iPhone stacks up, by the numbers.

Table 3.1   iPhone Specifications

Feature	Detail
Screen size	3.5" widescreen
Screen resolution	320x480 pixels
Operating system	OS X
Compatibility	Windows and Macintosh computers
Storage medium	Flash memory
Storage capacity	4GB or 8GB
Digital camera resolution	2 megapixels
Cellular system	Quad-band GSM (850MHz, 900MHz, 1800MHz, 1900MHz)
Cellular service provider	Cingular

Table 3.1   iPhone Specifications

Feature	Detail
Wireless technologies	Bluetooth, WiFi, EDGE (2.5G networks)
Web browser	Safari
Email client	Yahoo! Mail
Battery life	5 hours (talk/video/Internet) 16 hours (music playback)
Dimensions	4.5"x2.4"x0.46"
Weight	4.8 ounces
Price	$499 (4GB), $599 (8GB)

PREVIOUS ITUNES PHONES

The iPhone is not the first mobile phone with iTunes compatibility. In September 2005, Motorola released the ROKR E1, a candy bar–style phone with 512MB of Flash memory. The ROKR had a built-in music player called the iTunes Client, which enabled it to play back songs downloaded from the iTunes computer music player program and the iTunes Music Store. Unfortunately, the ROKR lacked the iPod's Click Wheel navigation (instead using a joypad-type controller) and held less music than even the iPod shuffle; storage was capped (supposedly at Apple's request) to a paltry 100 songs. Priced at $349, it was not an attractive proposition for consumers and didn't sell well.

Later Motorola models also sported iTunes compatibility. The SLVR L7, like the ROKR, was a candy bar–style phone (only thinner), whereas the RAZR V3i was a variation on Motorola's stylish flip phone. Neither was well promoted, and neither found acceptance in the marketplace.

Using the iPhone

Now that you know what the iPhone is, let's take a quick tour of what it does.

The iPhone Home Screen

Everything starts on the home screen. As you can see in Figure 3.2, the home screen provides access to major functions via the buttons along the bottom of the screen—Phone, Mail, Web, and iPod. Subsidiary functions are accessed via buttons in the middle of the screen—Text, Calendar, Photos, Camera, and the like.

FIGURE 3.2

The iPhone home screen. (Courtesy of Apple.)

To access a function, simply press the button on the touchscreen display. For example, to make a phone call, press Phone; to listen to music, press iPod.

Making Phone Calls

When you press the Phone button, you see the screen displayed in Figure 3.3. Press Keypad to "dial" a number using the onscreen keypad, or press Contacts to make a call to one your stored contacts. Press a contact name and the call is dialed.

To talk on the iPhone, just hold it to your face as you would any other candy bar–style mobile phone. The screen automatically blanks when you're talking, and then comes back on when you move the phone away from your face. To end a call, press End Call on the touchscreen.

Then there's voicemail. On a traditional phone, you have to call into the voicemail service and listen through all your waiting messages. Not so on the iPhone. The iPhone voicemail system, shown in Figure 3.4, lets you view all your waiting messages onscreen. You only have to listen to those messages you want; just touch a message to play it back.

FIGURE 3.3
Using the iPhone as a phone. (Courtesy of Apple.)

FIGURE 3.4
Viewing voicemail messages on the iPhone. (Courtesy of Apple.)

Sending Text Messages

As with most mobile phones today, the iPhone can also be used to send text messages. This is facilitated by an onscreen touch keyboard, shown in Figure 3.5. This virtual keyboard is a lot easier to use than a normal phone's numeric keypad; just tap out your message then press Send.

FIGURE 3.5

Using the iPhone to send text messages. (Courtesy of Apple.)

Taking Photos

The iPhone includes a built-in 2 megapixel digital camera. Just select Camera from the home screen, aim the camera, and shoot.

Viewing Photos

The photos you take with the iPhone, and any photos you transfer from your computer, are stored in the unit's Flash memory and can be viewed on the unit's widescreen display. Just select Photos on the home screen, and then navigate to the photo(s) you want to view—or select the Slideshow option to view all your photos in an automated slideshow.

Listening to Music

Of course, most people will be buying the iPhone to listen to music. In this respect, the iPhone is like a widescreen iPod with touchscreen operation. Instead of using a Click Wheel to navigate the iPod menus, you just touch the item you want onscreen.

Figure 3.6 shows the iPhone operating in iPod mode. You get the normal album cover display, with track information above the art. Below the art are navigation controls—Play/Pause, Forward, and Reverse. Tap a control to use it.

FIGURE 3.6
Using the iPhone as an iPod to listen to music. (Courtesy of Apple.)

Watching Videos

Similarly, it's easy to use the iPhone to watch videos. Again, you enter iPod mode, but when you start playback, you turn the iPhone on its side. In this horizontal orientation, the screen automatically flips so that you can watch movies and TV shows in all their widescreen glory, as shown in Figure 3.7.

FIGURE 3.7
Watching The Office in iPhone's widescreen mode. (Courtesy of Apple.)

Sending and Receiving Email

The iPhone is more than just a cell phone or media player, however. The most innovative part of the iPhone feature set is its ability to be used for web browsing and email.

The iPhone uses Yahoo! Mail as its HTML email client. As you can see in Figure 3.8, you get full HTML email onscreen, including picture attachments and the like. Yahoo! Mail can be configured to "push" email from any other service (including traditional POP email) to the iPhone. You compose email messages using an onscreen touch keyboard, similar to the one used to send text messages; you can also attach photos and music files to your emails.

FIGURE 3.8
Reading email messages on the iPhone.

Browsing the Web

The iPhone includes the Safari web browser, which lets you quickly and easily browse the Web, using either an EDGE or WiFi connection. As you can see in Figure 3.9, web pages display normally in a vertical orientation; you can also flip the iPhone horizontally to display any page wider, for easier reading.

FIGURE 3.9
Surfing the Web with the iPhone's Safari web browser.

Viewing Maps

One of the many applications included with the iPhone is a special version of Google Maps, shown in Figure 3.10. Google Maps on the iPhone lets you easily map out a route, get driving directions, and find nearby businesses. As with the regular version of Google Maps, you can view any map in traditional map view or satellite view—or, if you're searching for businesses, in a special list view. You can also make phone calls directly from Google Maps; just highlight a business and press to phone.

> **note** The iPhone defaults to WiFi for its Internet connectivity. If no WiFi network is available, it uses Cingular's EDGE network—which comes at a relatively high cost for data transfer. When the iPhone moves into range of a WiFi network, it automatically switches from EDGE to WiFi.

FIGURE 3.10
Viewing Google Maps on the iPhone.

Using Other Widgets

Finally, the iPhone lets you install all manner of small web-based applications, called *widgets*. A widget typically does one thing and one thing only. For example, widgets are available that display real-time weather reports, news headlines, sports scores, and stock data (shown in Figure 3.11). You can download additional widgets from Apple's website.

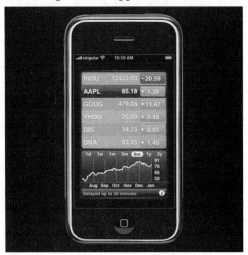

FIGURE 3.11
The iPhone's stock ticker widget.

Is the iPhone for You?

The introduction of the iPhone introduces a bit of complexity to your choice of iPod models. Should you replace your current iPod with an iPhone? It all depends.

Pros

The iPhone may be appealing if you meet some or all of the following criteria:

- You're currently using an iPod nano.
- You're currently a Cingular subscriber.
- You want to reduce the number of portable electronic devices you carry.
- You want to access the Web and email while you're on the go.
- You want to view movies on a larger screen than offered on the traditional iPod.
- You want to improve your on-the-go functionality.

Cons

On the other hand, the iPhone isn't for everybody. Here are some factors that may cause you *not* to embrace this new device:

- You're currently using a 30GB, 60GB, or 80GB iPod—and need the extra storage capacity.
- You're not a Cingular subscriber and don't want to become one.
- You like your current cell phone—or have more than a few months left on your current contract.
- You don't care about or even want continuous access to email and the Web.
- You already have web and email access with a notebook PC or BlackBerry device.

Bottom Line

In other words, the iPhone is a bit of a compromise. As a music player, it's not the biggest-capacity iPod available; so if you carry a ton of tunes with you, it's no good. As a cell phone, it's rather pricey and limited to use on the Cingular network. And as an Internet device, it replicates functionality that you might already have with a notebook PC or BlackBerry.

On the plus side, although the iPhone might offer less functionality than three separate devices, it is a single device. Instead of carrying around an iPod, cell phone, and notebook PC, you can carry around a single iPhone. And, let's face it, the iPhone is just plain cool. So there's that.

Is the iPhone for you? The slim amount of storage might be a deal breaker for some; the exclusive tie-in to Cingular could exclude many more consumers from the potential marketplace; and the hefty price might limit the market to well-heeled users. That said, I know a few people who are willing to spend the bucks to use the iPhone as nothing more than a touch-screen iPod—the phone capability is unimportant to them. And I know other folks who think the iPhone will make a stylish (if overpriced) cell phone, even if it is limited in its music and video storage.

The iPhone definitely breaks new ground, and does so in Apple's inimitably stylish fashion. It's safe to say that the iPhone redefines the mobile phone market in several ways; expect other cell phone manufacturers to eventually adopt many of the same features that Apple has crammed into the iPhone. The future will be interesting.

TRADEMARKS

The iPhone trademark is actually owned by Cisco, who acquired it when it purchased InfoGear Technology Corp. in 2000; InfoGear had registered the trademark in 1996. Three weeks before Apple's iPhone announcement, Cisco used the name for a new VoIP (Voice over Internet Protocol) phone marketed by its Linksys division.

Apple was negotiating with Cisco for rights to the name up until the evening before the MacWorld announcement. When Apple proceeded with the announcement without a signed agreement, Cisco filed suit in federal court to protect its trademark.

In its complaint requesting an injunction against Apple's use of the iPhone name, Cisco claimed that Apple had attempted to get rights to the iPhone name several times, starting in 2001. When Cisco refused, Apple purportedly created a front company called Ocean Telecom Services to try to acquire the rights another way. As Apple's iPhone product came closer to reality, Apple again began open negotiations with Cisco to use the iPhone name.

Mark Chandler, Cisco senior vice president, noted that the two companies were close to finalizing a deal the night before MacWorld that would have allowed both Cisco and Apple to use the iPhone name. One aspect of the agreement called for some sort of technical interoperability between Apple's iPhone and Cisco's Linksys Internet telephone products. The companies left the negotiating table at 8:00 that evening, with Cisco indicating that it was important that negotiations be completed before Apple's launch of its product. Obviously, that didn't happen, and according to Cisco, Apple never resumed talks.

"Cisco entered into negotiations with Apple in good faith after Apple repeatedly asked permission to use Cisco's iPhone name," Chandler said in an interview. "There is no doubt that Apple's new phone is very exciting, but they should not be using our trademark without our permission."

Apple, not surprisingly, is fighting the lawsuit, claiming the two iPhone products are decidedly different.

"We think Cisco's trademark suit is silly," said Apple spokesperson Natalie Kerris. "We believe (their) trademark registration is tenuous at best. There are already several companies using the iPhone name for VoIP products. We're the first company ever to use iPhone for a cell phone. If Cisco wants to challenge us on it, we're confident we'll prevail."

Buttressing Apple's point, it should be noted that British company Orate Telecommunications Services has been selling a VoIP phone called the iPhone. In addition, California company Teledex offers a product called iPhone for hotel rooms.

That said, Apple's appropriation of the iPhone name without proper agreement or compensation was somewhat brazen—especially considering Apple's history of overlitigating alleged exploiters of its own trademarks. It came as no surprise, then, when Apple and Cisco announced on February 22, 2007, that they had come to an agreement (out of court) that let both companies share the iPhone name, and market products that use that moniker. Details of the settlement were not made public, but the agreement cleared the path for the official release of Apple's iPhone—with no legal impediments pending.

Operation

Using the iPod

U sing an iPod is relatively simple, at least at the most basic level; and all iPods work in pretty much the same fashion. But there are some operational differences between models, and some features that are buried beneath one menu or another.

So, whichever model of iPod you own, it pays to drill down beneath the main menus and learn about all available features. Which is what this chapter is all about.

Using the 5G iPod

Thanks to Apple's unique Click Wheel, operating an iPod is a snap. Just run your fingers around the wheel ring to move up and down through the menus and increase or decrease the volume. Press the center button to select the current menu item, or press one of the four outlying buttons (on the spokes of the wheel) to perform other operations. Whatever you're doing is displayed onscreen—unless you're using an iPod shuffle, of course, which is screenless.

Using the Click Wheel

The Click Wheel on the 5G iPod, shown in Figure 4.1, has five embedded buttons. The buttons are located in the center of the Click Wheel and at the 12 o'clock, 3 o'clock, 6 o'clock, and 9 o'clock positions, as detailed in Table 4.1.

note The color display of the fifth-generation iPod is a joy to use. It's a high-resolution (320x240 pixel) display that shows not only the iPod's menus, but also album art, digital photos, and videos.

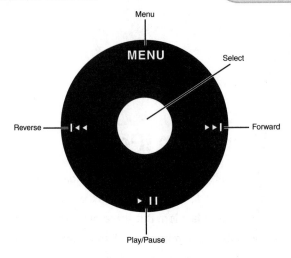

FIGURE 4.1
The iPod Click Wheel.

Table 4.1	Control Wheel Buttons	
Button	**Position**	**Function**
Select	Center	Selects the current menu item.
Menu	12 o'clock (top)	Moves backward through the menus; on older iPods, also toggles the backlight.
Play/Pause	6 o'clock (bottom)	Toggles between Play and Pause modes; press and hold to turn the iPod on and off.
Forward	3 o'clock (right)	Press once to skip to next track; press and hold to fast forward through the current track.
Reverse	9 o'clock (left)	Press once to skip to the start of the current track; press twice to skip to the previous track; press and hold to reverse through the current track.

Performing Basic Operations

To turn on your iPod, press and hold the Play/Pause button until the screen display appears. To turn off your iPod, press and hold the Play/Pause button until the screen goes blank.

To start playback, press the Play/Pause button. To pause playback, you also press the Play/Pause button; to resume playback, press the Play/Pause button again.

Use the Forward and Reverse buttons to move to the next or previous track, respectively. Press and hold these buttons to fast-forward or reverse through the current song. To go directly to any point in the current song, press the center Select button to display the "scrubber" bar, and then rotate the Click Wheel to move forward and back.

To display the iPod's menus, press the Menu button. To scroll through any onscreen menu, run your finger around the Control Wheel itself. Move clockwise to scroll down through a menu; move counterclockwise to scroll up.

You also use the Click Wheel to control the volume level of your playback. Scroll clockwise to increase the volume or counterclockwise to decrease the volume.

To prevent accidental button presses, use the Hold switch located on top of the iPod. Slide the switch to the right to lock the front controls; slide the switch back to the left to unlock and use the controls. This is especially useful if you carry your iPod in your pocket or use your iPod while exercising. It's also a good idea to press the Hold switch when you are not using your iPod (and when it's not connected to your computer), to prevent battery-draining accidental playback.

Navigating the Menus

The 5G iPod has a deceptively simple menu system. It's deceptive because there's a lot of functionality buried beneath the main menus.

As you can see in Figure 4.2, the main menu has the following options: Music, Photos, Videos, Extras, Settings, Shuffle

tip Your iPod will automatically pause playback whenever you unplug your earphones from the earphone jack. When you replug your earphones, you'll have to resume playback manually by pressing the Play/Pause button.

tip If, for whatever reason, your iPod becomes is frozen, you can easily reset it. Just move the Hold switch on then off, and then press and hold the Menu and Select buttons (together) for 6 to 10 seconds. (On older 1G, 2G, and 3G iPods, press the Menu and Play/Pause buttons instead.)

Songs, and (when a song is queued up) Now Playing. Navigate to a menu item and press the Select button to view the submenu for that item. For example, if you select Settings, you see a submenu with the choices About, Main Menu, Shuffle, Repeat, and so on, as shown in Figure 4.3.

FIGURE 4.2

The top menu on the 5G iPod.

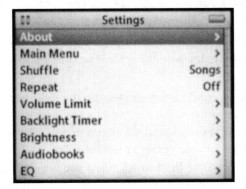

FIGURE 4.3

The iPod's Settings menu.

Menu items with a right arrow have submenus; those with no right arrow have toggled options. For example, the Settings > Shuffle option is a toggled item; press the Select button to toggle between Songs, Albums, and Off options.

Table 4.2 details all the menus and submenus on the 5G iPod.

Table 4.2   5G iPod Menus

Top Menu	Submenu	Submenu	Submenu	Submenu	Submenu
Music	Playlists	Playlist 1 Playlist 2 …	(Songs in selected playlist)		
	Artists	All Artist 1 Artist 2 …	(Songs by selected artist)		
	Albums	All Album 1 Album 2 …	(Songs on selected album)		
	Compilations	All Compilation 1 Compilation 2 …	(Songs on selected compilation album)		
	Songs	Song 1 Song 2 …			
	Podcasts	Podcast 1 Podcast 2 …			
	Genres	All Genre 1 Genre 2 …	(Artists in selected genre)	(Albums by selected artist)	(Songs on selected album)
	Composers	Song 1 Song 2 …			
	Audiobooks	Audiobook 1 Audiobook 2 …			
	Search	(Search screen)			
Photos	Slideshow Settings	Time Per Slide	Manual 2 Seconds 5 Seconds		

4

Top Menu	Submenu	Submenu	Submenu	Submenu	Submenu
Table 4.2	**5G iPod Menus**				
		10 Seconds			
		20 Seconds			
		Music	Now Playing		
			Off		
			Playlist 1		
			Playlist 2		
			. . .		
		Repeat	Off/On		
		Shuffle Photos	Off/On		
		Transitions	Off		
			Random		
			Cube across		
			Cube down		
			Dissolve		
			Page flip		
			Push across		
			Push down		
			Radial		
			Swirl		
			Wipe across		
			Wipe down		
			Wipe from center		
		TV Out	Off/On/Ask		
		TV Signal	NTSC/PAL		
	Photo Library	(Picture selection screen)			
Videos	Video Playlists	Playlist 1			
		Playlist 2			
		. . .			
	Movies	Movie 1			
		Movie 2			
		. . .			
	Music Videos	All	(Videos by selected artist)		
		Artist 1			
		Artist 2			
		. . .			

Table 4.2   5G iPod Menus

Top Menu	Submenu	Submenu	Submenu	Submenu	Submenu
	Video Podcasts	Podcast 1 Podcast 2 …			
	Video Settings	TV Out	Off/On/Ask		
		TV Signal	NTSC/PAL		
		Widescreen	Off/On		
Extras	Clock	Date & Time	Alarm Clock	Alarm	Off/On
				Time	Set time
				Sound	Beep Playlist 1 Playlist 2 …
			Change City	Continent 1 Continent 2 …	City 1 City 2 …
			Daylight Saving Time	Off/On	
			Delete This Clock		
			Sleep Timer	Off 15 Minutes 30 Minutes 60 Minutes 90 Minutes 120 Minutes	
		New Clock	Continent 1 Continent 2 …	City 1 City 2 …	
	Games	Brick Music Quiz Parachute Solitaire New game 1 New game 2 …	(Play game)		

Table 4.2   5G iPod Menus

Top Menu	Submenu	Submenu	Submenu	Submenu	Submenu
	Contacts	Contact 1 Contact 2 ...	(Contact info)		
	Calendar	All	(Selected calendar)		
		To Do	(To do list)		
		Alarms	Beep/Silent/Off		
	Notes	Note 1 Note 2 ...			
	Stopwatch	Timer	(Timer screen)		
	Screen Lock	Set Combination	(Enter New Code screen)		
Settings	About	(iPod info)			
	Main Menu	Menu item 1 Menu item 2 ...	Off/On		
	Shuffle	Songs/Albums/Off			
	Repeat	One/All/Off			
	Volume Limit	(Set maximum volume)			
	Backlight Timer	Off 2 Seconds 5 Seconds 10 Seconds 15 Seconds 20 Seconds Always On			
	Brightness	(Set screen brightness)			
	Audiobooks	Slower Normal Faster			

4

Table 4.2   5G iPod Menus

Top Menu	Submenu	Submenu	Submenu	Submenu	Submenu
	EQ	Off			
		Acoustic			
		Bass Booster			
		Bass Reducer			
		Classical			
		Dance			
		Deep			
		Electronic			
		Flat			
		Hip Hop			
		Jazz			
		Latin			
		Loudness			
		Lounge			
		Piano			
		Pop			
		R&B			
		Rock			
		Small Speakers			
		Spoken Word			
		Treble Booster			
		Treble Reducer			
		Vocal Booster			
	Compilations	Off/On			
	Sound Check	Off/On			
	Clicker	Off/On			
	Date & Time	Set Time Zone	Time zone 1		
			Time zone 2		
			. . .		
		Set Date & Time	(Set date and time)		
		Time	12-hour/ 24-hour		
		Time in Title	Off/On		
	Contacts	Sort	First Last/ Last, First		
		Display	First Last/ Last, First		

4

Table 4.2   5G iPod Menus

Top Menu	Submenu	Submenu	Submenu	Submenu	Submenu
	Language	Language 1 Language 2 …			
	Legal	(Apple legal notice)			
	Reset All Settings	Cancel Reset			
Shuffle Songs					
Now Playing	(Currently playing song)				

For example, to navigate to and select a specific song by a specific artist, select Music > Artists > *artist* > *song*. To play an iPod game, select Extras > Games > *game*. And so forth.

Evaluating Battery Life

The 5G iPod uses a lithium-ion battery. The charged life of this battery depends on the model of iPod you have and how you're using your iPod, as detailed in Table 4.3.

Table 4.3   5G iPod Battery Life

Function	30GB iPod	80GB iPod
Listening to music	14 hours	20 hours
Viewing digital photos	4 hours	6 hours
Viewing videos	4.5 hours	6.5 hours

Battery life is also affected by some of the settings you use. For example, the more you use the backlight, the faster you'll drain the battery; configure the backlight for a shorter duration to conserve your battery. In addition, use of the iPod's equalizer (EQ) will more quickly drain the battery. And the older your iPod, the less time you'll get on each charge.

note The later 5.5G iPods have longer battery life than the first fifth-generation models.

Ambient room conditions also affect battery life. The further your iPod is from normal room temperature, the more strain is put on the battery. Avoid using the iPod in extreme cold or hot conditions.

tip To keep your iPod's battery working properly, the electrons in the battery need to be moved from time to time. This means that you want to put your iPod through at least one charge cycle per month, just to keep the electrons moving.

You can gauge how much time you have left on a charge by observing the battery indicator in the iPod display. As you can see in Figure 4.4, a fully charged battery causes the indicator to display as all green. As the battery life decreases, the indicator changes to reflect the percent of charge left. When the indicator is near empty, it's time to recharge your iPod.

FIGURE 4.4

The iPod's battery indicator.

Syncing and Recharging the iPod

The 5G iPod syncs to your computer via the included USB cable. One end of this cable connects to the docking port at the bottom of the iPod; the other end connects to a USB port on your PC.

When the iPod is connected to your PC, it enters a special sync/charge mode, and the screen displays the "Do not disconnect" message shown in Figure 4.5. It's important that you heed this warning and do not prematurely disconnect your iPod.

note For more tips on how to extend your iPod's battery life, see Chapter 20, "iPod Tips and Tricks." For information on replacing a worn-out battery, see Chapter 24, "iPod Troubleshooting."

4

FIGURE 4.5

An iPod syncing to a PC—do not disconnect!

After you connect your iPod to your PC, your computer automatically launches the iTunes software and begins the sync process. During this process, new songs, playlists, and videos added to your PC are automatically transferred to your iPod. You can also use iTunes to manage the music already stored on your iPod.

caution Disconnecting your iPod while the "Do not disconnect" message is displayed could result in the corruption of files on your iPod.

Connecting your iPod to your PC also recharges the iPod's battery. Even if you don't need to sync your iPod, you still need to connect it to your PC to recharge it.

When you want to disconnect your iPod, click the Eject iPod button at the bottom right of the iTunes software window, shown in Figure 4.6. When the iPod display changes from the "Do not disconnect" message to the normal display, it's safe to disconnect the cable connecting the iPod to your PC.

note To learn how to use the iTunes software to sync the iPod with items on your computer, turn to Chapter 5, "Using the iTunes Software."

FIGURE 4.6

Click the Eject iPod button in iTunes to safely disconnect your iPod.

Playing Music on Your iPod

Far and away the most popular use for an iPod is to play music. You can choose to play the music stored on your iPod in a number of different ways:

- To shuffle randomly through all the songs stored on your iPod, select Shuffle Songs from the main menu.
- To play a specific song, select Music > Songs, and then select a song.
- To play an entire album, select Music > Albums, highlight a particular album, and then click the Play button on the Click Wheel.
- To play all songs on a compilation album, select Music > Compilations, highlight a particular album, and then click the Play button.
- To play all songs by a specific artist, select Music > Artists, highlight the artist, and then click the Play button.
- To play all songs written by a particular composer, select Music > Composers, highlight the composer, and then click the Play button.
- To play all songs in a specific genre, select Music > Genres, highlight the genre, and then click the Play button.
- To play all songs in a playlist, select Music > Playlists, highlight the Playlist, and then click the Play button.

You can also search for specific songs and artists. Just select Music > Search to display the Search screen. Use the Click Wheel to spell out the artist or song name; results start to appear onscreen, as shown in Figure 4.7. The iPod displays a mix of songs, albums (with an album icon), and

> **note** When you choose the Shuffle Play option, it stays on until you turn it off. That means if you choose to shuffle play one playlist, all your playlists will shuffle.

artists (with an artist icon) in the results list. Select Done when you've entered the complete keyword, and then scroll through the list and press the Select button to select a specific item.

FIGURE 4.7

Searching for music on the iPod.

When a song is playing, the iPod screen displays information about the song. Actually, there are several different views possible on the iPod display; you toggle between the views using the center Select button on the Click Wheel. The available views are shown in Figures 4.8 through 4.12.

FIGURE 4.8

The iPod's default music display—album cover, album title, artist name, and song name, with played and remaining time at the bottom.

FIGURE 4.9
The same display, for those songs without album art.

FIGURE 4.10
Click the Select button once and then scroll the Click Wheel to move back and forth through a song.

FIGURE 4.11
The third display mode—full-screen album cover.

FIGURE 4.12

The final display mode, used to set a song's rating; scroll the Click Wheel to change the number of stars.

Viewing Photos on Your iPod

note Learn more about playing music on your iPod in Chapter 7, "Music."

If you copy digital photos from your PC to your iPod, you can view those photos on the iPod display. You can display photos individually or as part of a slideshow.

To go to any individual picture, select Photos > Photo Library. This displays your photo thumbnails in a grid, as shown in Figure 4.13. Scroll to the picture you want to view and click the Select button on your iPod's Click Wheel; this displays the photo full-screen, as shown in Figure 4.14. To move to the next photo in order, press the Forward button on the Click Wheel—or press the Reverse button to display the previous photo.

FIGURE 4.13

The iPod's photo grid.

FIGURE 4.14
Viewing a digital photo on the iPod display.

To display your photos in an automatic slideshow, select Photos from the main menu, highlight the Photo Library option (but don't click it), and then click the Play button on the Click Wheel. This will start the slideshow.

> **note** Learn more about viewing photos on your iPod in Chapter 10, "Photos."

To adjust slideshow settings, select Photos > Slideshow Settings. You can adjust how much time is allowed per slide, what music plays during the slideshow, whether your photos are automatically shuffled, and so on.

Viewing Videos on Your iPod

New to the fifth-generation iPod is the ability to play back videos—TV shows, music videos, even full-length movies. You can transfer existing movies from your PC or download commercial videos from the iTunes Store.

To view a video on your iPod, select Videos from the main menu and then select the type of video you want to watch—Movies, Music Videos, or Video Podcasts. You can also assemble multiple-video playlists, which you access from the Video Playlists option. When you select a video, it automatically begins playback on the iPod screen, as shown in Figure 4.15. You can use the Click Wheel controls to pause and restart playback or to move back and forth through the videos in a playlist.

FIGURE 4.15
Viewing a video on the iPod.

Using Your iPod's Extras

The fifth-generation iPod also comes with a variety of "extras," special features that some users might find interesting or useful. Table 4.4 details these extras.

note Learn more about viewing videos on your iPod in Chapter 11, "Videos."

Table 4.4	5G iPod Extras	
Extra	**Location**	**Description**
Clock	Extras > Clock	Displays current time and date
Games	Extras > Games	Plays iPod games
Contacts	Extras > Contacts	Displays contact information (either manually entered or imported from another program)
Calendar	Extras > Calendar	Displays a monthly calendar
Notes	Extras > Notes	Lets you enter notes for storage and display on your iPod
Stopwatch	Extras > Stopwatch	Lets you use the iPod as a timer or stopwatch
Screen Lock	Extras > Screen Lock	Lets you lock your iPod so that others can't use it

For example, to use your iPod as a timer, select Extras > Stopwatch > Timer. This displays the timer screen, shown in Figure 4.16. Click Start to start the timer; the time now starts counting. Click Pause to stop the timer, or Lap to start timing a new lap. (This is a useful feature for runners and joggers.)

FIGURE 4.16

Using the iPod's built-in timer.

Configuring the 5G iPod

To get the most out of your iPod, you need to delve into the unit's Settings menu. It's here that you can configure the iPod to look, sound, and act precisely the way you want.

Here are some of the more common configuration options you may want to make to your iPod:

- To set or reset the date and time on your iPod, select Settings > Date & Time > Set Date & Time, and then use the Click Wheel to change the settings, as shown in Figure 4.17. To set your iPod's time zone, select Settings > Date & Time > Set Time Zone. To change the iPod from 12-hour to 24-hour (military) time display, select Settings > Date & Time > Time. And to display the current time as part of the general now playing display, select Settings > Date & Time > Time in Title > On.

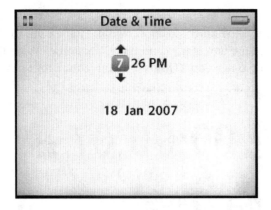

FIGURE 4.17

Setting the date and time on your iPod.

■ To configure how long the iPod's backlight stays lit after making a selection or playing a new song, select Settings > Backlight Timer, and then select a duration—from 2 seconds to Always On. (Remember, the longer the backlight is lit, the faster your iPod battery will be drained.)

■ To adjust the brightness of the iPod display, select Settings > Brightness, and then use the Click Wheel to set the brightness level.

■ To turn the iPod's "click" sound on or off, select Settings > Clicker.

■ To set the maximum volume level of your iPod (to prevent hearing damage), select Settings > Volume Limit, and then use the Click Wheel to set a specific volume level, as shown in Figure 4.18.

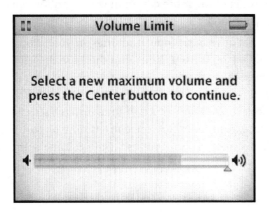

FIGURE 4.18

Setting the maximum volume level for your iPod.

■ To standardize the volume level between songs, select Settings > Sound Check > On. (Setting this option to Off will cause each song to play at its original level—which might vary wildly between tracks.)

caution Volume leveling may negatively impact the audio quality of some songs—particularly those that need their volume levels lowered.

■ To use the iPod's built-in equalizer to fine-tune the iPod's sound quality, select Settings > EQ, and then select a specific EQ curve from the list shown in Figure 4.19.

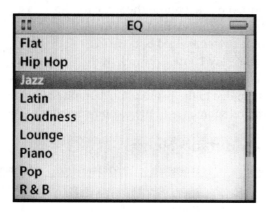

FIGURE 4.19

Choosing an EQ setting for your iPod.

■ To set your iPod for shuffle play (random playback of songs or albums), select Settings > Shuffle, and then select either Songs (to shuffle individual songs) or Albums (to shuffle complete albums).

■ To organize songs from compilation albums, select Settings > Compilations > On. (Setting this option to Off will organize the songs separately by song title or artist, rather than by album.)

■ To hide or redisplay items on the main menu, select Settings > Main Menu, and then toggle Off or On specific items.

■ To change the language used in the iPod display, select Settings > Language, and then choose a new language.

■ Finally, to reset your iPod to its factory default settings, select Settings > Reset All Settings > Reset.

tip You might want to play around with the various EQ settings; this is definitely a personal taste sort of setting. In addition, an EQ setting that sounds good through one set of earphones might not sound so good through a different set of earphones—or through an external speaker.

Using the iPod nano

The iPod nano operates much like the larger iPod, but with slightly fewer features. In particular, the nano lacks the iPod's video viewing capabilty; it also has a smaller (176x132 pixel) display.

caution Resetting your iPod will delete all customization you've performed to this point.

Menu Options

Basic operation of the nano is the same as with the traditional iPod; the Click Wheel has the same five embedded buttons (Select, Menu, Play/Pause, Forward, and Reverse). What is different, however, is the

note Battery life on the iPod nano is longer than on the standard iPod. You'll get 24 hours when playing music, or 5 hours when viewing photos.

menu system, due to the reduced functionality of the nano. Table 4.5 details the menus and submenus of the second-generation iPod nano.

Table 4.5   2G iPod nano Menus

Top Menu	Submenu	Submenu	Submenu	Submenu	Submenu
Music	Playlists	Playlist 1 Playlist 2 …	(Songs in selected playlist)		
	Artists	All Artist 1 Artist 2 …	(Songs by selected artist)		
	Albums	All Album 1 Album 2 …	(Songs on selected album)		
	Compilations	All Compilation 1 Compilation 2 …	(Songs on selected compilation album)		
	Songs	Song 1 Song 2 …			
	Genres	All Genre 1 Genre 2	(Artists in selected genre)	(Albums by selected artist)	(Songs on selected album)

4

Table 4.5   2G iPod nano Menus

Top Menu	Submenu	Submenu	Submenu	Submenu	Submenu
	Composers	Song 1 Song 2 ...			
	Search	(Search screen)			
Photos	Slideshow Settings	Time Per Slide	Manual 2 Seconds 5 Seconds 10 Seconds 20 Seconds		
		Music	Now Playing Off Playlist 1 Playlist 2 ...		
		Repeat	Off/On		
		Shuffle Photos	Off/On		
		Transitions	Off Random Cube across Cube down Dissolve Page flip Push across Push down Radial Swirl Wipe across Wipe down Wipe from center		
	Photo Library	(Picture selection screen)			
Extras	Clock	Date & Time	Alarm Clock	Alarm	Off/On
				Time	Set time
				Sound	Beep Playlist 1 Playlist 2 ...

Table 4.5	**2G iPod nano Menus**				
Top Menu	Submenu	Submenu	Submenu	Submenu	Submenu
			Change City	Continent 1 Continent 2 ...	City 1 City 2 ...
			Daylight Saving Time	Off/On	
			Delete This Clock		
			Sleep Timer	Off 15 Minutes 30 Minutes 60 Minutes 90 Minutes 120 Minutes	
		New Clock	Continent 1 Continent 2 ...	City 1 City 2 ...	
	Games	Brick Music Quiz Parachute Solitaire New game 1 New game 2 ...	(play game)		
	Contacts	Contact 1 Contact 2 ...	(Contact info)		
	Calendar	All	(Selected calendar)		
		To Do	(To do list)		
		Alarms	Beep/Silent/Off		
	Notes	Note 1 Note 2 ...			
	Stopwatch	Timer	(Timer screen)		
	Screen Lock	Set Combination	(Enter New Code screen)		

Table 4.5	**2G iPod nano Menus**				
Top Menu	**Submenu**	**Submenu**	**Submenu**	**Submenu**	**Submenu**
Settings	About	(iPod info)			
	Main Menu	Menu item 1 Menu item 2 ...	Off/On		
	Shuffle	Songs/Albums /Off			
	Repeat	One/All/Off			
	Volume Limit	(Set maximum volume)			
	Backlight Timer	Off 2 Seconds 5 Seconds 10 Seconds 15 Seconds 20 Seconds Always On			
	Brightness	(Set screen brightness)			
	Audiobooks	Slower Normal Faster			
	EQ	Off Acoustic Bass Booster Bass Reducer Classical Dance Deep Electronic Flat Hip Hop Jazz Latin Loudness Lounge Piano Pop			

4

		R&B Rock Small Speakers Spoken Word Treble Booster Treble Reducer Vocal Booster	
Compilations	Off/On	
Sound Check	Off/On	
Clicker	Off/On	
Date & Time	Set Time Zone	Time zone 1 Time zone 2 …
	Set Date & Time	(Set date and time)
	Time	12-hour/ 24-hour
	Time in Title	Off/On
Contacts	Sort	First Last/ Last, First
	Display	First Last/ Last, First
Language	Language 1 Language 2 …	
Legal	(Apple legal notice)	
Reset All Settings	Cancel Reset	
Shuffle Songs		
Now Playing	(Currently playing song)	

Basic Operations

Using the nano is identical to using the larger iPod. Use the Music menu to play music, the Photos menu to view digital photos, and so on. All configuration options are identical between the two units, as well. Syncing is also the same; the nano both recharges and automatically syncs files when connecting to your PC.

Using the iPod shuffle

The one iPod that's significantly different in operation from the rest of the family is the iPod shuffle. The second-generation shuffle has no display and uses a five-button control pad rather than the traditional Click Wheel.

> **tip** The only thing you might want to do differently when syncing your iPod nano, depending on the size of your Music library, is manually sync your music within iTunes. If your Music library is larger than the capacity of your nano, you'll need to manually select which songs to copy. Learn more in Chapter 5.

Using the Control Pad

As you can see in Figure 4.20, the control pad on the iPod shuffle consists of five buttons, with no scrolling surface.

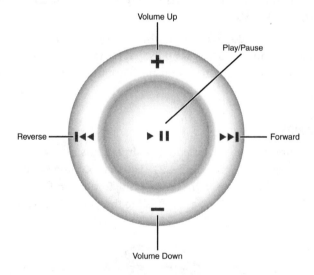

FIGURE 4.20
The iPod shuffle control pad.

Table 4.6	2G iPod shuffle Control Pad Buttons	
Button	**Position**	**Function**
Play/Pause	Center	Toggles between play and pause modes.
Volume Up	12 o'clock (top)	Raises the volume level.
Volume Down	6 o'clock (bottom)	Lowers the volume level.
Forward	3 o'clock (right)	Press once to skip to next track; press and hold to fast-forward through the current track.
Reverse	9 o'clock (left)	Press once to skip to the start of the current track; press twice to skip to the previous track; press and hold to reverse through the current track.

The iPod shuffle needs only these five buttons because it only does one thing—play music. Unlike the iPod and iPod nano, the iPod shuffle does not display photos or play videos, nor does it let you manage contacts, play games, or use it as a stopwatch. All it does is play music, so all you need are basic music transport controls.

And, because it doesn't have a display, you don't need a scroll wheel to scroll through menu options or song lists. It plays songs in random order, with no input from you other than starting, stopping, or moving back and forth from song to song.

Basic Operations

In addition to the control pad, the shuffle has two switches on the bottom of the unit, as shown in Figure 4.21. The first of these switches is the On/Off switch, on the bottom right of the unit. To turn on the shuffle, slide the On/Off switch to the right. To turn it off, slide the On/Off switch to the left.

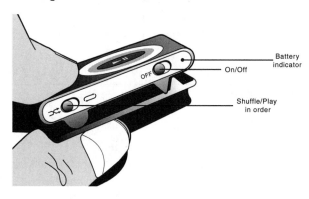

FIGURE 4.21

The switches on the bottom of the iPod shuffle.

To play songs on the shuffle, just plug in your earphones and click the Play/Pause button on the control pad. To stop playback, press the Play/Pause button again. Use the top and bottom buttons to raise or lower the volume.

Playback can be random, or in order (as determined by the playlist order you arranged within the iTunes software). To shuffle in random order, move the Shuffle switch on the bottom left of the unit to the left. To play songs in playlist order, move the Shuffle switch to the right.

Syncing, Charging, and Battery Life

Like the other iPod models, you recharge the iPod shuffle by connecting it to a USB port on your PC. The connecting cable plugs into the docking unit shown in Figure 4.22. Insert the shuffle into the dock, and then plug the docking unit to your PC's USB port.

FIGURE 4.22

The iPod shuffle sitting in its dock—it actually inserts upside down! (Photo courtesy of Apple.)

The shuffle also syncs to your PC when it's connected. As with the nano, you'll want to manually determine which songs you transfer to the shuffle; the 1GB second-generation model can hold about 240 songs.

The 2G iPod shuffle gets about 12 hours per battery charge. There's a battery indicator light (actually a small LED) on the bottom of the shuffle, next to the power switch. It glows green when the battery is fully charged, orange when the charge is about half-spent, and red when the battery is dangerously low. Unfortunately, the LED

> **tip**
>
> iTunes offers an Autofill function that's ideal for randomly adding tunes to your iPod shuffle. Learn more in Chapter 5.

only lights for a few seconds after you turn on the shuffle—which means you have to turn it off and then back on to check the battery life during playback.

Using the iPod with the iTunes Software

As you can see, much of the functionality of the iPod is dependent on the accompanying iTunes software. You use iTunes to sync all the media files on your computer with your iPod; the iTunes software is also used to create playlists, manage the files on your iPod, and purchase and download music and videos from the iTunes Store.

In fact, the iTunes software is so important, it commands a whole chapter by itself. So, turn the page to learn more about using the iTunes program—and getting the most out of your iPod!

4

5

Using the iTunes Software

The iPod is a great little portable music player—once it's loaded up with music. The job of managing the music on your iPod is handled by the iTunes software program that runs on both the Windows and Mac platforms. The iTunes software organizes all the digital media on your PC, facilitates the ripping of music from CD and the burning of music to CD, manages the downloading of music and videos from Apple's iTunes Store, and handles the transfer of digital media files from your PC to your iPod. It's all accomplished with easy-to-use operation and a very elegant interface.

To manage the music, photos, and videos on your iPod, therefore, you have to master the iTunes software. Fortunately, it's easy to do.

Navigating the iTunes Software

The iTunes program is free; you download it from Apple's website (www.apple.com/itunes/download/). Separate versions are available for both Windows and Macintosh computers.

The current version of the iTunes software, as of this writing, is iTunes 7. If you're using an older version of the program, you should go to Apple's website to download the latest version.

> **note** iTunes also drives the music function of Apple TV. Learn more about using Apple TV to play music on your home entertainment system in Chapter 14, "Using Your iPod in the Living Room."

The iTunes Interface

As you can see in Figure 5.1, the basic iTunes interface is relatively simple. The interface is divided into six main areas:

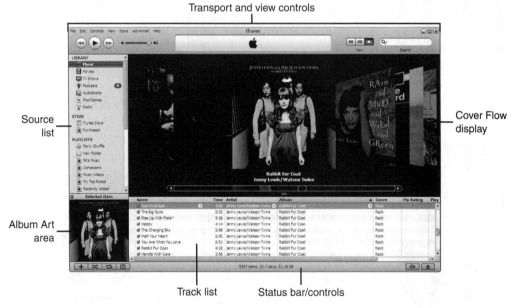

Transport and view controls

Source list

Cover Flow display

Album Art area

Track list

Status bar/controls

FIGURE 5.1
The iTunes program window.

- ■ **Transport and view controls**, located at the top of the iTunes window, also hosts the program's menu bar, now playing display, and search box.
- ■ **Source list**, located at the left of the window, used to access various parts of your iTunes media library—and the iTunes Store.
- ■ **Album Art area**, an optional area at the bottom of the Source pane that displays cover art for the currently-playing song.

■ **Cover Flow display**, available in
the Cover Flow view only (enabled
by clicking the rightmost view button next to the Search box), displays album covers for all the tracks
in your iTunes library.

> **note** The window shown
> in Figure 5.1 is just
> one "look" presented by the
> iTunes software. As you'll learn
> later in this chapter, what you see
> in the iTunes window depends on
> what view you've selected and on
> what type of media you're viewing.

■ **Track list**, below the album art display, displays all the tracks in your
library.

■ **Status bar/controls**, located at the very bottom of the iTunes window,
hosts a variety of auxiliary controls.

Let's look at each of these parts of the window separately.

Transport and View Controls

At the very top of the iTunes window are the transport and view controls,
shown in Figure 5.2. From left to right, here's what you find in this section:

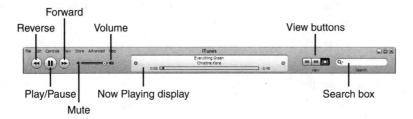

FIGURE 5.2

iTunes' transport and view controls.

■ **Transport controls—reverse, play/pause, forward**. Use these buttons
to control music and video playback. The Play/Pause button starts and
pauses playback, and the reverse and forward controls move you back
and forward through the tracks.

■ **Volume controls**. The slider controls volume up (right) and down (left).
The little speaker icon to the left of the volume control is the mute control; click it to quickly mute the sound. The speaker icon to the right of
the volume control quickly raises the sound to the maximum level.

■ **Now Playing display**. This display, in the center of the top section, displays information about the currently playing track—song title, artist,
album, elapsed time, and time remaining. This section can also display
a graphic equalizer, as shown in Figure 5.3; just click the right-arrow
on the left side of the display.

FIGURE 5.3

iTunes' graphic equalizer display.

■ **View buttons**. These buttons let you switch between three distinct program views. The right button displays the cover flow view, which was shown in Figure 5.1. The middle button displays the album view, where tracks are grouped by album. The left button displays the list view, where tracks can be sorted by name, time, album, artist, genre, and so forth.

■ **Search box**. This is where you search for media in your library; just enter one or more keywords, then press Enter. (Click the down arrow on the left side of the box to restrict your search to artist, album, composer, or song—or, when searching videos, to titles only.)

At the top of the iTunes window is a standard menu bar. Click any menu item to display a corresponding pull-down menu.

Source List

You navigate the sections of your iTunes collection via the Source list at the left of the iTunes window, shown in Figure 5.4. By default, the Source list is divided into three sections:

FIGURE 5.4

iTunes' Source pane.

■ **Library**, which lets you access various types of media files stored on your PC—music, movies, TV shows, Podcasts, and the like

> **note** A fourth section, for *your* iPod, appears in the Source pane when your iPod is connected to your computer.

■ **Store**, which provides access to the online iTunes Store

■ **Playlists**, which displays all the music playlists you've created

The main iTunes window changes when you make different selections in the Source pane. For example, selecting Music in the Library section displays a list of your stored songs; selecting iTunes Store in the Store section displays the main page of the iTunes Store; and selecting any playlist in the Playlists section displays the contents of that playlist.

> **tip** By default, the Library section of the Source list only shows items for Music, Movies, TV Shows, Podcasts, and Radio. To display additional items (Audiobooks and iPod Games), select Edit > Preferences, select the General tab, and then click the desired items.

Album Art Area

At the bottom of the Source list, you can opt to display the Album Art or Now Playing window. This is a small area that displays the cover for the currently playing song or album, or a thumbnail preview of the selected video file. You turn this area on or off by View > Hide Artwork or View > Show Artwork.

Cover Flow Display

When you're viewing music, movies, or TV shows in the iTunes library, you can opt to view album art for each item in iTunes' Cover Flow view. We talk more about this view later in this chapter. When you select the Cover Flow view (by clicking the Cover Flow button at the top of the iTunes window), you can "flip" through the albums in your media library, much as you would in a real-world record store. Click any album in the flow to highlight that album, or use the scrollbar beneath the display to scroll through all the albums.

> **tip** You can change the size of the Cover Flow display by using your mouse to grab the small resizing handle beneath the Cover Flow slider and drag it up or down. You can also resize the Source list by dragging the right side of the panel with your mouse and moving it left or right.

5

Track List

Below the album art display (in Cover Flow view), or displayed in the full window in other views, you see a list of all the tracks in your library. This list can be sorted by name, time, artist, album, genre,

tip You can edit which columns are displayed by right-clicking any column header and then checking the columns you want to see.

and so forth, by clicking the appropriate column header. You can also manually resize any column by clicking and dragging the edge of the desired column header with your mouse.

Status Bar/Controls

At the bottom of the iTunes window is the status bar, shown in Figure 5.5. In addition to display information about your entire media collection (number of songs, how many hours or days it would take to play all the tracks, and how much total disk space is used), the area of the program window houses a few key controls:

Repeat

Create a playlist

Library data

Eject disc

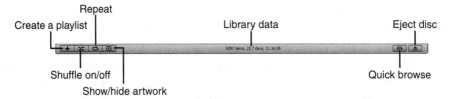

9297 items, 23.7 days, 31.16 GB

Shuffle on/off

Quick browse

Show/hide artwork

FIGURE 5.5

iTunes' status bar.

- **Create a playlist**. Click this button to create a new playlist. A new playlist will appear as "untitled playlist"; click to name the playlist however you like.

- **Shuffle on/off**. Click this button on or off to activate or deactivate iTunes' shuffle (random play) function.

- **Repeat**. Click once to repeat an entire playlist, or click twice to repeat a single item.

- **Show/hide artwork**. Click this button to display the album artwork for the currently playing track. This opens the Album Art area at the

note When your iPod is connected to your PC, the eject disc control is replaced with an eject iPod button. And when you're viewing a playlist, the status bar displays a Burn Disc button.

lower left of the iTunes window. If you're viewing a video, this displays the currently playing video in the same panel. (Click the button a second time to hide the artwork panel.)

- **Quick browse.** Click this button to display a series of panels (Genre, Artist, Album) at the top of the iTunes window, as shown in Figure 5.6. Use these panels to drill down through the contents of your iTunes library; select a genre, then an artist within that genre, then an album by that artist, and then the contents for that album are displayed in the track list below. (Click the button a second time to hide the quick browse panels.)

FIGURE 5.6
The quick browse panels in the iTunes window.

> **caution** The Quick Browse option is not available in Cover Flow view. You'll still see the button there, but it's not operational.

- **Eject disc.** Click this button to eject a CD or DVD from your computer's drive.

Displaying the Mini Store

If you're a frequent visitor to the iTunes Store, you can have constant access to store contents via the Mini Store pane in the iTunes window. As you can see in Figure 5.7, the Mini Store is a short pane at the bottom of the iTunes window that offers quick access to the most popular iTunes Store sections—or, if you have a track selected in your iTunes library, other songs and albums by that artist.

FIGURE 5.7
The iTunes Mini Store.

To display the Mini Store, select View > Show Mini Store. To hide the Mini Store, select View > Hide Mini Store.

Displaying the Mini Player

Here's something else neat about the iTunes program—it doesn't have to be maximized on your desktop to work. You can minimize iTunes into a special Mini Player configuration that floats on your computer desktop.

tip You can also switch between the Mini Player and full iTunes player by pressing Ctrl+M on your keyboard.

To switch to the Mini Player, select Advanced > Switch to Mini Player. As you can see in Figure 5.8, the Mini Player contains a bare minimum of controls and information—play/pause, reverse, forward transport controls along with the now playing display. Return to the full iTunes window by clicking the maximize button on the left side of the Mini Player.

FIGURE 5.8

The iTunes Mini Player.

Configuring the iTunes Program

Most consumers can use the iTunes program with its default settings and be quite satisfied. However, for full control over your media collection, you might want to play with some configuration settings.

You configure the iTunes program by selecting Edit > Preferences. This displays the multiple-tabbed dialog box shown in Figure 5.9. Table 5.1 details the configuration options for each tab.

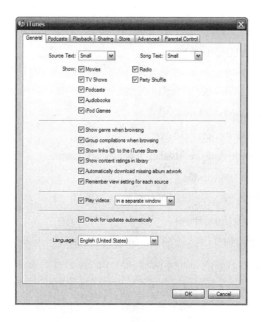

FIGURE 5.9
Configuring the iTunes software.

Table 5.1	iTunes Configuration Options
Tab	**Configuration Options**
General	Text size
	Items displayed in Library section of Source pane (Movies, TV Shows, Podcasts, Audiobooks, iPod Games, Radio, Party Shuffle)
	Show genre when browsing
	Group compilations when browsing
	Show links to the iTunes Store
	Show content ratings in library
	Automatically download missing album artwork
	Remember view setting for each source
	Play videos in the main window, in a separate window, full screen, or full screen with visuals
	Check for updates automatically
	Display language
Podcasts	Check for new episodes every hour, every day, every week, or manually

Table 5.1   iTunes Configuration Options

Tab	Configuration Options
	When new episodes are available, download the most recent one, download all, or do nothing
	Keep all episodes, all unplayed episodes, most recent episode, or the last 2–10 episodes
Playback	Activate crossfade playback
	Activate the Sound Enhancer
	Activate Sound Check (standardized playback volume)
	Adjust Smart Shuffle
	Shuffle songs, albums, or groupings
Sharing	Look for shared libraries
	Share iPod library on local network (entire library or selected playlists)
Store	Buy and download using 1-click (automatically charges your account)
	Buy using a shopping cart (lets you add or remove items before purchasing)
	Automatically download pre-purchased content (for season pass TV episodes)
	Automatically create playlists when buying song collections
	Load complete preview before playing (for slow Internet connections)
Advanced	**General tab:**
	iTunes Music folder location
	Keep iTunes Music folder organized
	Copy files to iTunes Music folder when adding to library
	Use iTunes as default player for audio files
	Streaming buffer size
	Look for remote speakers connected with AirTunes
	Keep Mini Player on top of other windows
	Show iTunes icon in system tray
	Visualizer size
	Display visualizer full screen
	Importing tab:
	On CD insert, show CD, begin playing, ask to import CD, import CD, or import CD and eject
	Import using AAC Encoder, AIFF Encoder, Apple Lossless Encoder, MP3 Encoder, or Wave Encoder (determines file types for ripped music)

5

Tab	Configuration Options
Table 5.1 iTunes Configuration Options	
	Setting (audio quality for ripped music)
	Play songs while importing or converting
	Automatically retrieve CD track names from Internet
	Create filenames with track number
	Use error correction when reading Audio CDs (for problem rips)
	Burning tab:
	Preferred speed
	Disk format: Audio CD, MP3 CD, or Data CD or DVD (for Audio CD—gap between songs)
Parental Control	Disable sources (Podcasts, radio, iTunes Store, shared music)
	Restrict iTunes Store content (explicit content, movies by rating, TV shows by rating)

We address specific configuration options as necessary throughout this book consumers can use the iTunes program.

Managing Your Music Collection

Most consumers can use the iTunes program users use iTunes most of the time to manage their digital music collection—and to sync that collection with their iPods. Even if you don't use iTunes with an iPod, the program is an elegant music manager and player, one of the best available today.

Listening to Music

As consumers can use the iTunes program just noted, iTunes functions quite well as a standalone music player program. You can use iTunes to organize all the music on your computer's hard drive and to play that music on your PC.

To play a song in the iTunes library, you can either navigate to the track (by genre, artist, album, or song name) and click the Play button or just double-click the track. Playback now starts, with the track info display in the now playing area at the top of the iTunes window.

Alternatively, you can play an entire album by switching to Album or Cover Flow view and double-clicking the album cover. You can also play all the tracks by an artist by switching to List view, sorting by artist, and then double-clicking the first song by that artist. The same technique is used to play all tracks in a particular genre; sort by genre, and then double-click the first song in the list. For any of these approaches, make sure you have the shuffle feature turned off; otherwise, iTunes will next jump to a random track not by the same artist, album, or genre.

After you begin playback, you can pause that playback by clicking the Pause button. Click the Play button to resume playback.

To move to the next track in a list, click the Forward button in the transport controls. To return to a previous track, click the Reverse button. You also can use the forward and back arrows on your keyboard to advance and return to tracks.

To repeat one or more tracks, select the track(s), and then click the Repeat button at the bottom of the iTunes window. To shuffle through selected tracks (or a playlist) in random order, select the tracks or playlist, and then click the Shuffle button.

Adjust playback volume with the volume control slider at the top of the iTunes windows. To quickly mute the sound, click the speaker icon to the left of the volume slider.

caution If iTunes only plays one song at a time (that is, never advances to a second track when you're playing a list of songs), chances are you've inadvertently *unchecked* all the songs in your library; you need all your tracks checked for them to be played. To remedy this situation, select Music in the Library section of the Source pane, and then select Edit > Select All. (And watch for tracks you've unchecked in a particular playlist; uncheck a song in one place in iTunes, and it becomes unchecked throughout the entire library.)

tip You can also choose to play songs by playlist. Learn more about playlists in Chapter 7, "Music."

Viewing Your Music Collection

As previously noted, iTunes lets you view your music collection in a number of ways. Which view you use is purely a personal preference.

The coolest view, in my opinion, is the new Cover Flow view shown in Figure 5.10. This displays your music as a series of album covers, which you can then "flip" through

tip You can select multiple tracks by highlighting them with your mouse (hold down the Ctrl key when selecting multiple tracks) or by checking the check boxes next to each track name. Pressing Shift+Alt while selecting tracks will allow you to select a large group of tracks quickly.

using your mouse. Click any album to highlight it, or use the slider beneath the covers to flip back and forth. The tracks of the current album display at the top of the Track list below the cover flow; if you select a song from another album in the Track list, the cover flow switches to highlight that track's album.

> **note** In iTunes version 7.1, click the button next to the cover flow slider to view the cover flow artwork full screen.

FIGURE 5.10

Cover Flow view.

As cool-looking as Cover Flow view is, it isn't always the most useful view. Many users prefer to group their music by album, while displaying more track information. This is possible in the Album view, shown in Figure 5.11. In this view, each album displays separately (sorted by album name), with the contents of each album listed to the side.

> **tip** By default, the Cover Flow view displays tracks grouped by album. However, if you select a different column header in the track list, the covers will be rearranged by that option. For example, to display tracks by track name, click the Name column; covers for each song in order will now display in the Cover Flow pane.

5

FIGURE 5.11

Album view.

Then there's the standard List view, shown in Figure 5.12. In this view there's no artwork to be seen, just basic track information. You can sort this view by any column, which makes it perhaps the most useful of the three views. Use this view if you want to sort tracks by name, artist, genre, and so on.

FIGURE 5.12

List view.

Finally, you can display information about
any item in your library by right-clicking
the item in the track list and selecting Get
Info. This displays an information dialog
box, like the one in Figure 5.13. The
Summary tab displays the basic information; click the other tabs to view more
details.

tip Multiple sorting is available by album. Click the
Album column once for a standard sort by album title; click
again to sort by album by artist;
click yet again to sort by album
by year.

FIGURE 5.13

Getting more information about a selected item.

Searching for Music

When your music collection gets really large, it becomes more and more difficult to simply browse for tracks. With large music collections, it's often easier
to search for specific tracks, albums, artists, or genres.

Searching in iTunes is accomplished via the search box at the top right of the
program window. Enter one or more keywords, and then press Enter.

By default, iTunes searches on all fields. So, for example, if you searched for
"country," you'd get a list of tracks with the word *country* in the title, and all
songs in the Country genre and artists with the word *country* in their name.
You can narrow the search to a specific field, however, by clicking the down
arrow next to the search icon on the left side of the search box; you can
search by artist, album, composer, or song.

When you press Enter, iTunes returns a list of matching tracks in the track list. To return to a full track list, click the X icon in the search box; this cancels the search process.

Using the Equalizer

The sound quality on many PCs is iffy, at best. Of course, you can improve the sound quality by upgrading your PC's speakers or switching to a set of quality earphones—or you can utilize iTunes' built-in equalizer.

An equalizer "equalizes" the sound by boosting or lowering specific frequency bands. For example, if your PC has speakers with a wimpy bass response, you can improve the bass by boosting the lower frequencies with the equalizer.

To use iTunes' equalizer, select View > Show Equalizer. This displays the floating equalizer window shown in Figure 5.14. By default, the equalizer is set for a flat response—that is, all frequencies set to their 0dB position.

FIGURE 5.14
iTunes' equalizer.

You adjust the equalizer by moving the sliders for each frequency band up or down. Move a slider up to boost that frequency band; move the slider down to cut or lower that frequency band. So if you want more treble, for example, raise the right-most sliders (typically for the 4K, 8K, and 16K frequency bands).

Alternatively, you can choose from a variety of equalization presets. Just click the blue arrow button in the top center of the equalizer (set to Flat by default); this dis-

tip iTunes also includes a Sound Enhancer feature. When activated, the Sound Enhancer widens the stereo soundfield, making your music sound "bigger" than it would normally. You activate the Sound Enhancer by selecting Edit > Preferences, selecting the Playback tab, and then checking the Sound Enhancer option. You can increase or decrease the size of the stereo soundfield by moving the slider to the left or right.

plays a menu full of equalization presets, from Acoustic to Vocal Booster. For example, the Rock preset looks a little like a *V*, with boosts to both the low and high frequencies, while the middle frequencies stay flat in the valley of the *V*.

Cross-Fading Songs

By default, iTunes works like most music player programs and plays each song as a separate audio file, putting a little empty space between each file played. This is fine when playing most albums and playlists, but not so good if you have an album where each song runs into the next—which is the case with many dance, live, and concept albums. When you want to play back an album with no gaps between the songs, you want to turn on the new cross-fade feature built in to iTunes 7.

iTunes' cross-fade control skips the gaps between songs and fades one song into the next. To activate cross-fade, select Edit > Preferences, select the Playback tab (shown in Figure 5.15), and then check the Crossfade Playback option. You can adjust the timing of the cross-fades with the accompanying slider.

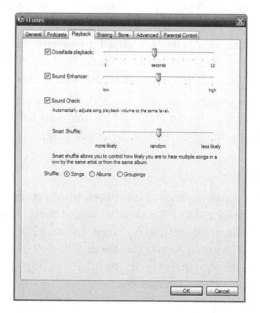

FIGURE 5.15

Adjusting iTunes' cross-fade setting.

Standardizing Playback Volume

If you're sometimes annoyed when one song plays considerably louder or softer than the next, you'll appreciate another useful setting found on the Playback tab of the Preferences dialog box. iTunes' Sound Check feature essentially balances the sound level for all songs played, so that no one song stands out as being louder or softer than the next. To turn on Sound Check, select Edit > Preferences, select the Playback tab, and then check the Sound Check option.

Changing the Way Songs Shuffle

Many users prefer to shuffle the playback of songs in random order. However, what you think of as random might differ slightly from how iTunes does it.

You see, pure random playback is just that—purely random. That means you're as likely to hear two songs from the same album or artist in a row as you are to hear two songs from completely different albums or artists. (It's like the odds of twice flipping a coin and getting heads both times; you're as likely to get two heads in a row as you are to get heads and then tails.) Unfortunately, when you hear two songs in a row from the same album or artist, it doesn't necessarily sound random to you.

For that reason, iTunes lets you adjust the perceived randomness of its shuffle mode via its Smart Shuffle feature. Smart Shuffle lets you determine the likelihood of hearing multiple songs in a row from the same artist or album.

To adjust the perceived randomness, select Edit > Preferences, select the Playback tab, then adjust the Smart Shuffle slider left (more likely to hear multiple songs) or right (less likely). The middle position offers true randomness.

Showing the Visualizer

When you're playing music with iTunes, what you see by default is what you normally see—the Cover Flow view or track listings. If you want to see something a little more interesting onscreen, check out iTunes' Visualizer. As you can see in Figure 5.16, the Visualizer is a trippy full-window visualization, reminiscent of 1960s-era light shows.

tip The Playback tab of the Preferences dialog box also includes settings for what exactly iTunes shuffles—individual songs, complete albums, or groupings of multiple selected songs.

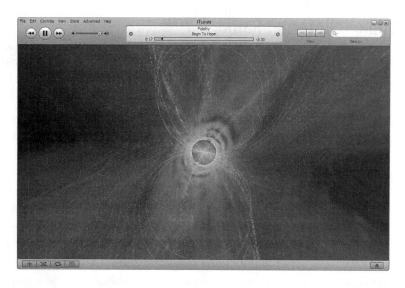

FIGURE 5.16
The iTunes Visualizer.

To activate the Visualizer, select View > Show Visualizer, or press Ctrl+T. To turn off the Visualizer, select View > Hide Visualizer, or press Ctrl+T again.

> **tip**
> You can adjust the size of the Visualizer, or opt to show it full screen, by selecting Edit > Preferences, selecting the Advanced tab, and then selecting the General tab.

Manually Adding Music to iTunes

By default, the iTunes software should recognize all new music you add to your PC. That's because iTunes automatically monitors your PC's music folders.

On the rare occasion when music stored on your PC doesn't appear in iTunes, you can manually add those music files to your iTunes library. You can add both individual files and complete folders.

To add an individual music track to the iTunes library, select File > Add File to Library. To add all the contents of a folder, select File > Add Folder to Library. You also can drag and drop tracks from My Documents or a similar folder to the music library.

Listening to Internet Radio

In addition to playing music stored on your hard disk, iTunes can also play music streamed from Internet radio stations. A variety of Internet radio stations are listed within the iTunes program; playing a station is as simple as selecting a station (while your computer is connected to the Internet, of course).

> **tip** Streaming Internet radio sounds best when you have a broadband cable or DSL Internet connection. Listening to Internet radio over a dial-up connection can sometimes result in lower-quality sound with intermittent stuttering and pauses.

To select an Internet radio station, select Radio from the Library selection of the Source pane. The iTunes window changes to show a list of radio formats—50s/60s Pop, 70s/80s Pop, Alt/Modern Rock, and the like. When you double-click a format name, you see all available stations within that format, as shown in Figure 5.17. Double-click a station name to begin streaming playback.

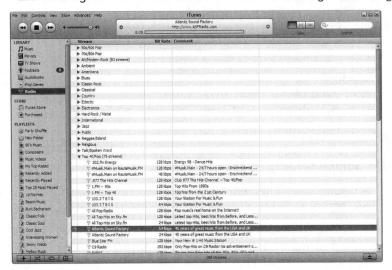

FIGURE 5.17
Internet radio via iTunes.

Viewing Videos

The iTunes program can also be used to play videos you've downloaded from the Internet or purchased from the iTunes Store. Videos are organized into one of two categories: Movies or TV Shows. Or, if you purchase a music video, it's categorized within the Music section of your iTunes library.

In the iTunes window, you can view your videos in any of the three standard views, including the cool-looking Cover Flow view. Within each view, individual episodes of a TV show are grouped together, as shown in Figure 5.18.

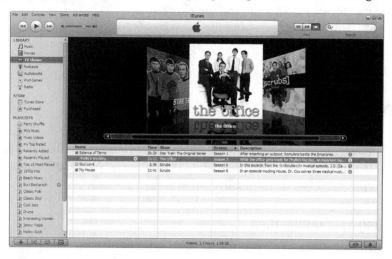

FIGURE 5.18

Displaying downloaded videos in iTunes.

To play a video, select Movies or TV Shows from the Library section of the Source pane (or select the appropriate music video from the Music section of your library), and then double-click the video. The video opens in a new window on your desktop, as shown in Figure 5.19.

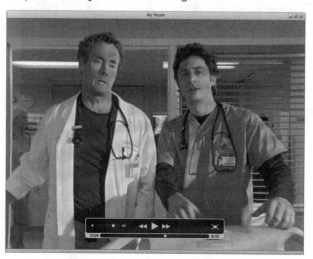

FIGURE 5.19

Viewing a video with iTunes.

To pause playback, hover your mouse over the window until the transport controls display, and then click the Pause button; resume playback by clicking the Play button. Fast-forward or rewind the video by clicking and holding down the forward or rewind buttons.

tip To view the video full-screen, click the full-screen button to the right of the transport controls. Return to window viewing by clicking the full-screen button again.

Syncing Your iPod

After you have music, movies, and more stored and organized in the iTunes library, you use the iTunes software to sync your media files with your iPod. The syncing process is automatic to some extent, although there are a lot of things you can do manually.

Displaying Basic Information

The basic sync process is the same for all iPod models. Connect the sync cable to the bottom of the iPod (or to the docking unit if you have an iPod shuffle) and to a USB port on your PC. Your PC should automatically recognize the iPod and launch the iTunes software. Within iTunes, a new Devices section appears in the Source pane, with your iPod listed. In addition, the main window changes to display information about your iPod in a series of tabs, as shown in Figure 5.20.

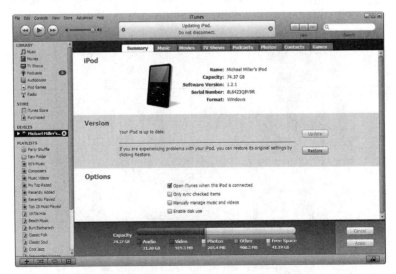

FIGURE 5.20
Viewing information about your connected iPod in iTunes.

The Summary tab displays the name, capacity, version information, serial number, and format (Windows or Mac) for your iPod. In addition, the Version section lets you update your iPod's firmware or restore the iPod to its factory condition (useful if you have corrupted data or some sort of operational problem).

At the bottom of the Summary tab is a visual representation of what's currently stored on your iPod. You'll see how much total space is available, how much space is devoted to each type of media (audio, video, photos, and other), and how much free space is left to use.

Configuring Sync Options

The Options section of the Summary tab determines how your iPod syncs to your PC. The following options are available:

- **Open iTunes when this iPod is connected**, the default operational mode.
- **Only sync checked items**, which is useful when you're syncing an iPod nano or iPod shuffle that has less storage capacity than you have songs stored on your PC. When this option is selected, only those tracks you've checked in your iTunes library are copied to your iPod. When this option is not selected, all the songs in your library are automatically transferred to your iPod—which works well if you have a larger-capacity iPod (or a smaller music library).
- **Manually manage music and videos**, which should be checked if you want to delete files already stored on your iPod.
- **Enable disk use**. Check this option if you want to use your iPod as a portable data storage device. (Learn more about this option in Chapter 16, "Using Your iPod as a Portable Storage Device.")

If you have a large-capacity iPod and you want to transfer all the songs on your PC to the iPod, uncheck all but the first option. If you have a smaller-capacity iPod nano or shuffle or want to transfer only selected songs to your iPod, check the first and second options. If you want to manage the music already stored on your iPod, check the first and third options.

Syncing Music

To configure what music files are synced, you need to access the Music tab, shown in Figure 5.21. From here, you can choose to sync all songs and playlists or just selected playlists (those playlists checked in your iTunes library). You can also choose to include music videos in your sync, and whether or not to copy album art from iTunes to your iPod.

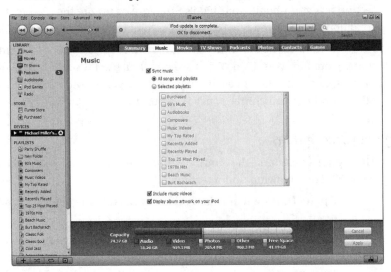

FIGURE 5.21

Selecting music sync options.

Autofilling the iPod shuffle

Syncing the iPod shuffle is slightly different from syncing the regular iPod or iPod nano. This is because the slim 1GB capacity of the shuffle is typically smaller than most music libraries; most users can't automatically load all their music onto the shuffle.

To that end, Apple offers an autofill option when iTunes is connected to an iPod shuffle. When you first connect your iPod shuffle to your computer, the Setup Assistant window (the one that prompts you to name your iPod) offers the option to "automatically choose songs for my iPod." Check this option and iTunes fills your iPod with a random assortment of songs from your library.

This initial autofill serves to fill up your iPod with music on its first connection. You can refill your shuffle with a different assortment of songs any time you connect the shuffle to your PC, however. As you can see in Figure 5.22, the device screen for

tip After you make a change on the Music, Movies, or similar tabs, click the Apply button to register the change and make the new sync.

the shuffle is different from the one for the iPod and iPod nano. There are only two tabs; the Settings tab is the same, but the Contents tab shows the current contents of the shuffle and allows you to autofill the device.

FIGURE 5.22
Autofill options for the iPod shuffle.

To refill your iPod shuffle with music, click the Autofill button at the bottom of the Contents tab. You can opt to autofill from your complete Music library or click the Autofill From button to autofill from a selected playlist. You can also opt to have iTunes choose tracks randomly or weight higher-rated items more heavily in the autofill queue. Check the Replace All Items when Autofilling option to completely change the shuffle's music when syncing.

Alternatively, you can opt to manually select which tracks to sync to your iPod. Go to the Settings tab and select Only Update Checked Songs, and then return to your Music library and check those songs you want to transfer to the shuffle.

Syncing Movies

If you have a video iPod you can configure which movies are synced from the Movies tab, shown in Figure 5.23. From here you can choose to sync all movies, selected movies, or a selected number of unwatched movies. This last option is good if you want to view movies on your iPod that you haven't yet watched.

FIGURE 5.23

Selecting movie sync options.

Syncing TV Shows

If you have a video iPod you can configure which TV shows are synced from the TV Shows tab, shown in Figure 5.24. From here you can choose to sync all episodes of all or selected TV shows, only the most recent episodes, or only a selected number of unwatched episodes.

Syncing Podcasts

Your iPod can also play podcasts downloaded from the iTunes Store. When you select the Podcasts tab, shown in Figure 5.25, you can choose to sync all episodes, all unplayed episodes, or the most recent episodes of all or selected podcasts.

note Which tabs are displayed for your player depends on which type of iPod you have connected. For example, an iPod nano will not display the Movies or TV Shows tabs because it doesn't have video playback capability.

FIGURE 5.24

Selecting TV show sync options.

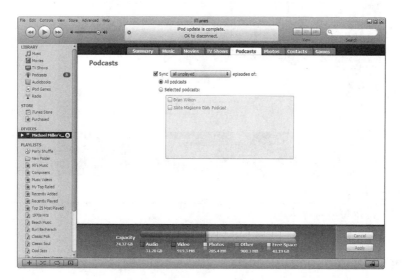

FIGURE 5.25

Selecting podcast sync options.

> **note** Learn more about listening to podcasts in Chapter 8, "Podcasts."

Syncing Photos

If you have an iPod or iPod nano and want to display digital photos on your device, you use the Photos tab to determine which photos are synced to your iPod. But first you want to organize the photos on your PC so that all the photos you want to transfer are stored in the same folder; iTunes can only transfer photos from a single folder to your iPod.

After your photos are organized, select the Photos tab, shown in Figure 5.26. From here, you select which photos to transfer—those organized in Photoshop Elements, those organized as iPod Photos, or those stored in a specific folder on your PC's hard drive. You can also opt to copy full-resolution photos to your iPod; if you don't select this option, iTunes automatically resizes photos to best match the iPod's smaller display (which saves storage space, by the way).

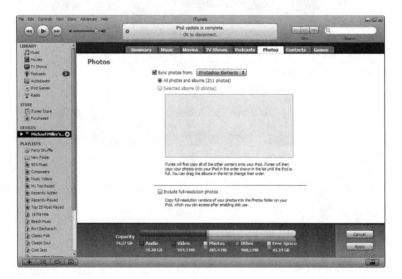

FIGURE 5.26
Selecting photo sync options.

Syncing Contacts and Calendars

If you use your iPod or iPod nano to store contacts or calendars, select the Contacts tab, shown in Figure 5.27 to configure which items are automatically synced. From here you can choose to sync all or selected con-

note Learn more about using your iPod to store and display photos in Chapter 10, "Photos."

tacts from Microsoft Outlook or your Windows Address book, as well as selected calendars created with Microsoft Outlook. (You can also choose whether to include photos with your contacts.)

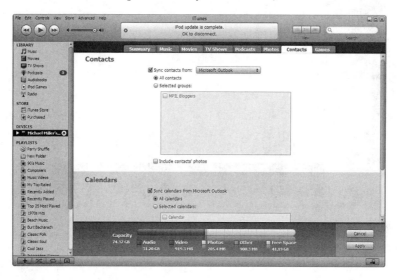

FIGURE 5.27
Selecting contact and calendar sync options.

Syncing Games

Finally, if you use your iPod or iPod nano to play games, you need to select the Games tab, shown in Figure 5.28, to determine which games are automatically synced. From here, you can choose to sync all games or just selected games.

note Learn more about using your iPod with contacts and calendars in Chapter 19, "Using Your iPod as a Calendar/Scheduler."

5

FIGURE 5.28

Selecting sync options for iPod games.

Managing Files on Your iPod

> **note** Learn more about playing games on your iPod in Chapter 12, "Games."

You also use the iTunes software to delete or otherwise manage files already stored on your iPod. It's easy to do, after you have your iPod connected to your PC.

First, you have to configure your iPod for manual syncing. You do this by going to the Summary tab in iTunes and checking the Manually Manage Music and Videos option. Then you click the Apply button.

Next, click the small arrow to the left of your iPod name in the Devices section of the Source pane. This expands the device listing to show all the media stored on your iPod, organized by media type (Music, Movies, and so on) and playlist. Select an item to show all the tracks or videos stored on your iPod in the main iTunes window, as shown in Figure 5.29.

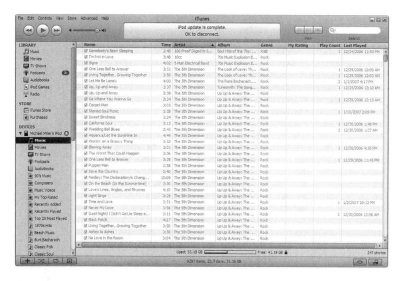

FIGURE 5.29
Managing the iPod's contents in iTunes.

To delete an item from your iPod, simply select it in the Track listing and then press the Del key on your computer keyboard. To edit a track name or other information, click the desired field for the selected track, and then enter new information.

When you're done deleting or editing files on your iPod, it's best to return to the Summary screen and uncheck the Manually Manage Music and Videos option. Remember to click the Apply button when done.

Visiting the iTunes Store

The other important thing that the iTunes software does is provide access to the iTunes Store. In fact, the only way to access the iTunes Store is with the iTunes software. And the iTunes Store is a whole other topic, big enough to warrant its own chapter. So, turn the page and start iTuning in Chapter 6, "Using the iTunes Store."

caution If you delete an item from your iPod but still have the item stored in your computer's iTunes library (and have iTunes configured for automatic sync), the item will be automatically transferred back to your iPod the next time you sync the device. You'll want to delete the track from both your iPod and your iTunes library—or configure iTunes for manual sync and leave the unwanted item unchecked.

Using the iTunes Store

There are several different ways to get music for your iPod. You can rip songs from the CDs you own, you can download MP3 files from file-trading websites, and you can purchase music from Apple's iTunes Store.

The iTunes Store (iTS) has become immensely popular. You can purchase music, movies, TV shows, and more from the store, with music priced at just 99 cents per track. The iTS offers more than 4 million songs, 350 television shows, 250 feature films, and 100,000 podcasts for download.

Navigating the iTunes Store

You access the iTunes Store with the iTunes software, as discussed in Chapter 5, "Using the iTunes Software." After you launch the iTunes software, select iTunes Store in the Store section of the Source pane.

As you can see in Figure 6.1, the main page of the iTS offers access to just about everything the Store offers. Main sections of the main page include the following:

FIGURE 6.1
The main page of the iTunes Store.

- **iTunes Store contents**. Quick links to Music, Movies, TV Shows, Music Videos, Audiobooks, Podcasts, iPod Games, and the new iTunes Latino subsidiary store.

- **New Releases by category**. Music, Movies, TV Shows, Rock, Pop, and R&B/Soul. Click the See All link to view all new releases.

- **Quick Links to key operations**. Browse, Power Search, Account, Buy iTunes Gifts, Redeem (gift cards), and Support.

- **Staff Favorites**. Regular picks by iTunes staffers in the Music, Movies, TV Shows, Audiobooks, and Podcasts categories.

- **Free on iTunes**. The most current free content on the iTunes site.

- **Exclusively on iTunes**. The most recent exclusive content to the iTunes Store.

- **Top Movies**. iTunes' 10 best-selling movie downloads.

- **Top TV Episodes**. iTunes' 10 best-selling television show downloads.

- **Top Music Videos**. iTunes' 10 best-selling music video downloads.

- **Top Songs**. iTunes' 10 best-selling song downloads.

- **Top Albums**. iTunes' 10 best-selling whole-album downloads.

- **Top Audiobooks**. iTune's five best-selling audiobook downloads.

- **Top Podcasts**. iTunes' top five podcast downloads.

There are three navigational buttons at the top left of the main iTunes Store window. Click the back button to return to the previous store page, click the forward button to go to the next store page (after you've clicked the back button), and click the home button to return to the store's main page. In addition, there is a Sign In button at the top right of the window; click this button to sign in to your Apple account.

Creating an Apple Account

Before you can purchase items from the iTunes Store, you have to create an Apple account. You might be prompted to do this the first time you click to purchase, or you can create your account manually, at any time.

To create an Apple account, click the Sign In button at the top right of the iTunes window. When prompted, click the Create New Account button. (If you already have an Apple account, you should instead enter your account ID and password.)

tip Different versions of the iTunes Store are available for different countries. Go to the bottom of the iTS main page, click the My Store button, and select a country from the list. At this writing, the iTunes Store is available in country-specific versions for Austria (Österreich), Australia, Belgium (Belgique), Canada, Denmark, Finland, France, Germany (Deustchland), Greece, Ireland, Italy (Italia), Luxembourg, the Netherlands (Nederland), New Zealand, Norway, Portugal, Spain (España), Switzerland (Schweiz), Sweden, the United Kingdom, and, of course, the United States. The look and feel of the iTS main page differs from country to country. (And, while you can browse stores in other countries, you may not be able to make purchases from them, due to country-specific availability and copyright issues.)

There are three steps to creating an Apple account:

1. Agree to the iTunes Store terms of service.

2. Enter your email address, desired password, security question and answer, and month and date of birth, as shown in Figure 6.2. (And choose whether you want to receive Apple's email promos, of course.)

3. Enter your credit card, debit card, or PayPal information—which is how you'll be billed for your iTS purchases.

caution You also need an Apple account before the iTunes software can download album art from the iTunes Store.

6

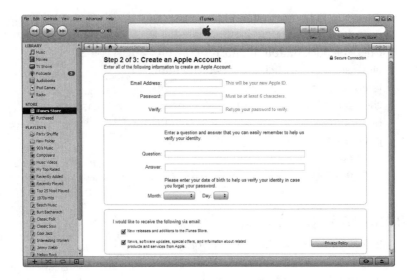

FIGURE 6.2
Creating an Apple account—necessary to use the iTunes Store.

There is no cost to create your Apple account. The only charges billed to your credit card come when you make purchases from the iTunes Store.

tip If you're an AOL subscriber, you can also log in to the iTunes Store with your AOL account info.

To manage your Apple account, click the Account link in the Quick Links box on the iTS home page. From here, you can change your method of payment, nickname, and so forth. You can also use the Apple Account Information page to view your purchase history from the iTunes Store.

iTunes Store Pricing

How much does it cost to purchase items from the iTunes Store? Table 6.1 details the pricing for available products.

Table 6.1 iTunes Store Pricing	
Product	**Price**
Music (single track)	99 cents
Music (complete album)	$7.99 to $14.99

Table 6.1 iTunes Store Pricing	
Product	**Price**
Music videos	$1.99
TV shows (single episode)	$1.99
TV shows (full-season pass)	$29.99 to $39.99
Movies	$9.99 to $14.99
Audiobooks	$4.95 to $31.95
Podcasts	Free
iPod games	$4.99

note The prices in Table 6.1 are for the U.S. iTunes Store. Prices differ by country.

99 CENTS AND NO PROFIT

You know the old marketing adage, give away the razors to sell the blades? This is a tried-and-true strategy, actually adopted by Gillette and Schick, where they give away (or sell for a low price) refillable razors, and then make all their money selling the more-profitable razor blades. You get a razor for free, but you have to keep purchasing blades week-in and week-out. It's a valid strategy.

Apple, however, has embraced a contrary strategy for the iPod. Instead of giving away the iPod (the refillable razor) and making money on all the music sold via the iTunes Store (the high-profit razor blades), Apple essentially gives away the music/blades to make a high profit on its iPod/razor.

Give away the blades? Apple sells all the music in its iTunes Store for 99 cents each. That's not nothing, but it might as well be, in terms of profit. Although Apple collects your 99 cents, it doesn't keep it all. The majority of that 99 cent fee goes directly to the record company that supplies the track—analysts estimate that record labels make any-where from 65 cents to 85 cents per track.(And they're not satisfied

6

with that; the labels have constantly put pressure on Apple to raise its prices.)

In fact, Apple CEO Steve Jobs has admitted that Apple makes virtually no profit from its online download service. ("We would like to break even/make a little bit of money," Jobs said, "but it's not a money maker.") Yes, Apple does make a small gross profit per track sold, but that money goes to pay for the servers and bandwidth that host and serve the tracks in the iTunes Store.

Instead, Apple makes its money where it always has—on its hardware. The iPod is a profitable product, with Apple making more than 50% gross margin on the core product. (Research firm Jeffries and Company estimates that a $299 30GB iPod costs Apple about $143.50 in parts, before manufacturing, marketing, and the like.) Obviously, Apple's margins are cut a tad when it sells through the traditional retail channel, but even then Apple allows retailers very slim profit margins, when compared to similar consumer electronics products.

Even if Apple retained all the revenue from its iTunes Store sales, which it doesn't, it would have to sell 150 tracks to a consumer to equal the profit generated by the sale of the host iPod. Given that Apple realizes less than 20 cents profit per track sold, that's more like 600 tracks necessary to equal the profit from a single iPod. (And, surveys have shown, most users only have 20-30 iTunes-purchased tracks on their iPods—which means that the majority of iPod music comes from ripping CDs, not from purchasing from the iTunes Store.)

So the iTunes Store, the darling of the digital media industry, is nothing more than a loss leader for Apple. It offers tunes in the store purely as a come-on to entice consumers to buy more iPods—and the iPod is where Apple makes its real money. Give away the blades, make a ton of money on the razors! That's Apple's strategy.

Searching the iTunes Store

To find items for download, you can either browse through the categories presented in the main page iTunes Store box or you can search for specific items. Given the millions of items available in the iTS, searching is often the most efficient method.

The easiest way to search the iTunes Store is to use the search box in the upper-right corner of the iTunes software window. (Yes, this is the same search box you use to search your own music library; when you have the iTunes Store selected in the search pane, it reverts to an iTS-specific search.) Just enter one or more keywords (such as a song or artist name) and press Enter. If you're searching for music, tracks that match your query display in the bottom half of the main iTunes window, with albums and other media by that artist in the top half of the window, as shown in Figure 6.3.

FIGURE 6.3

The results of an iTunes search by artist.

More sophisticated searching can be had by clicking the Power Search link in the Quick Links section of the iTS home page. This displays the search page screen shown in Figure 6.4, where you can search by artist, composer, song, album, or genre. Enter the appropriate keywords into the desired boxes, and then click the Search button.

6

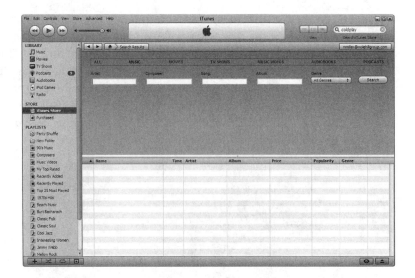

FIGURE 6.4
iTunes' Power Search screen.

You can use the Power Search screen to conduct fairly detailed searches. For example, to search for all songs written by Burt Bacharach and recorded by Dionne Warwick, enter **dionne warwick** into the Artist field and **burt bacharach** into the Composer field; the results displays in a Track list below the search form.

Browsing the iTunes Store

Some days you feel more like browsing than searching. Fortunately, the iTunes Store can accommodate your different moods.

To browse the iTunes Store, start by clicking the Browse link in the Quick Links box on the iTS home page. This displays the browse screen, shown in Figure 6.5. From here, it's a matter of narrowing down your browsing.

6

FIGURE 6.5

Browsing for items in the iTunes Store.

Start by selecting a type of media in the first column—Audiobooks, Movies, Music, Music Videos, Podcasts, or TV Shows. Then select a genre from the second column; the genre choices vary by type of media.

What you see next depends on what type of media you're browsing:

> **tip** To display more information about an artist, including available albums, double-click the artist name in the Artist list. You can also double-click a genre or subgenre to view an iTunes page devoted to that type of music.

- If you're browsing music, you'll be faced with additional choices—subgenre, artist, album, and the like. Keep narrowing down your choices until you see a track list on the bottom half of the screen.

- If you're browsing movies, when you select a genre you see a list of films within that genre listed in the bottom half of the window.

- If you're browsing TV shows, you can select the specific TV show and season within a genre. Episodes for that season are then listed in the bottom half of the window.

- If you're browsing music videos, you select the desired artist after you select a genre. All music videos for that artist are listed in the bottom half of the window.

6

- If you're browsing audiobooks, you select an author/narrator after you select a genre. Matching books are listed in the bottom half of the window.

- If you're browsing podcasts, select a subcategory after you select the main category. Podcasts in that subcategory are then listed in the bottom half of the window.

> **tip** To display more information about a TV show, including the option to order an entire season's worth of episodes, double-click the show name in the TV Shows list. You can also double-click a genre to view an iTunes page devoted to shows within that genre.

Purchasing Items from the iTunes Store

The primary reason to visit the iTunes Store, of course, is to purchase media to download to your iPod. Apple makes this very easy to do.

> **tip** You can preview most items in the iTunes Store by double-clicking that item in any Track list. For example, most songs have a short (30-second) preview that plays via the iTunes player software.

Purchasing Music

First and foremost, the iTunes Store is an online music store. As described previously, you can either search or browse for music, by track or by artist.

Whether you browse or search for music, you eventually end up with either a track list or an artist page, like the one shown in Figure 6.6. The artist page is particularly useful, because this page enables you to purchase complete albums. To view information about an album, click the album title; to purchase the album, click the Buy Album button.

> **tip** Many items in the iTunes Store can be purchased as gifts for other users. Look for the Gift This Music button to send a link to the gift purchase to the intended recipient—and see Chapter 19, "Using iTunes to Manage Your Music Purchases" for more information.

6

FIGURE 6.6
An artist page in the iTunes Store.

When you select an album, iTunes displays all the tracks for that album in a track list. Alternatively, you can display all tracks for an artist by clicking the See All Songs for This Artist link on the artist page. You can then purchase individual tracks; just click the Buy Song button next to the desired track.

When you choose to purchase a track or album, you're prompted as to whether you really want to make the purchase. (This ensures you don't click the Buy button by mistake.) When you confirm your intention, iTunes automatically charges your credit card and begins downloading the purchased music.

All items you purchase from the iTunes Store (music and other items) are listed when you click Purchased in the iTunes Store section of the iTunes Source pane, as shown in Figure 6.7. Items are also categorized in the appropriate section(s) of your iTunes library; for example, purchased music shows up in the Music section of your library.

6

FIGURE 6.7

Viewing a list of all items purchased from the iTunes Store.

Purchasing Videos

Purchasing videos is similar to purchasing music. The big difference is choosing which type of video you want to purchase—movies, TV shows, or music videos.

When you search or browse for movies, you typically end on either a movie list or individual movie page, like the one shown in Figure 6.8. (You can display a movie page by double-clicking the movie name on a list page.) The individual movie page is nice in that it displays information about the movie and offers the opportunity to watch the movie's trailer. To purchase and download the movie, click the Buy Movie button.

FIGURE 6.8

View the trailer or purchase the movie from an iTS movie page.

When you search or browse for TV shows, you want to click through to the page for a particular season of a given show, like the one shown in Figure 6.9. That's because the season page typically offers two options for purchasing. You can purchase individual episodes (for $1.99 each) or a "season pass" for all episodes from that season, typically at a discounted price. Click the Buy Episode to purchase and download a single episode, or the Buy Season or Buy Season Pass button to purchase all of that season's episodes.

> **tip** Movies and other videos take a lot longer to download than do music tracks because the files are much larger. If you can't complete a download in a single setting, go to the download screen in iTunes and click the Pause All button. You can resume the download the next time your computer is connected to the Internet.

FIGURE 6.9
Purchase individual episodes or entire seasons of a given television show.

When you search or browse for music videos, you end up either on a track listing or an artist page. Click the Buy Video button to purchase and download a video.

Purchasing Audiobooks

The iPod is actually a great device for listening to audiobooks, and the iTunes Store offers a wide variety of audiobooks for

> **tip** A season pass is for a season that is still in progress. You'll be able to download new episodes as they become available.

6

purchase and download. Click the Audiobooks link on the iTunes Store home page and you can browse for audiobooks by category—fiction, nonfiction, mystery, romance, and so forth. When you find an audiobook you want to purchase, double-click the title to open the book's page, as shown in Figure 6.10. From here, you can listen to a preview from the book or click the Buy Book button to make your purchase.

FIGURE 6.10

Preview and purchase an audiobook from the book's page in iTunes.

Purchasing iPod Games

If you have a fifth-generation iPod, you can use your device to play games while you're on the go. A number of iPod games are available from the iTunes Store.

When you click the iPod Games link on the iTS home page, you see the list of available games, as shown in Figure 6.11. Click any game to see that game's description. From here, you can preview the game or

note Learn more about audiobooks on your iPod in Chapter 9, "Audiobooks."

caution The current games available from the iTunes Store can only be played on fifth-generation iPods. They cannot be played on older iPods or the iPod nano, mini, or shuffle.

click the Buy Game button to purchase it. After you have purchased and downloaded it, the game is then transferred to your iPod the next time you sync your device.

note Learn more about iPod games in Chapter 12, "Games."

FIGURE 6.11

Viewing available iPod games from the iTunes Store.

Downloading Podcasts

Finally, the iTunes Store lets you subscribe to and download a variety of audio podcasts, all for free. To view available podcasts, click the Podcasts link on the iTS home page. From here, you can browse podcasts by category—arts, business, comedy, and the like.

When you find a podcast that interests you, click through to the page for that podcast, like the one shown in Figure 6.12. You now have a choice—you can download individual podcast episodes (click the Get Episode button) or subscribe to a feed of all future episodes (click the Subscribe button). Subscribing is the way to go if you're really interested in this podcast; this way you'll have all future episodes downloaded to your PC (and then synced to your iPod) when you connect to the iTunes Store over time.

note Learn more about podcasts in Chapter 8, "Podcasts."

6

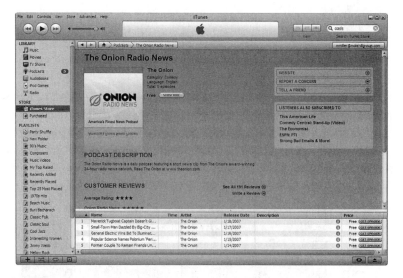

FIGURE 6.12
Viewing a podcast in the iTunes Store.

Dealing with DRM

Here's the thing about the music you download from the iTunes Store—you don't actually own it. What you purchase for your 99 cents is a license to use the music, in a manner prescribed by Apple (and the corresponding recording label). That means what you can do with the music you download is limited, to some degree, by some form of copy protection.

The technology used to protect digital media files from copyright infringement or illegal copying is generally referred to as *digital rights management*, or DRM. DRM schemes use a form of content encryption to keep the files from being used in a nonprescribed manner.

FairPlay Restrictions

In terms of music files downloaded from the iTunes Store, the DRM scheme Apple uses is called FairPlay. FairPlay is an encryption process used on the iTunes Store's AAC-format files, which effectively wraps the music file within an M4A format encrypted file. The decoding of the M4A format file is performed by Apple's QuickTime plug-in, which operates behind the scenes in the iTunes software.

> **note** Learn more about digital audio file formats in Chapter 7, "Music."

In practical terms, Apple imposes the following DRM-managed restrictions on all music downloaded from the iTunes Store:

- Can be played on any number of Apple iPod music players, but not on any non-iPod player.

- Can be played on only five authorized computers—although a computer can be deauthorized so that a new computer can then be authorized in its place.

- Can be copied to any number of standard audio CDs. The resulting CD has no DRM protection and can then be played, copied, and ripped like any normal CD.

In addition, a specific iTunes playlist that contains a DRM-protected track can be copied to CD only up to seven times; after that, the playlist cannot be burned to CD unless or until some part of the playlist has been changed.

In other words, Apple limits which portable devices and how many PCs on which you can play your purchased music, and how you can use your purchased music within playlists designed for CD burning. This is the primary reason why you can't play encrypted Advanced Audio Coding (AAC) files on non-Apple music players, such as those from Creative and SansaDisk; those players do not offer FairPlay decryption, so FairPlay-encrypted tracks simply won't play.

Authorizing Computers for Playback

As noted, songs purchased from the iTunes Store can be played on only five computers at a time. To add a new computer (beyond the original five) to your authorized list, you first have to deauthorize one of the original computers. Of course, you should also deauthorize any computer that you intend to sell or give away.

To authorize a computer to playback your iTunes purchases, you must have the iTunes software installed on that computer. When you first play a song that's been purchased from the iTunes Store, iTunes asks you to enter the Apple ID and password you used to purchase the song. Enter this info, and your computer is automatically authorized for playback. (You can also select Store > Authorize Computer to initiate this process manually.)

note For what it's worth, Steve Jobs has called for the music industry to remove DRM protection from their digital music, and some record labels are reportedly considering doing just that. Most experts believe that online music sales will increase significantly if DRM restrictions are removed.

6

To deauthorize a computer, open the iTunes software and select Store > Deauthorize Computer. When prompted, enter your Apple ID and password, and then click OK; this computer will now be deauthorized, and playback of purchased tracks halted.

> **tip** Another workaround for dealing with DRM restrictions is to use a third-party utility called QTFairUse. This software program removes the DRM wrapping from iTunes-purchased music files. You can download QTFairUse for free from www.hymn-project.org/download.php.

The DRM Workaround

So, what do you do if you want to play a track you purchased from the iTunes Store on your non-Apple music player? Although such an action is technically prohibited, there is a workaround.

Essentially, what you have to do is burn the protected track to CD and then rip it back to your PC (in a format other than AAC). When you burn the track to CD, the encrypted wrapper is removed as the file is converted from AAC to CD Audio format. Then when you rip the track from CD back to your hard drive, there's no DRM encryption to worry about.

OTHER ONLINE MUSIC STORES

Apple's iTunes Store isn't the only online music store on the Web—even if it does have an 82% market share. It is, however, the only store that sells music in AAC format for use on iPods; most other online stores (such as Napster, Rhapsody, and URGE) sell tracks in Microsoft's WMA format, which can't be played on an iPod.

There are, of course, some online music stores and sites that offer songs in the universal MP3 format, which *can* be played on an iPod. The most popular MP3 download services is eMusic (www.emusic.com), which offers more than two million MP3-format audio files for download. The eMusic service is a subscription service that lets you download a set number of tracks for a set monthly price. Three subscription plans are offered: $9.99/month for 30 downloads, $14.99/month for 50 downloads, or $19.99/month for 75 downloads. That's substantially less per song than you pay with the iTunes Store; in addition, eMusic's downloads are DRM-free, which means you can play them on any number of players and make any number of copies.

The only drawback to eMusic is that it doesn't offer a lot of major-label product. If you want the top commercial acts, the iTunes Store is a better bet. But if you're into indie music, eMusic might have just what you're looking for—at a fraction of the price per track.

PART

Applications

Music

Whatever else they do, most people use their iPods to play music. As you've learned, you can get music on your iPod in a number of ways—you can purchase songs from the iTunes Store, download MP3 files from other online music sites, and rip music from CDs that you own. All of these operations are managed by the iTunes software, which also helps you manage the music stored on your PC and your iPod (and use the music stored on your PC to burn custom mix CDs).

Although the iTunes software might appear easy enough to use at first glance, there's a lot of complexity and power under the surface—all of which you need to learn to best manage all your digital music.

Understanding Digital Audio File Formats

Before we get into using iTunes to manage your digital music collection, it helps to know a little bit about what you're managing—the digital audio files that comprise your Music library.

In the world of computers and the Internet, and on the iPod, all data is stored in digital format. (In a digital file, information is assembled from a series of 0 and 1 bits.) Digital music is better than its analog counterpart in that noise and distortion aren't introduced into the process. A digital copy of a song, if recorded properly, can be an exact copy of the original. It's impossible to make an exact copy using analog methods.

In the world of audio, music used to be recorded and stored nondigitally, in the form of vinyl records and magnetic recording tape. However, with the advent of compact discs (CD) and computer-based music players, music is now stored digitally.

When music is digital, it's easy to incorporate it into the computer environment. To a computer, one digital file is pretty much the same as another. It's all the same to your computer whether you're saving or copying an MP3 music file or a Word document—they're both collections of bits and bytes, and are both managed in a similar fashion.

How Digital Sampling Works

All digital recordings—starting in the recording studio—are made by creating digital samples of the original sound. The way it works is that special software "listens" to the music and takes a digital snapshot of the music at a particular point in time. The length of that snapshot (measured in bits) and the number of snapshots per second (called the sampling rate) determine the quality of the reproduction. The more samples per second, the more accurate the resulting "picture" of the original music.

Compact discs sample music at a 44.1kHz rate—in other words, the music is sampled, digitally, 44,100 times per second. Each sample is 16 bits long. When you multiply the sampling rate by the sample size and the number of channels (two for stereo), you end up with a *bit rate*. For CDs, you multiply 44,100 x 16 x 2, and end up with 1,400,000 bits per second—or 1,400Kbps.

All these bits are converted into data that is then copied onto some sort of storage medium. In the case of CDs, the storage medium is the compact disc itself; you can also store this digital audio data on hard disk drives or in Flash memory, as used in various iPod models.

Of course, the space taken up by these bits starts to add up quickly. If you take a typical three-minute song recorded at 44.1kHz, you end up using 32MB of disk space. Although that song can easily fit on a 650MB CD, it's much too large to download over a standard Internet connection or to store on an iPod.

7

This is where audio compression comes in. By taking selected bits out of the original audio file, the file size is compressed. If the right bits are excised, you'll never miss them.

Understanding File Compression

When you copy a digital audio file, you can either copy the file exactly (in noncompressed format) or you can use some sort of compression to reduce the otherwise-huge file sizes. If you choose a compressed format, you can opt for formats that use either *lossy* or *lossless* compression. Lossy compression loses some of the original audio information to create a smaller file, resulting in music that isn't quite as good sounding as the original. Lossless compression doesn't affect the original sound quality, but results in larger file sizes—although not near as big as noncompressed files.

If you want to rip your music for playback on your computer or iPod, you'll likely use a lossy compression format, such as MP3 or AAC. If you want to archive your CD collection for playback on a home audio or home theater system, you'll probably want to use a lossless compression format, such as Apple Lossless, or copy your CDs in noncompressed format.

Lossy Compression

Lossy compression works by sampling the original file and removing those ranges of sounds that the average listener can't hear. A lossless encoder uses complex algorithms to determine what sounds a human is able to hear, based on accepted psychoacoustic models, and chops off those sounds outside this range. You can control the sound quality and the size of the resulting file by selecting different sampling rates for the data. The less sampling going on, the smaller the file size—and the lower the sound quality.

The problem with shrinking files to this degree, of course, is that by making a smaller file, you've dramatically reduced the sampling rate of the music. This results in music that sounds compressed; it won't have the high-frequency response or the dynamic range (the difference between soft and loud passages) of the original recording. To many users, the sound of the compressed file will be acceptable, much like listening to an FM radio station. To other users, however, the compression presents an unacceptable alternative to high-fidelity reproduction.

The most popular lossy compressed format today is the MP3 format, which is pretty much a universal format that plays on virtually all music player hardware and software. The AAC file format used in the iPod and iTunes Store is also a lossy format.

Lossless Compression

For listening on an iPod or on a computer, lossy formats such as AAC sound good enough to most people. If you're listening to music on a home audio system, however, lossy compression doesn't sound quite as good as the originals. (Remember that word *lossy*—you lose something in the translation!)

If you want to create a high-fidelity digital archive, a better solution is to use a lossless compression format. These formats work more or less like Zip compression for computer data; redundant bits are taken out to create the compressed file, which is then uncompressed for playback. So, what you hear has exact fidelity to the original, while still being stored in a smaller file.

Of course, a lossless compressed file isn't near the size of a file with lossy compression; it is much larger. Whereas an MP3 file might be 10% the size of the original, uncompressed file, a file with lossless compression is typically about 50% the original's size. This is why lossless compression isn't recommended for iPods, where storage space is limited. If you're storing your CD collection on hard disk, however, it works just fine—especially with today's cheap hard disk prices. You can easily store 1,000 CDs on a 300GB hard disk, using any lossless compression format.

If you want to rip your CDs with lossless compression, you can configure the iTunes software to rip to the Apple Lossless format. Although Apple Lossless uses the same .M4A extension as Protected AAC files, the results are much better sounding—virtually identical to the original recording.

Uncompressed Audio

Compressed audio is the way to go when you're ripping your own music or creating a digital media archive. But the original digital music files you find on a CD are uncompressed, as are digital sounds used by your computer's operating system. If you insist on archiving your music in its original unaltered form, you'll want to use either the AIFF (for Macs) or WAV (for Windows PCs) file formats, which store music in a bit-for-bit identical format to the original CD audio files.

Compatible File Formats

So, of all these available digital audio formats, which ones can you use with the iTunes software and iPod music player? Table 7.1 details the compatible formats.

Table 7.1 Digital Audio Formats Playable with iPod and iTunes

Format	File Extension(s)	Type of Compression
Advanced Audio Coding (AAC)	.AAC, .M4A	Lossy
Protected AAC	.M4A	Lossy
MPEG Audio Layer III (MP3)	.MP3	Lossy
Variable bit rate MP3 (MP3 VBR)	.MP3	Lossy
Audible Audiobook	.AA	Lossy
Apple Lossless	.M4A	Lossless
Audio Interchange File Format (AIFF)	.AIF, .AIFC, .AIFF	Uncompressed
Windows Audio	.WAV	Uncompressed
Compact Disc Digital Audio (CDDA)	.CDA	Uncompressed

When you're using the iTunes software, the default format for music ripped from CD is AAC; the default format for music downloaded from the iTunes Store is Protected AAC. (The difference is the DRM wrapping applied to iTunes Store purchases.) iTunes assigns the same .M4A file format to both file types.

note Learn more about DRM in Chapter 6, "Using the iTunes Store."

Incompatible File Formats

What audio formats *aren't* supported by iTunes and the iPod? Here's the short list:

- Free Lossless Audio Codec (FLAC)
- MPEG Audio Layer II (.MP2, .MPA)
- Musical Instrument Digital Interface (.MID, .MIDI, .RMI)
- RealNetworks (.RA, .RM, .RAM)
- UNIX Sound Files (.AU, .SND)
- Windows Media Audio (.WMA)

Of these noncompatible formats, the most problematic is WMA, which is the format used by Microsoft in all its music player software (including the Windows Media Player) and in most non-Apple online

note Just as AAC files can be both protected (with DRM) and unprotected, so can WMA files. WMA files you rip on your own are unprotected; WMA files you download from an online music store, such as URGE or Napster, are protected.

music stores. If you download a WMA-format file from Napster, for example, you can't play it in iTunes or on your iPod. For that matter, you can't play AAC-format tracks downloaded from the iTunes Store with Windows Media Player, or with non-Apple portable music players, such as the Creative ZEN Vision:M. Apple and Microsoft just don't play well together.

IMPORTING UNPROTECTED WMA-FORMAT FILES INTO ITUNES

Even though Apple's iTunes is incompatible with Microsoft's WMA format, you can easily import unprotected WMA files into iTunes. This is useful if you have a lot of WMA-format files you've previously ripped from CD using Windows Media Player or some similar program.

All you have to do is launch the iTunes software and select either File > Add File to Library (to import a single track) or File > Add Folder to Library. Identify the file or folder full of WMA files to import, and iTunes will do the rest. The original WMA files remain as-is in their original location, while new AAC-format files for these tracks are created and added to the iTunes Music library.

If you have protected WMA files (such as those downloaded from Napster or URGE), you will need to first burn them to an audio CD, and then rip the tracks on that CD back to your hard drive using iTunes.

Understanding Bit Rates

Besides compressing the data in an audio file, the AAC and MP3 file formats also let you choose the rate at which the original music is sampled. The lower the sampling rate, the smaller the file size; the higher the sampling rate, the better the sound quality. It's a trade-off.

For example, if you choose to encode an MP3 file at a 128Kbps bit rate, a three-minute song that takes up 32MB in uncompressed format will compress to just 3MB of storage. That's small enough to download easily, even on a dial-up connection.

iTunes lets you rip songs at a variety of bit rates, from 16Kbps to 320Kbps. Obviously, the lower bit rates are appropriate only for spoken word or low-fidelity recordings; the higher bit rates are more appropriate for higher-fidelity recordings.

note Sound quality is highly subjective, as you can imagine. Some "golden-eared" audiophiles find it difficult to listen to any audio files created with lossy compression—no matter what the bit rate.

The default bit rate in iTunes is 128Kbps, which is a decent compromise between sound quality and file size. Know, however, that while some refer to this bit rate as "CD quality," it really isn't; the quality is more like that of a good FM radio station—which, as I said, is good enough for most listeners.

Ripping Music from CD

When you want to transfer music you have on CD to your iPod, you first have to copy that music from CD to your computer's hard disk. This process is called *ripping*, and you can do it with the iTunes software.

Setting File Format and Bit Rate

Before you rip any music, you need to tell iTunes what file format and bit rate you want the resulting files to have. Follow these steps:

1. From iTunes, select Edit > Preferences.

2. Select the Advanced tab, and then select the Importing tab, as shown in Figure 7.1.

3. Pull down the Import Using list and select the appropriate encoder for the desired file format. To rip to Apple's AAC format, select AAC Encoder; to rip to MP3 format, select MP3 Encoder.

4. Pull down the Setting list and select the desired bit rate for your ripped files. The High Quality (128Kbps) setting is selected by default. To see more options, select Custom to display the dialog box shown in Figure 7.2, and then select a new Stereo Bit Rate from the pull-down list.

5. Back in the main dialog box, check the second and third options (Automatically Retrieve CD Track Names from the Internet and Create Filenames with Track Number).

6. Click OK.

tip If you're ripping exclusively for use with iTunes or an iPod, use the AAC Encoder. If you're ripping tracks that will also be played on non-Apple music players, use the MP3 Encoder.

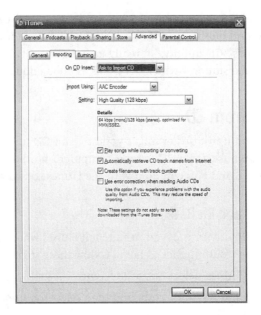

FIGURE 7.1

Setting file format and bit rate.

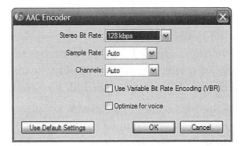

FIGURE 7.2

Selecting a custom bit rate.

Ripping the CD

After you've set your file format and bit rate preferences, you can start ripping. Make sure your computer is connected to the Internet (to retrieve track names and album art), and then follow these steps:

1. Insert the CD you want to copy into your PC's CD drive.

2. As you can see in Figure 7.3, all the tracks from the CD are now listed in the iTunes window. Check those tracks you want to copy.

3. Click the Import CD button at the bottom of the iTunes window.

CD tracks

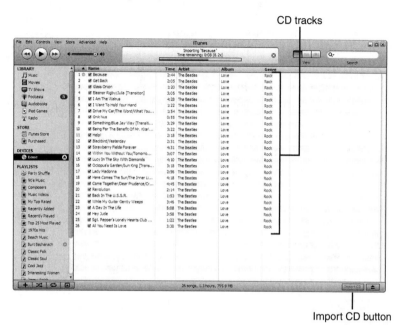

Import CD button

FIGURE 7.3

Getting ready to rip a CD using iTunes.

iTunes now extracts the selected tracks from the CD and converts them from their original CD audio format to the file format you selected, sampled at the bit rate you selected. The converted files are now written to your PC's hard disk and added to the iTunes library.

Burning Music to CD

Burning music from your PC to a blank CD is also easy with iTunes. Here's how to do it:

1. In iTunes, create a new playlist containing all the songs you want to burn to CD. Make sure that your playlist is less than 74 minutes (for a normal CD) or 80 minutes (for an extended CD) long.

> **tip**
> Most users are well served by the default filenames and track information provided by iTunes when you rip music from a CD. However, some exacting users might want to rename the ripped files to conform to a particular naming scheme, or edit the default track information to include different or more correct data. To make these types of changes, you'll need to use a tag-editing program, as described in the "Third-Party Tag Editors" section, later in this chapter.

7

2. Insert a blank CD-R disc into your PC's CD drive.

3. Select the playlist that contains the songs you want to burn, as shown in Figure 7.4, and make sure that all the songs in the playlist are checked.

4. Click the Burn Disc button at the bottom of the iTunes window.

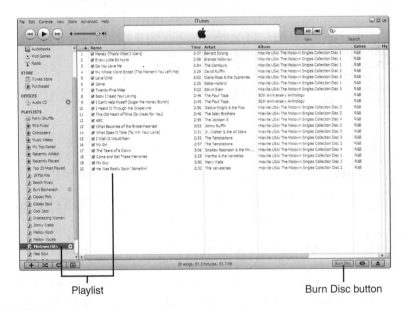

Playlist   Burn Disc button

FIGURE 7.4
Burning a playlist of songs to CD.

iTunes converts the selected files to CDDA format and copies them to your CD. When the entire burning process is done, iTunes displays a message to that effect and ejects the newly burned CD from the disc drive.

Playing CDs

As you've probably figured out on your own, if you can use the iTunes software to rip and burn CDs, you can also use it to play CDs directly from disc. In fact, iTunes ends up being a pretty good little CD player.

7

When you insert a CD into your PC's CD drive, that CD automatically appears in the iTunes window, as shown in Figure 7.5. To start playback, all you have to do is click the Play button. You can then use the transport controls to pause the CD or go backward and forward through the tracks. Naturally, the volume control adjusts the playback level.

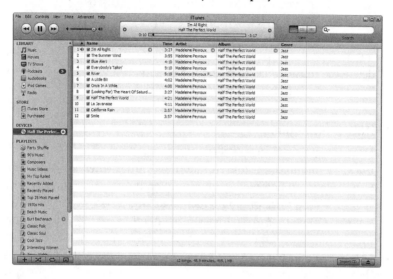

FIGURE 7.5

Playing a CD with iTunes.

To play the songs on a CD in a random order, click the Shuffle button at the lower left of the iTunes window. iTunes also offers a repeat function, which repeats the selected song(s) over and over. You activate this function by clicking on the Repeat button, which is next to the Shuffle button.

Managing Music in iTunes

After you've ripped music from your CDs to your PC, you can then use iTunes to manage that music. You can delete tracks, edit tracks, even add or change album art for selected tracks. Read on to learn how.

tip On some Windows PCs, Windows Media Player is configured as the default CD player, not iTunes. To configure Windows so that iTunes plays all your CDs, open the Windows Control panel and select Appearance and Themes > Folder Options. When the Folder Options dialog box appears, select the File Types tab, then scroll down and select the CDA extension. Click the Change button, then select iTunes and click OK. Repeat this last process for the CDDA file extension, and iTunes will now be used to play any CD you insert.

7

Deleting Tracks

Deleting a track from your Music library is as easy as selecting the track and pressing the Del key on your computer keyboard. Alternatively, you can select the track and then select Edit > Delete, or right-click the track and select Delete from the pop-up menu. iTunes will ask whether you want to delete the music track itself and the link to it in iTunes. The choice is yours.

Editing Track Information

Most of the time iTunes retrieves the correct track, album, and artist information for a track when it rips the track from CD. Sometimes, however, the information it retrieves is incorrect (title misspelled, wrong track or album identified, and so on) or incomplete. And other times, a CD you insert isn't recognized at all, meaning you will have to input the track info by hand. (This happens most frequently with obscure CDs or CDs that are brand new and haven't yet been entered by someone else.) In these instances, you can edit the track info manually.

To edit the info for any individual track, select the track in iTunes and then select File > Get Info. This displays the dialog box shown in Figure 7.6. The Summary tab, which is not editable, displays all the known information about the track—file format, file size, bit rate, date modified, when it was last played, and the like.

The information you can edit is contained on the Info tab, shown in Figure 7.7. Table 7.2 details what each field means.

FIGURE 7.6

Summary track info in iTunes.

FIGURE 7.7

Editing track information.

7

Table 7.2   Editable Track Information

Field/Option	Description
Name	The title of the song
Artist	The name of the performing artist for this track
Album Artist	The name of the performing artist for the host album; Artist and Album Artist may not be the same for some compilation albums
Year	The year the track was released (or, in some instances, the year the CD was released—which might not be the same for CD reissues of older albums)
Album	The title of the host album
Track Number	The track number on the album (along with the optional total number of tracks on the album)
Disc Number	For multiple-disc releases (boxed sets), the disc number of the host album (along with the optional total number of discs in the set)
Grouping	Used in classical works, the movement or piece of the work from which this track is taken
BPM	Beats per minute (typically used in dance music)
Composer	The composer of the track (not the same as the performing artist)
Comments	Any additional (and optional) comments about the track
Genre	The musical genre of the track (pop, rock, dance, soul, and so on)
Part of a compilation	Checked if this track is part of a compilation CD (typically a CD with tracks by various artists)

Editing information is as simple as entering new information into any field. Click OK to save the new information.

tip Not all fields are always filled in, nor do they need to be. The important fields are Name, Artist, and Genre; everything else is optional.

Editing Multiple Tracks

This process is fine when you have a limited number of tracks to edit, but what do you do when you have a ton of music that needs new information?

Editing Within iTunes

If you're talking about editing the title, artist, or genre of a multitrack album, you can do so from within iTunes. All you have to do is select the multiple tracks (hold down the Shift or Ctrl keys while selecting with your mouse) and select Edit > Get Info. You're asked if you're sure you want to edit multiple tracks; click Yes and you see the Multiple Item Information dialog box, shown in Figure 7.8. Note that you can't edit individual track titles from this dialog box, but you can edit just about anything else—including the art for the entire album.

FIGURE 7.8

Editing information for multiple tracks.

Third-Party Tag Editors

tip   You can also use the Multiple Item Information dialog box to configure an album for gapless playback, or as a compilation album.

Alternatively, you can use a third-party tag editor to edit multiple tracks. This is a software program that edits the metadata "tags" found in most digital audio files. Most of these tag editor programs work with all types of audio files—MP3s and WMAs, in addition to Apple's AAC files. Most also let you edit attributes for multiple files at one time; for example, you can change the genre or artist name for dozens of albums in a single edit. Some programs also let you change the album cover art for selected tracks and to rename the track files.

The most popular of these tag-editing programs include the following:

- AudioManage Audio Library (www.audiomanage.com)
- AudioShell (www.softpointer.com/AudioShell.htm)
- FixTunes (www.fixtunes.com)
- mp3Tag (www.maniactools.com/soft/mp3tag)
- Tag Clinic (www.kevesoft.com)
- Tag&Rename (www.softpointer.com/tr.htm)

Of these programs, my favorite is FixTunes. Even though it costs $24.95, it offers more flexibility and editing power than the other programs; it will do just about anything you want it to do, and quite easily.

> **tip** Third-party tag-editing programs are typically more versatile than the tag-editing features built in to the iTunes software. Check them out if you can't get iTunes to do what you want to do.

Adding and Editing Album Art

All color iPods can display album covers when playing music. The album cover artwork is transferred from your computer to your iPod, via iTunes, at the same time the audio files are transferred.

> **note** You don't have to bother with importing artwork for tracks you purchase from the iTunes Store—the proper cover art is downloaded along with the audio file when you make your purchase.

By default, iTunes accesses the iTunes Store to find album art for all tracks you rip to your PC's hard disk. The unfortunate fact is that the iTunes Store doesn't have art for all albums. Depending on your musical tastes, you could end up with a significant portion of your Music library without any accompanying artwork. In addition, iTunes doesn't always add the right art to your tracks, which means you might need to change the cover art that iTunes automatically assigns.

Fortunately, there are several different ways to add or change album art in iTunes.

Adding Art to a Single Track

If you're just missing artwork, the first thing to do is let iTunes try to find it for you. Select the track in your Music library, and then click Advanced > Get Album Artwork. iTunes will now connect to the Internet and attempt to download the artwork from the iTunes Store. If the artwork is there, great; if not, you'll have to use another approach.

You can add or change album art for a single track from the Get Info dialog box. Select the track in your Music library, click File > Get Info, and then select the Artwork tab, shown in Figure 7.9. Any existing artwork is already displayed in this dialog box; to delete an incorrect cover, select it

> **caution** iTunes is rather picky about finding cover art—especially if you rename your track files or change the artist information. For example, if you rename "The Cure" to "Cure, The" (for alphabetization purposes), iTunes won't recognize the artist and won't find the album art.

with your mouse and then click the Delete button. To add new artwork, click the Add button, and then browse your hard disk for the replacement art file. (You can also copy and paste or drag and drop artwork directly onto the Artwork tab.)

caution Make sure your new artwork is at least 200 x 200 pixels, or it won't fill the allotted area in iTunes or on your iPod.

FIGURE 7.9

Adding new album art for a single track.

Adding Art to Multiple Tracks

To add or change artwork for all the tracks of an album, select all the tracks in your Music library, and then select File > Get Info to display the Multiple Item Information dialog box. Check the Artwork option, and then double-click the large Artwork box. This lets you browse your hard disk for the new art file.

tip iTunes and the iPod can display multiple album art files (sequentially) for any single track. You can add multiple covers from the Get Info dialog box, and then scroll through the covers within the dialog box.

Dragging and Dropping Artwork

An even easier way to add album artwork is to use the Album Art area in the iTunes software—the small area in the lower left of the main window, shown in Figure 7.10. (If this area is not visible, click the Show/Hide Item Artwork button in the bottom left of the iTunes window.) You'll also want to have a folder open on your desktop (in Windows, this is probably the Pictures or My Pictures folder), with the new artwork visible. In the iTunes window, select the track you want to edit, and then drag the new artwork from the other window

7

and drop it onto the Album Art area. (You can also copy and paste artwork
into the Album Art area.)

FIGURE 7.10
The Album Art area in iTunes.

FINDING ALBUM ART

I'm a stickler for good album art. I want high-quality reproductions, and
I want the art to be the right art (which is sometimes difficult when
you're talking CD reissues of classic vinyl albums). Where do I find
album art that meets my needs?

The first place I look is Amazon (www.amazon.com). The world's largest
online retailer of CDs has, not surprisingly, the largest library of CD artwork. Just search Amazon for the CD in question, and the resulting
product page should display the album art—but as a thumbnail. Click
the thumbnail to display a larger version, and then right-click the larger
picture and copy or save the file. It's this file you then add to iTunes for
the album artwork.

If Amazon doesn't have the right artwork, there are several other sites
worth searching. Wal-Mart (www.walmart.com) and AllMusic (www.
allmusic.com) both have large databases of albums and album art; the
latter is especially good for hard-to-find albums.

Of course, nothing beats a good Google search for finding all sorts of
album artwork. Use Google Image Search (images.google.com) and
type in the artist and album name. You can even sort your results by
file size, if that's important to you.

Finally, if you can't find any cover art for an album online, you can
always scan in a copy of the actual CD cover—assuming you have the
CD, that is. You can then import the scanned cover into iTunes, as you
would any album artwork.

Using Album Art Importing Programs

Several third-party programs can help you add album art to your iTunes tracks. Most of these programs search your iTunes library for tracks without art, go online to find appropriate cover artwork, and then add those covers to the tracks in question. The best of these programs include the following:

- FixTunes (www.fixtunes.com)
- iArt (www.ipodsoft.com)
- iAutoArtwork (www.jtasoftware.com/iAutoArtwork)
- iTunes Art Importer (www.yvg.com/itunesartimporter.shtml)
- TuneSleeve (tunesleeve.googlepages.com)

Using the art4iTunes Website

You can use a website to add album art to your iTunes tracks. The art4iTunes.com (www.art4itunes.com) site, shown in Figure 7.11, lets you add artwork for an entire playlist or list of songs in one batch operation.

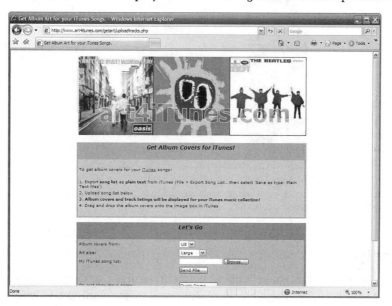

FIGURE 7.11

art4iTunes.com—a website for adding iTunes album art.

The operation itself involves several steps:

1. In iTunes, select a playlist to export, and then select File > Export. When the Save As dialog box appears, pull down the Save as File Type list and select Text Files (.txt). Then click Save.

2. Go to the art4iTunes site, click the Browse button, and select the text file you just created. Click Send File to upload the file to the site.

3. The art4iTunes site will now use your music list to find the appropriate album covers, and generate a series of web pages with all those covers displayed, like the one shown in Figure 7.12.

4. Return to the iTunes window, display the Album Art area, and select the first track you want to add artwork to. Then use your mouse to drag the album cover from the art4iTunes page to the Album Art area in iTunes.

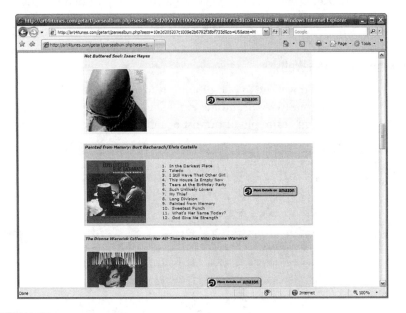

FIGURE 7.12
The results of an art4iTunes cover art search.

Adding Lyrics

What else can you edit about your iTunes music tracks? Well, if you're into karaoke (or you're a big words fan), you might want to add lyrics to your iTunes tunes.

You add lyrics to any track by selecting the track, selecting File > Get Info, and then selecting the Lyrics tab, shown in Figure 7.13. You can then type in the lyrics, or paste the lyrics copied from another source. Click OK when done.

FIGURE 7.13
Adding lyrics to an iTunes track.

Where can you find lyrics for your iTunes songs? There are several song lyrics sites on the Web, including the following:

- Absolute Lyrics (www.absolutelyrics.com)
- A-Z Lyrics Universe (www.azlyrics.com)
- Lyrics On Demand (www.lyricsondemand.com)
- Lyrics Search Engine (lyrics.astraweb.com)
- Lyrics.com (www.lyrics.com)
- MetroLyrics (www.metrolyrics.com)

In addition, there are two third-party software programs that can search the Web for song lyrics and then automatically import them into iTunes for downloading to your iPod. These programs (both free and Windows only) are EvilLyrics (www.evillabs.sk/evillyrics) and Songbook24 (www.songbook24.com).

Setting Playback Volume and Equalization

Don't like the way a particular song sounds when you play it back? Or maybe the track plays back too loud—or too soft?

tip By the way, to view song lyrics on your iPod, start playing the song and then press the center Select button a few times. If there are lyrics stored, they should eventually appear in the display.

7

iTunes lets you adjust the playback volume and equalization for each individual track in your Music library. So if one track stands out from the rest, you can deal with it without affecting the other tracks in your library.

To adjust the volume and equalization for a given track, simply select the track in your Music library, select File > Get Info, and then select the Options tab, shown in Figure 7.14. To adjust the volume, use the Volume Adjustment slider. To apply equalization, pull down the Equalizer Preset list and make a selection. Click OK when done.

FIGURE 7.14

Adjusting volume and equalization for a single track.

Rating Tracks

One feature of iTunes that most people either don't know about or don't use enough is the ability to rate each track, on a scale of one to five stars. When your tracks are rated, that's one more criteria on which to sort and select music for playback. For example, you could build a playlist of your highest-rated tracks. (The iPod shuffle's Autofill feature can also be configured to fill your shuffle with only your highest-rated tracks—which only works when you've taken the time to rate them.)

To rate a track or group of tracks, select the track(s), select File > My Rating, and then select a star rating. It's that easy.

Editing Track Length—and Splitting Tracks

Here's something else you probably didn't know iTunes could do. You can use the iTunes software to trim sections off the beginning or ending of a track, and to split a long track into several shorter tracks. (This proves particularly useful if you've dubbed a vinyl LP to a single digital audio file and want to separate that file into individual song tracks.)

tip To determine where you want to edit a track, first play back the track in iTunes and note the timing of the desired beginning or end in the track info area at the top of the iTunes window.

To trim a track, select it in your media library, select File > Get Info, and then select the Options tab. To trim the beginning of the track, check the Start Time option and enter the timing (from zero) where you want the track to start. To trim the end of a track, check the Stop Time option and enter the timing where you want the track to end.

To edit a long file into shorter segments, use the same procedure to set the start and stop time for the individual song segment. Click OK to close the dialog box, and then select Advanced > Convert Selection to AAC. This will convert the section of the track you just defined to a new AAC-format audio file.

Using Playlists

The next music-related item we'll discuss is the topic of playlists. A playlist is simply a list of songs, selected either by you or automatically by iTunes, based on criteria you've previously set. You can listen to playlists within iTunes or on your iPod, and you can use playlists to determine which songs are copied to your iPod or burned to CD.

All playlists you create are listed in the Playlists section of the iTunes Source pane, as shown in Figure 7.15. To play a playlist, select it in the Source pane and then click the Play button. The playlist will play in original track order—unless you click the Shuffle button to randomize the track playback.

7

FIGURE 7.15
Playlists displayed in the iTunes Source pane.

Creating Custom Playlists

You create playlists within the iTunes software. The playlists you create are then synced to your iPod when it's next connected to your PC.

To create a new playlist, follow these steps:

1. Select File > New Playlist, or click the + button in the lower-left corner of the iTunes window.

2. A new "untitled playlist" item appears in the Playlists section of the Source pane. Double-click this item and enter a title for the playlist.

3. Select Music in the Library section of the Source pane.

4. Select a song you want to add to the playlist, and then drag that item onto the name of the playlist in the Source pane.

5. Repeat step 4 as many times as you want to add more songs to your playlist.

Your playlist is automatically saved as you go, with tracks listed in the order added.

> **tip** You can also create a playlist from a previously selected group of tracks. Just select the tracks in your Music library, and then select File > New Playlist from Selection.

Creating Smart Playlists

For ultimate control over playlist content, you want to create custom playlists as just described. For ease of creation, however, you might want to take advantage of the iTunes Smart Playlist feature, which automatically creates playlists on-the-fly based on criteria you specify in advance.

For example, you might want to create a playlist of your favorite swing singers, or of all music released in a given year, or even of all dance tracks at a specific tempo. All you have to do is define the rules, and iTunes will find the matching tracks and use them to create a new playlist.

To create a Smart Playlist, follow these steps:

1. Select File > New Smart Playlist to display the Smart Playlist dialog box, shown in Figure 7.16.

FIGURE 7.16

Creating a new Smart Playlist.

2. Define a new rule that follows the form *field > matches > keyword*. Pull down the first list box to define the field (Album, Artist, Genre, and so on); pull down the second list box to define the match (contains, does not contain, starts with, ends with, and so forth); then enter one or more keywords into the final text box. For example, to include all songs by Frank Sinatra, select Artist > contains > Frank Sinatra.

3. To define another rule for this playlist, click the + button next to the first rule. This displays another set of selection controls. Repeat step 2 to add the new rule. Repeat this step to add even more rules for this playlist.

4. At the top of the dialog box, select whether you want songs to match Any or All of the rules you just created.

5. To limit the size of the playlist, check the Limit To option and enter the number of items desired.

7

6. To keep this playlist updated when you add new items to your Music library, check the Live Updating option.

7. Click OK when done.

caution When you create a smart playlist, you can't manually add other tracks to the playlist—songs can only be added via smart playlist rules.

iTunes will now search your Music library for items that match the rules you just defined and create the new playlist. The playlist is initially labeled "untitled playlist," so you'll need to select it in the Source pane and give it a proper name.

Using the Party Shuffle

iTunes comes with one playlist already created. This playlist, called Party Shuffle, is a short list of songs queued up for playback, kind of like a predetermined shuffle mix.

When you select Party Mix in the Playlists section of the Source pane, you see the list of songs, as shown in Figure 7.17. This list includes the last few songs you've played and a longer list of upcoming tracks. The nature of this list is determined by the controls at the bottom of the window. You can select the source of the tracks (your entire Music library or a specific playlist) and the number of recently played and upcoming songs displayed. You can also opt to play higher-rated songs more often.

FIGURE 7.17

Viewing and controlling the iTunes Party Shuffle.

To change the upcoming songs in the Party Shuffle, click the Shuffle button. Every time you click the Shuffle button, iTunes reloads the list with a different set of tracks.

Organizing Playlists into Folders

After you've created a ton of playlists, all those playlists can get to be a bear to manage. That's why smart iPodders organize their playlists into folders. For example, you might have created a half-dozen dance-related playlists, all of which you can organize under a top-level "Dance" folder, as shown in Figure 7.18.

FIGURE 7.18

Playlists organized by folder.

To create a folder in your Playlist library, select File > New Folder. This creates an "untitled folder" item in the Playlist section of the Source pane; enter a name for this new folder. To move an existing playlist into this folder, just drag and drop it onto the folder in the Source pane.

Sharing Playlists

If your friends like your taste in music, you can share your iTunes playlists with them. Essentially, iTunes lets you export the list of songs in a playlist as an XML-format file, which can then be imported by your friends into their copies of iTunes. (The XML list includes only track lists—not the audio files themselves.)

To export a playlist, select the playlist in the Source pane, and then select File > Export. When the Save As dialog box appears, pull down the Save As Type list, select XML, and then click the Save button.

To import a playlist, select File > Import, and then locate and select the XML file. The playlist will be added to this copy of iTunes; any tracks not residing on this computer will automatically be deleted from the playlist.

caution You can only move playlists and other folders into iTunes' playlist folders. You can't move individual tracks inside a folder.

Uploading iMix Playlists to the iTunes Store

Here's another neat way to share your playlists. You can upload your playlists to the iTunes Store, where other users can access and listen to the music in your playlists.

This type of shared online playlist is called an iMix. You can view others' iMixes by going to the Music section of the iTunes Store and clicking the iMix link in the More in Music box. As you can see in Figure 7.19, you can view the top-rated, most recent, and featured iMixes, or search for other iMixes using the top-of-page Search box. Click an iMix title to view the contents of the playlist, as shown in Figure 7.20. You even have the option of downloading individual songs in the playlist or purchasing all the playlist songs. (To purchase all the songs, just click the Buy All Songs button.)

FIGURE 7.19
Users' iMixes available at the iTunes Store.

To upload your own playlist as an iMix, highlight the playlist in the Source pane, click the arrow icon to the right of the playlist name, and then click the Create iMix button. When prompted, click the Create button. iTunes now generates an iMix file and connects to the iTunes Store.

caution iMix playlists can contain a maximum of 100 songs. Larger playlists won't be uploaded.

FIGURE 7.20

Viewing—and purchasing—the contents of a user's iMix.

The iTunes software now displays the screen shown in Figure 7.21. You're told which songs in your playlist are available in the iTunes Store and prompted to give the iMix a name and a description. Click the Publish button to finish the process and publish the iMix.

FIGURE 7.21

Uploading a playlist as an iTunes iMix.

After you've published an iMix, you can choose to let others know about your uploaded playlist. Go to the iMix playlist page and use the Tell a Friend link to send a notification email, or click Publish to the Web link to generate HTML code that can insert the iMix into any web page, as shown in Figure 7.22.

tip You can specify whether to create a regular iMix or a special Sport iMix. Sport iMixes are organized into a separate section on iTunes for sports enthusiasts looking for workout music. Learn more about Sport iMixes in Chapter 17, "Using Your iPod for Running and Exercise."

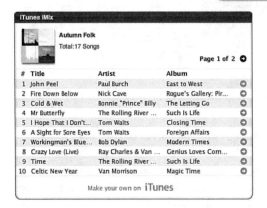

FIGURE 7.22
Displaying an iMix playlist on another web page.

And, if you like, you can update your published iMixes at any time from within the iTunes Store. Just go to the iMix page and click the Go to My iMixes button. Your uploaded playlists are available for editing on the following page.

Using Third-Party Playlist Software

Apple's iTunes isn't the only way to create playlists for your iPod. Several third-party programs exist that help you create more sophisticated playlists from the tracks stored in your iTunes Music library.

For example, **The Filter** (www.thefilter.com) is a plug-in for iTunes that automates playlist creation based on songs you select. That is, you select one or two songs, and the Filter creates a playlist

tip If you like the iMix concept, check out **Goombah** (www.goombah.com). Goombah is a combination software/service that analyzes your iTunes Music library and then matches you with 20 of its members who have similar musical tastes—so that you can hopefully find more music that you'll like. Also similar to iMix is **iLike** (www.ilike.com), which helps you discover new music from other users with similar musical tastes.

with tracks similar to your selection(s). It can also create playlists for specific activities, such as going to work or working out at the gym. It's a free download for the Windows version of iTunes.

Soundflavor DJ (www.soundflavor.com) works in a similar fashion. Specify a song or existing playlist in your library, and the DJ software picks other songs from your library to complement your selection, based on overall sound, style, or era. Like the Filter, Soundflavor DJ is a free download for the Windows version of iTunes.

A comparable program is **MusicIP Mixer** (www.musicip.com), although with a few more options for tweaking your playlists. Select a song and have the program generate a playlist, which you can then fine-tune ("more like this," "less like this," and so forth). The basic program is a free download for both Windows and Mac platforms; a $19.95 Premium version is also available, with more customization.

Bossa (www.mybossa.com) is an iPod management program with a lot of different features, most interesting being the Generator playlist generator. The Generator lets you create timed playlists—that is, playlists with a certain feel that fit within a designated time span. You designate what you want to hear and how long. So, if you want a half hour of dance music followed by 45 minutes of ballads followed by an hour of techno-chill, this program will do it. Bossa is a Windows-only program, with a free trial available.

Other popular playlist creation programs include **Playlist Creator** (www.oddgravity.de) and the Mac-only **Tangerine** (www.potionfactory.com).

Printing Your Music Library List

Want to share a list of your music collection with a friend? iTunes lets you do it—in a number of different ways.

Printing a Song List

To print a list of individual tracks in your library, select Music in the Source pane and then select File > Print. When the Print dialog box appears, select Song Listing, as shown in Figure 7.23. Then pull down the Theme list and select one of the following:

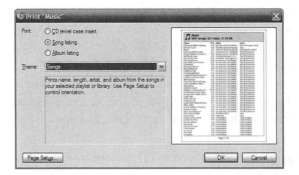

FIGURE 7.23
Printing a list of songs in your Music library.

■ **Songs**, which prints song title, length, artist, and album for each track

■ **User ratings**, which prints song title, length, artist, album, and rating for each track, in landscape format

■ **Dates played**, which prints song title, length, artist, album, play count, and most recent date played for each track, in landscape format

■ **Custom**, which prints the current view of songs as displayed in the iTunes library list

When you've made your selections, click OK to print the list.

Printing an Album List

To print a list of albums or tracks by album, select Music in the Source pane, and then select File > Print. When the Print dialog box appears, select Album Listing, as shown in Figure 7.24. Then pull down the Theme list and select one of the following:

> **tip** Alternatively, you can choose to print a list of tracks in a specific playlist rather than your entire Music library. Just select the playlist name in the Source pane before you select File > Print.

■ **Songs by album**, which prints the album name, artist, and album tracks (along with cover art) for each album in your library

■ **List of albums**, which prints a text list of albums, organized by artist, without listing album tracks

Again, click OK to print the list.

FIGURE 7.24

Printing a list of albums in your Music library.

Exporting a Music Library List

Alternatively, you can export a data file containing your Music library track list, which can then be imported into other applications. To export your track list, select Music in the Source pane, and then select File > Export. When the Save As dialog box appears, pull down the Save As Type list and select either Text Files (.txt) or XML Files (.xml). Click Save to create the text or XML file.

> **tip**
> Text files are the most universally useful because they can be imported into virtually any other program, including both Word and Excel. XML files are used to create web pages, and therefore are readable in any web browser.

7

Podcasts

Songs are only one type of audio file you can listen to on your iPod. Your iPod is also a great device for listening to podcasts—those online audio programs that help you keep up with current news and opinions.

Understanding Podcasts

Despite the name, a podcast doesn't necessarily have anything to do with Apple's iPod. A podcast is essentially a homegrown radio program, distributed over the Internet, that you can play on any portable audio player—iPods included.

Anyone with a microphone and a computer can create her own podcasts. That's because a podcast is nothing more than a digital audio file (typically in MP3 format) posted to the Internet. Most podcasters deliver their content via an RSS feed, which enables users to easily find future podcasts by subscribing to the podcaster's feed. The podcasts are then downloaded to the listener's portable audio player and listened to at the listener's convenience.

What kinds of podcasts are out there? It's an interesting world, full of all sorts of basement and garage productions and more professional recordings. Probably the most common form of podcast is the amateur radio show, where the podcaster assembles a mixture of personally selected music and commentary. But, there are also professional podcasts by real radio stations and broadcasters, interviews and exposés, and true audio blogs that consist of running commentary and ravings. The variety is staggering, and the quality level ranges from embarrassingly amateurish to surprisingly professional.

> **note** Many blogs offer a *feed* of their posts, to which users can subscribe. This is an updated list of all new posts; a feed subscription uses Real Simple Syndication (RSS) technology to notify subscribers of all new posts made to that blog.

Finding and Downloading Podcasts from the iTunes Store

Podcasting hit the mainstream in 2005 when Apple released version 4.9 of its iTunes software, which added podcast capability to the iPod. Now you can browse for and subscribe to podcasts directly from iTunes, and then easily sync them to your iPod.

All current iPods and iPod nanos have a Podcasts item on the main menu. This lets you dial up all your stored podcasts, and then play them back in any order, just as you can with music tracks.

Browsing the iTunes Podcast Directory

The easiest way to find podcasts is to use the Podcast Directory in the iTunes Store. Unlike everything else in the iTunes Store, all podcasts are free to download.

To access the Podcast Directory, click iTunes Store in the Source pane of the iTunes software, and then click the Podcasts link. As you can see in Figure 8.1, you can browse or search through the available podcasts, download the ones you like, and subscribe to the ones you want to hear again. Most of the podcasts here are relatively professional, including programs from ABC News, ESPN, and podcast guru Adam Curry.

FIGURE 8.1

Browsing the iTunes Podcast Directory.

When browsing for podcasts (which is probably the best way to get started), you can browse by the following The:

- **New Releases**. Today's newest podcasts

- **What's Hot**. The most buzzworthy podcasts on iTunes

- **Staff Favorites**. Some of the favorite podcasts from the iTunes staff

- **Top Podcasts**. iTunes' 30 most popular podcasts

- **Categories**. Arts, Business, Comedy, Games & Hobbies, Government & Organizations, Health, Kids & Family, Music, News & Politics, Religion & Spirituality, Science & Medicine, Society & Culture, Sports & Recreation, Technology, and TV & Film

- **Featured Providers**. ABC News, American Public Media, BBC, BusinesssWeek, CBC Radio, CBS News, CNN, Comedy Central, Discovery Networks, ESPN, G4, HBO, Indiefeed.com Community, KCRW, Mondo Mini Shows, MTV News, National Geographic, NBC News, The New York Times, NPR, PBS, PRI, Revision3, TPN The Podcast Network, TWiT TV, The Wall Street Journal, VH1, and WNYC

- **Video Podcasts**. Links to video (not audio) podcasts, which we discuss in the "Watching Video Podcasts" section, later in this chapter

In addition, the center portion of the Podcasts page offers quick links to special categories. For example, a recent page had two special sections, one for Macworld Expo coverage and the other for Iraq War coverage.

Of course, you can also search for podcasts as you can search for any item on iTunes. Use either the search box at the upper-right corner of the iTunes window or click the Power Search link (in the Quick Links box) for more advanced searching by podcast title or author.

> **caution** You don't always know what you're getting until you listen to a podcast. That said, podcasts with known explicit language are listed with an "EXPLICIT" icon; those with known nonexplicit language are listed with a "CLEAN" icon.

Downloading and Subscribing to Podcasts

When you find a podcast you like, you can easily download it to your computer, and then transfer it to your iPod. Each podcast "series" has its own page, like the one shown in Figure 8.2. To download a specific episode, just click the Get Episode link. Podcast downloads work just like music downloads, except without the charge to your credit card. (All podcast downloads are free, remember.)

FIGURE 8.2

Viewing information about a podcast series—and individual episodes.

When you find a podcast series that you like, you can have iTunes automatically download all new podcast episodes. Just go to the podcast page and click the Subscribe button. When you subscribe to a podcast, iTunes automatically checks for updates and downloads new episodes to your computer. (By default, iTunes checks for podcast updates once each day.)

> **tip** To view more podcasts from a given author, click the author's name on the podcast page. This displays a new page with all of that author's podcasts listed.

To access all the podcasts you've downloaded, click Podcasts in the Library section of the iTunes Source pane. (If there's a number next to the Podcasts item, that indicates how many new podcasts are available for you to listen to.)

Finding and Subscribing to Other Podcasts on the Web

Even though the iTunes Store offers many thousands of podcasts, that's still a small fraction of all the podcasts available on the Web. Fortunately, Apple still lets you manage non-iTunes podcasts from the iTunes software.

Finding More Podcasts

First things first. Where can you find more podcasts on the Web?

The best way to find more podcasts is to use a podcast directory. Some of the most useful sites are as follows:

- Digital Podcast (www.digitalpodcast.com)
- iPodder (www.ipodder.org)
- Podcast Alley (www.podcastalley.com)
- Podcast Bunker (www.podcastbunker.com)
- Podcast Directory (www.podcastdirectory.com)
- Podcast.net (www.podcast.net)
- Podcasting News Directory (www.podcastingnews.com/forum/links.php)
- Podcasting Station (www.podcasting-station.com)
- PodCastZoom (www.podcastzoom.com)
- Podfeed.net (www.podfeed.net)
- Syndic8 Podcast Directory (www.syndic8.com/podcasts/)
- Yahoo! Podcasts (podcasts.yahoo.com)

You might have to use more than one podcast directory to find any specific podcast; not all directories list all podcasts from all authors.

Subscribing to Other Podcasts

When you find a podcast you like outside of iTunes, it's relatively easy to add a subscription to that podcast to the iTunes software. iTunes will then track that podcast series and automatically download new episodes as they come available.

The easiest way to subscribe to a non-iTunes podcast is to use your web browser to open the page for that specific podcast. Use your mouse to drag the URL for that page onto the Podcasts item in the Library section of the iTunes Source pane. The podcast is now added to your podcast subscription list.

Alternatively, you can select Advanced > Subscribe to Podcast in iTunes. This displays the Subscribe to Podcast dialog box, shown in Figure 8.3. Enter the URL for the podcast into the URL box, and then click OK.

FIGURE 8.3

Subscribing to a non-iTunes podcast.

Playing Podcasts

After you've downloaded a podcast or two, it's time to give them a listen. Read on to learn how.

Listening to—and Managing—Podcasts in iTunes

To listen to podcasts on your computer—and to manage your downloaded podcasts—you use the iTunes software. As you can see in Figure 8.4, all your downloaded podcasts display when you click Podcasts in the Library section of the Source pane. Click the arrow to the left of the podcast title to view all downloaded episodes from a series.

FIGURE 8.4
Viewing—and listening to—downloaded podcasts with the iTunes software.

To play a particular podcast episode, just double-click it (or select it and then click the Play button). Episodes you've not yet played appear with a blue dot to the left of the title. The blue dot disappears when you start playing the podcast—which is a reminder that the episode will be removed from your iPod the next time you sync your iPod to your PC. If you want that episode to remain on your iPod, you have to manually mark it as not yet played, which you do by right-clicking the episode title and selecting Mark as Unplayed.

One of the neat things about how iTunes handles podcasts is how it handles longish episodes. If you can't get through an entire episode in one setting, iTunes makes it easy to pick up where you left off. When you pause playback of a podcast, iTunes remembers your playback position. Resume playback at your convenience.

Some podcasts come with text notes or information that accompanies each episode. To view the podcast notes, click the *i* icon in the podcast's description column; this displays a notes window, like the one in Figure 8.5.

> **tip**
> To disable the blue-dot auto-remove feature for a particular podcast series, right-click one of the podcast episodes and select Do Not Auto Delete from the pop-up menu. This will retain all episodes of the podcast series until you manually delete them.

FIGURE 8.5

Viewing podcast show notes.

By default, downloaded podcast episodes are stored indefinitely on your computer. As you might suspect, this could rapidly result in an overwhelmingly large podcast library. To change how long podcasts are stored, click the Settings button at the bottom of the Podcasts window to display the iTunes preferences dialog box, and then select the Podcasts tab. From here, pull down the Keep list and make a new selection—All episodes, All unplayed episodes, Most recent episode, or Last *X* episodes.

As previously noted, iTunes searches for new podcast episodes once a day, which is fine for most podcasts. If you subscribe to a podcast that issues new episodes more frequently, however, you can change iTunes' update frequency. Click the Settings button, select the Podcasts tab, and then pull down the Check for New Episodes list and select Every Hour.

Finally, if you get tired of a podcast series and want to unsubscribe, all you have to do is highlight that podcast and click the Unsubscribe button at the bottom of the iTunes window. To delete stored episodes of a podcast, highlight the episode(s) and press the Del key on your computer keyboard.

Listening to Podcasts on Your iPod

On your iPod, you access all stored podcasts by selecting Music > Podcasts.

tip Want to email a podcast episode to a friend? Start by dragging the podcast episode from the iTunes software to your computer desktop. This creates a .pcst file on your desktop for that podcast. You can then attach this file to an email message and send it to whomever you like. If your email recipient has the iTunes software installed, opening the .pcst file will automatically subscribe them to the podcast and download the most recent episode.

Navigate to and select the podcast you want to listen to, and then press the Play button. It's that simple.

As with the iTunes software, your iPod automatically remembers your play-back position when you pause or stop playback of a podcast. Return to the podcast at any future time and press Play, and your iPod resumes playback at the point you previously left off.

Watching Video Podcasts

Not all podcasts are audio podcasts. There is now such a thing as a video pod-cast, which is—as you might suspect—a short podcast-like video broadcast. Video podcasts are typically a bit more professional than audio ones, due sim-ply to the higher production costs of creating videos. Audio podcasts can be created by anybody with a cheap microphone and a computer; video podcasts require a video camera and video recording and editing equipment.

The iTunes Store includes a good selection of video podcasts, located near the bottom of the Podcasts Directory page. You can download and subscribe to video podcasts the same way as you do their audio siblings; downloaded video podcasts are also stored in the Podcasts section of your iTunes library, and automatically transferred to your iPod—assuming you have a video-capable iPod, that is. (Figure 8.6 shows a series page for a typical video podcast.)

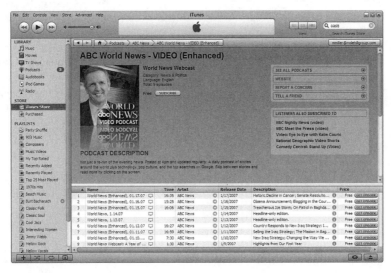

FIGURE 8.6

A video podcast, available from the iTunes Store.

To play a video podcast in iTunes, high-light the podcast and click Play. (Or just double-click the podcast title.) This opens a new playback window, as shown in Figure 8.7, which operates like iTunes' other video playback windows.

caution Video podcasts do not play on iPod nanos or shuffles.

FIGURE 8.7

Viewing a video podcast in iTunes.

tip To find other video podcasts, check out PodGuide.TV (www.podguide.tv), a directory of iPod-compatible video podcasts. Click any link to open a page for the selected podcast in iTunes. You can then download individual episodes or subscribe to the entire video podcast series.

Audiobooks

I travel a lot, and nothing takes the boredom out of a long car trip than listening to a good audiobook. An audiobook is just what the name says, a book on tape or disc or in a digital audio file that you listen to rather than read.

Acknowledging the popularity of audiobooks, Apple has added audiobook capability to both iTunes and the iPod. You can download audiobooks from the iTunes Store and then play them on your computer with the iTunes software, or on the go with your iPod.

Downloading Audiobooks from the iTunes Store

Apple devotes an entire section of the iTunes Store to audiobooks. When you click the Audiobooks link in the iTunes Store box, you see the Audiobooks home page, shown in Figure 9.1. From here you can browse or search for specific titles.

FIGURE 9.1
Audiobooks in the iTunes Store.

Browsing and Searching for Audiobooks

The iTunes Store lets you browse for audiobooks in a number of different
ways:

- **New Fiction**—The latest fiction audiobooks
- **New Nonfiction**—The latest nonfiction audiobooks
- **Top Audiobooks**—iTunes' top 25 best-selling audiobooks
- **Books That Inspired the Movie**—A selection of books on which
  recent movies were based
- **What's Hot**—The most buzzworthy audiobooks
- **Staff Favorites**—Titles chosen by iTunes' staffers
- **Categories**—Audiobooks by major category: Arts & Entertainment,
  Biography & Memoir, Business, Classics, Comedy, Drama & Poetry,
  Audiobooks Latino, Fiction, History, Kids & Young Adults, Languages,
  Mystery, News, Nonfiction, Periodicals, Religion & Spirituality,
  Romance, Sci Fi & Fantasy, Science, Self Development, Speakers &
  Storytellers, Sports, Technology, and Travel & Adventure
- **Popular Authors**—Audiobooks by today's best-selling authors

- **Radio Programs**—Not books per se, but rather titles compiled from popular NPR and PRI radio programs
- **Learn a Language**—Links to language-learning audiobooks

tip The iTunes Audiobooks page also includes a link to podcasts about books—which should delight hardcore booklovers.

You can also search for specific audiobooks. General searches can be accomplished with the top-of-window Search box, or you can click Power Search in the Quick Links box for more advanced searching by title or author.

Purchasing Audiobooks

When you find a specific audiobook page, like the one in Figure 9.2, you can preview the audiobook or go ahead and make your purchase. Purchasing is as easy as clicking the Buy Book button.

FIGURE 9.2
Reading about—and purchasing—a specific audiobook.

Listening to Audiobooks

Listening to an audiobook is pretty much like listening to a music track—with one important exception.

tip To view more audiobooks by a given author, click the author's name on any specific audiobook page. Alternatively, you can click the narrator's name to view all books narrated by this person. (Did you know that Stephen Hoye narrated books by Tom Clancy, James Ellroy, and Kinky Friedman?)

Playing Audiobooks in iTunes

All audiobooks you purchase are downloaded to the Audiobooks section of your iTunes library. (Go to the Library section of the Source pane and click Audiobooks.) To play an audiobook in iTunes, just highlight the title and click the Play button— or just double-click the title.

And here's where audiobook playback is somewhat different from normal audio playback. iTunes *bookmarks* the audiobook—actually, places a marker where you paused—so that it remembers where you last stopped playback. This makes it easy to listen to longer audiobooks in multiple settings. Click the Pause button to pause playback, and the next time you start playing this audiobook, playback resumes from the point where you paused.

Playing Audiobooks on Your iPod

On your iPod, you can browse and play back audiobooks by selecting Music > Audiobooks from the main menu. As with iTunes playback, your iPod bookmarks all audiobooks you play, so future playback is resumed from the last point you paused.

To skip to the next chapter in the audiobook, press the center Select button several times, until the playback indicator changes to a diamond shape. Then you can use the Click Wheel to scroll to any chapter in the audiobook.

There's one more difference between playing back audiobooks and regular music tracks. Some people like to accelerate their audiobook listening by increasing the playback speed—which the iPod lets you do. You can change audiobook playback speed on your iPod by selecting Settings > Audiobooks and choosing either Faster or Slower. Alternatively, while you're playing an audiobook, click the center Select button three times, and then scroll the Click Wheel clockwise to speed up the playback, or counterclockwise to slow down the playback.

tip If a particular audiobook isn't holding its bookmarks, it might not be configured correctly. Select the audiobook in the iTunes software, select File > Get Info, and select the Options tab. To enable bookmarks, make sure the Remember Playback Position option is checked.

Using Non-iTunes Audiobooks on Your iPod

Although the iTunes Store offers thousands of audiobook titles for purchase, lots of other audiobooks are available for download from the Internet. In addition, you can always rip CD-based audiobooks to your PC, and then transfer those files to your iPod for on-the-go listening.

> **tip** Both the iPod and iPod nano offer audiobook playback from the menu system. You can also play back audiobooks (and podcasts) on the iPod shuffle, although the Autofill feature doesn't automatically transfer these spoken-word files along with music files. Instead, you have to manually sync audiobooks and podcasts to the shuffle, using the iTunes software.

Audiobooks at Audible.com

One of the largest distributors of audiobooks is Audible.com (www.audible.com), shown in Figure 9.3. All audiobooks downloaded from Audible.com are in the Audible Audiobook format and offer the same resume-play bookmarking as audiobooks downloaded from the iTunes Store; with more than 35,000 titles available, Audible.com is one of the top sources for audiobooks for your iPod.

FIGURE 9.3

Audible.com—a great source of audiobooks for your iPod.

In addition, Audible.com offers a subscription service that lets you download one audiobook per month, along with other selected audio downloads, for just $14.95 per month. You can also subscribe to audio versions of various newspapers and magazines, such as the *Wall Street Journal*, *Forbes*, and the *New Yorker*.

> **tip**
> One advantage to downloading a title from Audible.com rather than from the iTunes Store is that Audible.com lets you download your audiobooks again in case your lose them. The iTunes Store doesn't let you redownload purchased titles; so if you accidentally erase an audiobook you've purchased, you're out of luck.

Ripping Audiobooks from CD

Ripping an audiobook from CD is pretty much the same as ripping a music CD—but with two major differences.

Before you rip the audiobook, you should reduce the bit rate used to create the resulting audio file. That's because a spoken word recording doesn't require the same playback quality as does a music recording. Select Edit > Preferences in the iTunes window, and then select the Advanced tab and then the Importing tab. Pull down the Setting list and select Spoken Podcast—or select the Custom option and then select 64Kbps, which is the same rate used by both Audible and Apple for their downloadable audiobooks.

Next, know that most audiobooks are divided into multiple tracks on multiple CDs, which result in ripping multiple tracks for a single audiobook. You'll probably want to join these tracks into a single track, or at least one track per CD. To do this, insert the CD you want to rip, check all the tracks on the CD in the iTunes window, and then select Advanced > Join CD Tracks. When you click the Import button, all the tracks on the CD will be ripped to a single file on your PC's hard disk.

Using Audiobook Software

The only problem with listening to ripped and downloaded non-Audible audiobooks is that these titles—in either MP3 or AAC format—don't have the bookmark resume-play capabilities of the audiobooks you download from the iTunes Store. Fortunately, several software solutions are available to solve this problem.

For Windows users, MarkAble (www.ipodsoft.com) lets you merge multiple-track audiobooks into a single file, and then convert that file into bookmark-able format. This gives your ripped audiobooks the same functionality as those you download from Audible.com or the iTunes Store. The software is downloadable for $15.

If you're a Mac user, Audiobook Builder (www.splasm.com/audiobookbuilder) is the program for you. Audiobook Builder lets you organize a multiple-track audiobook into a single file, and then imports that file into a playlist in the Audiobooks section of iTunes and your iPod. Individual tracks become chapter stops in the new combined audiobook file, for easier browsing. The software is downloadable for $9.95.

Manually Changing Ripped Files

As an alternative to using one of these third-party programs, some users have noted success in manually altering their ripped files to appear as audiobook files. After you rip your audiobook in AAC format, use My Computer, Windows Explorer, or a similar file-editing utility to change the extensions on all the ripped files from .M4A to .M4B. (The .M4B file extension enables book-marking by iTunes and the iPod.)

After you've changed the file extensions, you might have to manually re-add the changed files to iTunes; it's also possible that iTunes will automatically recognize the changed files. In either case, the new file extensions should do the job—and let you play your files with all of the normal audiobook play-back features.

Photos

Starting with the iPod Photo, introduced in mid-2005, all iPods with color screens have been capable of displaying digital photos. You might think that viewing photos has little to do with listening to music (and you might be right), but the fact remains that the iPod is a handy little portable photo viewer.

About Photos and Your iPod

The iPod and iTunes are capable of storing and displaying digital photos in the following formats:

- JPG, JPEG
- TIF, TIFF
- GIF
- PNG
- BMP
- PSD
- SGI

■ PICT (Mac-only version of iTunes)

■ JPG2000, JP3 (Mac-only version of iTunes)

Naturally, you use the iTunes software to transfer your digital photos to your iPod. iTunes can sync photos stored in Adobe Photoshop Album, Photoshop Elements, iPhoto (on the Mac), or in any specified folder on your hard drive.

By default, iTunes rescales your photos to better match the display of the iPod. That means that the versions of your photos stored on your iPod are of lower resolution than the original photos—which remain in their original locations on your hard disk.

The photos that iTunes rescales are stored in their own folder on your computer. In essence, iTunes creates a new photo database on your hard drive, which makes photo syncing to your iPod faster than it would be otherwise.

Transferring Photos to Your iPod

Syncing photos to your iPod is a bit different than syncing music. Although you can select individual music tracks to transfer, iTunes can only sync entire folders of photos—not individual photos. iTunes doesn't even display a list of your photos, as it does with music tracks; there's no "Photos" item in the Library section of the Source pane.

In fact, unless you're using iPhoto (on the Mac) or one of the Adobe photo management programs, the best procedure is to create a single folder on your hard drive to store the photos you want to sync to your iPod. This requires a bit of forethought and planning, so be forewarned.

To transfer photos to your iPod, start by connecting your iPod to your computer, and then select the iPod item in the iTunes Source pane. Select the Photos tab (shown in Figure 10.1), make sure the Sync Photos From option is checked, and then click the button to select which photos you want to sync. Your options are as follows:

caution iTunes cannot sync photos from multiple folders to your iPod. It can only sync photos from a single folder—unless you choose a master folder such as My Pictures, in which case you can select one or more subfolders from which to sync. If you select a different folder in iTunes at a later date, all photos from the original folder will be deleted from your iPod when the new photos are synced.

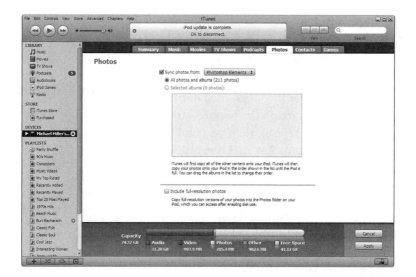

FIGURE 10.1
Preparing to sync photos in iTunes.

- iPhoto (if you have a Mac)
- Photoshop Album (if you have this program installed)
- Photoshop Elements (if you have this program installed)
- Choose Folder

If you select iPhoto or either of the Photoshop applications, you can choose to sync from selected albums within the program. If you choose to sync from a folder on your hard drive, you can choose to sync from selected subfolders within that folder. So, for example, you could select the Choose Folder option, select My Pictures as the folder to sync from, and then check selected subfolders within the My Pictures folder.

Make your selections (and make sure the Include Full-Resolution Photos option is left unchecked—which we discuss shortly), and then click the Apply button to begin the photo transfer to your iPod.

Viewing Photos on Your iPod

After your selected photos have been transferred to your device, you can use your iPod or iPod nano as a portable photo viewer. Here's how.

tip If you opt to sync selected subfolders within a master folder, those subfolders will display as separate photo albums when viewed on your iPod.

Viewing Single Photos

To view one photo at a time on your iPod, select Photos > Photo Library. As you can see in Figure 10.2, this displays all the photos stored on your iPod, in a tiled display. You can scroll through the photos using the iPod's Click Wheel; when you find the photo you want to view, click the center Select button. This displays the photo full screen—or as full screen as possible, given the individual photo's dimensions and orientation. (A standard landscape photo is shown displayed in Figure 10.3; a portrait photo is shown in Figure 10.4, with appropriate black space on either side.)

note Due to its lack of a screen, the iPod shuffle obviously cannot be used to view photos. Neither can older black and white iPods or iPod minis.

caution Since you need to have your iPod's screen on and backlit to see your photos, viewing photos results in a shorter battery charge for your iPod.

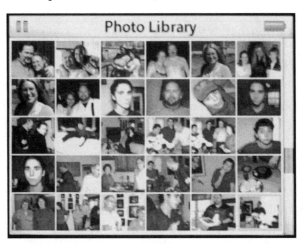

FIGURE 10.2
An iPod's library of tiled photos.

To view the next picture in your library, press the Forward button on your iPod's Click Wheel. To view the previous photo, press the Rewind button. To return to the tiled Photo Library display, press the Menu button. And to start playing a photo slideshow (discussed next), click the Play button.

FIGURE 10.3

A picture displayed in landscape mode.

10

FIGURE 10.4

A picture displayed in portrait mode.

Viewing a Photo Slideshow

As you just learned, your iPod can display all of your photos in an automated photo slideshow. Each photo is displayed onscreen for a short period of time, and then the display changes to show the next photo (either in order or in a random shuffle). The transitions between photos are automated with a variety of special effects.

There are two ways to start a photo slideshow. First, you can navigate to the tiled Photo Library list (Photo > Photo Library), click to select the starting photo, and then press the iPod's Play button. Second, you can select Photo from the iPod's main menu, highlight (but not click) the Photo Library option, and then press the iPod's Play button. Either method starts the slideshow—although only the first approach lets you signify which photo you start with.

When you're in a slideshow, you can pause it at any time (to view a particular photo longer) by clicking the Pause button. Resume the show by pressing Play.

You can move faster to the next photo by pressing the iPod's Forward button. Likewise, you can revisit the last photo displayed by pressing the Rewind button. And pressing the Menu button returns you to either the Photo Library or the previous menu.

Viewing a Slideshow with Music

Slideshows are definitely cool, but even cooler is viewing a slideshow while listening to music in the background. Apple lets you do this via an option on the iPod's Slideshow Settings menu. Here's how it works.

From the iPod's main menu, select Photos > Slideshow Settings > Music. From here, you can select which playlist you want to hear while you're viewing the slideshow. Just select a playlist (or select Off to turn off the background music), and then return to the Photos menu to start your slideshow.

Setting Slideshow Options

You can set several options for your iPod slideshows—how long each photo displays, whether photos display in order or randomly, which transitions are used between pictures, and so on. You access all these options by selecting Photos > Slideshow Settings on your iPod, which displays the Slideshow Settings screen shown in Figure 10.5.

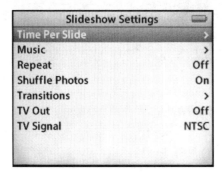

FIGURE 10.5

Configuring slideshow settings for your iPod.

Table 10.1 details each of the available settings.

Table 10.5	iPod Slideshow Settings
Setting	Description
Time Per Slide	Determines how long each photo is displayed in the slideshow; choose from 2 to 20 seconds per photo, or Manual to use manual advance only.
Music	Determines which playlist (if any) you want to play while viewing your slideshows.
Repeat	Turn On to repeat the slideshow over and over, or Off to view the pictures only once.
Shuffle Photos	Turn On to display photos in random order, or Off to display in the order in which they're stored in your photo library.
Transitions	Choose from a variety of slide-to-slide transitions (including cube across, cube down, dissolve, page flip, push across, push down, radial, swirl, wipe across, wipe down, or wipe from center), random transitions, or no transitions.
TV Out	Turns on or off the iPod's TV out function; turn On to view iPod photos on a connected television set, or Ask if you prefer to be prompted as to whether you want to view on your iPod or TV.
TV Signal	Toggle between NTSC (U.S.) or PAL (European) television standards.

Make your selections, and then start the slideshow whenever you want.

Viewing iPod Photos on Your TV

The last two options on the Slideshow Settings screen help you view your iPod photos on a television set. That's right, you're not limited to viewing your photos on the tiny iPod screen. If your TV has a video or S-Video input jack, you can pipe your photos from your iPod to your TV, for viewing on the big screen.

To connect your iPod to a television set, you need to purchase Apple's iPod AV Cable ($19), shown in Figure 10.6, or a similar cable from another manufacturer. You can purchase this cable from the Apple's iPod Store (www.apple.com/ipodstore) or wherever iPods are sold at retail.

Just connect one end of the cable to the dock connector on the bottom of your iPod, and the video plug on the other end to the video input jack on your television set. (Go ahead and connect the audio connectors, too, if you want to pipe music through your TV.) Then select Photos > Slideshow Settings on your iPod and set TV Out to On and TV Signal to NTSC (for U.S. use). Start the slideshow on your iPod, and it appears "big as life" on your TV screen.

tip Another option is to use Apple's iPod Universal Dock ($39), which lets you connect your iPod to the S-Video input on your TV—which results in a slightly sharper picture.

FIGURE 10.6

Use the iPod AV Cable to connect your iPod to your television set.

Using Your iPod as a Digital Photo Storage Device

As noted previously, by default the photos transferred to your iPod are of slightly lower resolution than the original photos stored on your PC. In addition, you can only sync photos one way—that is, you can transfer photos from your PC to your iPod, but not back again (or to another computer).

Unless, that is, you configure your iPod for portable data storage.

Configuring Your iPod for Photo Storage

The concept here is that you use your iPod as a portable hard disk. In this configuration, you can copy full-resolution photos from your computer to your iPod, and then from your iPod to any other computer. While stored on your iPod, the full-resolution photos are viewable the same as any photos, from the iPod's Photos menu. But you can still transfer those photos from one PC to another, using the iPod as the go-between device. It's a great boon for traveling photographers.

To use your iPod in this fashion, you first have to configure your iPod for data storage. You do this from within the iTunes software. Select your iPod in the Source pane, select the Summary tab, and then check the Enable Disk Use option.

Next, you have to instruct iTunes to copy your original photographs in their native resolution to your iPod. You do this from the Photos tab in iTunes. Just check the Include Full-Resolution Photos option.

note Learn more about using your iPod for data storage in Chapter 15, "Using Your iPod as a Portable Storage Device."

When you click Apply, iTunes syncs your selected photos to your iPod. In this instance, it actually transfers two copies of each photo to your iPod. The normal lower-resolution iPod-optimized photos are copied as normal, along with the full-resolution photos that are copied to the Photos folder on your iPod.

note The low-resolution, iPod-optimized photos are stored in a subfolder within the Photos folder, in special .ITHMB format files.

When you view photos on your iPod, the lower-resolution photos are used. But you can now access your iPod from any PC (using My Computer, for example), open

note For any of these devices to work, you have to configure your iPod for disk usage, as described previously.

the Photos folder, and copy the full-resolution photos to that PC's hard disk. It's a great way to store and transfer your digital photos when you're on the go!

Transferring Photos from Your Camera to Your iPod

What do you do when you're in the field and want to store your most-recent photos on your iPod—without first transferring them to PC? For this application, you need a third-party adapter that lets you transfer photos directly from your digital camera to your iPod.

iPod Camera Connectors

There are actually two different types of devices you can buy. The first type of device is a camera connector that lets you run a cable directly from your camera to your iPod. Once connected, you can transfer any and all photos from your camera to your iPod.

The most popular of these devices are Apple's iPod Camera Connector (www.apple.com/ipod/accessories.html, $29), shown in Figure 10.7, and Belkin's Digital Camera Link for iPod (www.belkin.com, $79.99). These devices connect to the dock connector on the bottom of your iPod, and then via USB to your digital camera.

FIGURE 10.7

Use Apple's iPod Camera Connector to connect your digital camera directly to your iPod.

iPod Memory Card Readers

The second type of device is a Flash memory card reader for the iPod. Insert your camera's memory card in the device, connect the device to your iPod, and start transferring photos.

The most popular such device is Belkin's Media Reader (www.belkin.com, $99.99), shown in Figure 10.8. It's essentially a freestanding media card reader that connects to the dock connector on the bottom of your iPod. The data from Flash memory cards inserted into the device are directly transferred to your iPod for storage.

FIGURE 10.8

Use the Belkin Media Reader to copy photos from your camera's memory card to your iPod.

Videos

The 30GB and 80GB fifth-generation iPods do more than just play music. The 5G iPods are full-featured media players, meaning they can play back both audio and video programming—movies, TV shows, and the like.

Watching video programming on the go is great, especially if you're a daily commuter, taking a long-distance trip, or just have a lot of free time on your hands. Read on to learn how to use your iPod for video viewing—and learn how to find and download videos for your iPod.

Understanding iPod Video

The 5G iPod is compatible with a limited number of video file formats, using two specific video codecs—MPEG-4 and H.264. Table 11.1 provides the details.

Table 11.1   iPod Video Codecs

	H.264	MPEG-4
File formats	MPEG-4 (.M4V, .MP4) or QuickTime (.MOV)	MPEG-4 (.M4V, .MP4) or QuickTime (.MOV)
Maximum resolution	320 x 240	480 x 480
Maximum bit rate	768Kbps	2.5Mbps
Maximum frame rate (frames per second)	30fps	30fps

In other words, the iPod can play videos in either the MPEG-4 or QuickTime file formats, encoded with either the MPEG-4 or H.264 video codecs. Videos using the MPEG-4 codec can be of higher quality (higher bit rate and higher resolution) than those using the H.264 codec; videos that use the H.264 codec, however, are more compact in size.

note A *codec* is a compression/decompression technology that compresses audio/video files for storage, and then decompresses them for playback. Different codecs have different performance and storage characteristics. Of the two codecs, H.264 produces smaller file sizes, whereas MPEG-4 offers higher-resolution video.

Because the iPod itself has a screen resolution of 320 x 240 pixels, videos that use the higher-quality MPEG-4 codec are automatically downsized from the maximum 480 x 480 resolution to the iPod's native screen resolution.

Whereas videos you download from the iTunes Store match these file requirements, most other videos you might want to use for iPod viewing don't. That means you must convert these other videos to the proper resolution, bit rate, and file format for iPod use, which we discuss later in this chapter.

Downloading Videos from the iTunes Store

The easiest way to find videos to play on your iPod is to visit the iTunes Store. What used to be called the iTunes *Music* Store has had the "music" removed from its name, thanks to the addition of videos to the store inventory.

What's Available in the Store

The iTunes Store offers three different types of videos available for purchase and download:

- **Music videos**, priced at $1.99 per video
- **TV shows**, priced at $1.99 per episode or $29.99 to $39.99 for a full season
- **Movies**, priced at $9.99 to $14.99, depending on age and studio

You access each of these three types of videos in separate sections of the iTunes Store by clicking the appropriate links in the iTunes Store box on the main page. (Figures 11.1 through 11.3 show the three video home pages in the iTunes Store.) When in a particular section, you can browse by genre, view the latest and hottest items, or perform a Power Search for specific titles.

FIGURE 11.1

Browsing music videos for purchase in the iTunes Store.

FIGURE 11.2

Browsing TV shows for purchase in the iTunes Store.

FIGURE 11.3

Browsing movies for purchase in the iTunes Store.

Purchasing Videos in the iTunes Store

Purchasing movies and music videos is fairly straightforward. Just click the Buy Music or Buy Video button. Purchasing TV shows, however, can be more complex.

note Learn more about purchasing from the iTunes Store in Chapter 6, "Using the iTunes Store."

Within the iTunes Store, television shows are organized by genre, series, and then by season. If you're a *Scrubs* fan, for example, you'd browse the Comedy genre, then *Scrubs*, then for a particular season of the show. When you navigate to the season page for a show, like the one shown in Figure 11.4, you have the option of purchasing individual episodes or of purchasing all episodes for that season. Click the Buy Episode button to purchase and download an individual episode; click the Buy Season button to purchase and download all of that season's episodes. (Or, if the show is currently midseason, click the Buy Season Pass button to download all current and future episodes from this season.)

FIGURE 11.4
Purchasing individual episodes of a TV show—or an entire season.

Transferring Videos to Your iPod

Syncing videos to your iPod is identical to syncing music and other types of files. The next time you connect your iPod to your computer, all recently downloaded videos (of all types) will automatically be transferred to your iPod. You can, if you want, go to the Movies or TV Shows tabs in the iTunes software to specify individual items to transfer; by default, however, all new videos are automatically transferred.

Playing iPod Videos

The videos you download from the iTunes Store can be played back in your iTunes Software, on your iPod, or even on a television set—assuming you have your iPod connected to your TV, that is.

Playing Videos in iTunes

To play a video in the iTunes software, select either Movies or TV Shows from the Library section of the Source pane, select the show you want to watch, and then click the Play button. (Music videos are stored in the Music section of the library, organized by artist with a little TV icon next to the name, as shown in Figure 11.5.)

Name	Time	Artist	
☑ Suddenly I See	3:21	KT Tunstall	
☑ Stoppin' the Love	4:02	KT Tunstall	
☑ Through the Dark	3:48	KT Tunstall	
☐ Suddenly I See ⊙ ☐	3:27	KT Tunstall ⊙
☑ Moonlight Serenade	4:22	Kurt Elling	
☑ Detour Ahead	5:34	Kurt Elling	

FIGURE 11.5

A music video listed in the iTunes Music library.

When you click the Play button, a new window appears on your computer desktop and the video begins playing. When you hover your mouse over the window, the video transport controls appear, as shown in Figure 11.6. You can use these controls to pause, rewind, and fast-forward the playback, and to change or mute the volume. To view the video full screen, click the full-screen button to the right of the transport controls, or press Ctrl+F on your computer keyboard. Click the full-screen button again (or press Ctrl+F again) to return to the video window.

FIGURE 11.6
Playing a video with iTunes.

Playing Videos on Your iPod

To access videos on your iPod, click the Videos item on the main menu. This displays the Videos screen, shown in Figure 11.7, which offers the following options:

> **tip** You can create video playlists within iTunes, just as you do music playlists. Simply create a new playlist item, and then drag individual videos from your library onto the new playlist.

FIGURE 11.7
Browsing videos stored on your iPod.

- **Video Playlists**, similar to music playlists, as created in iTunes
- **Movies**, sorted by title
- **Music Videos**, organized by artist
- **TV Shows**, with individual episodes organized by series
- **Video Podcasts**, as downloaded from the iTunes Store
- **Video Settings**, which provides quick access to key configuration settings—TV Out (On, Off, or Ask), TV Signal (NTSC or PAL), and Widescreen (On or Off)

When you navigate to a specific video, click the center Select button to begin playback. The video now begins to play on the iPod screen. You can pause playback by pressing the Play/Pause button; resume playback by pressing the Play/Pause button again.

To move backward or forward through a video, click the center Select button once to display the progress bar shown in Figure 11.8. With the progress bar displayed, use the Click Wheel to scroll to a specific point, and then click the Select button again.

FIGURE 11.8

Moving to a specific point in the video.

To increase or decrease the screen brightness, click the center Select button *twice* to display the adjustment bar shown in Figure 11.9. With the adjustment bar displayed, use the Click Wheel to adjust the brightness higher or lower, and then click the Select button again.

FIGURE 11.9

Adjusting screen brightness on the iPod.

To move to the next video in the queue, press the iPod's forward button. To return to the start of the current video, press the rewind button once; to move to the previous video in the queue, press the rewind button twice.

note Scrolling the Click Wheel without first pressing the Select button raises or lowers the video's volume level.

Playing iPod Videos on Your TV

If your TV has a video or S-Video input jack and accompanying audio input jacks, you can use your iPod to play movies on your TV. All you have to do is connect the proper cable between your iPod and your TV and set your iPod for TV playback.

First things first—and that's the cable. To connect your iPod to your TV, you need a special audio/video cable. Two of the most popular such cables are Apple's iPod AV Cable (store.apple.com, $19) and Belkin's AV Cable for 4G/5G iPod (www.belkin.com, $19.99), shown in Figure 11.10. These cables are functionally identical—one end of the cable connects to the dock connector on the bottom of your iPod; the other end features a composite video and R/L audio connectors, which connect to the corresponding inputs on your television set.

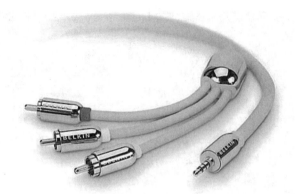

FIGURE 11.10

Belkin's audio/video connecting cable for iPod video.

If want to operate your iPod via remote control while you're watching videos on your TV, check out Apple's iPod AV Connection Kit (store.apple.com, $99). This kit includes the iPod AV Cable and an iPod Universal Dock and iPod Remote, all packaged in a single box.

Even better is Belkin's TuneCommand AV (www.belkin.com, $89.99), shown in Figure 11.11. This accessory includes a dock for your iPod, a wireless remote control, and the necessary connecting cables. It's a slightly more elegant solution than Apple's similar AV Connection Kit.

FIGURE 11.11

Use Belkin's TuneCommand AV to connect your iPod to your television.

After you have everything connected, you have to set your iPod for TV playback. You do this by selecting Videos > Video Settings > TV Out > On. Also, make sure TV Signal is set to NTSC (for North American viewing; European viewers should use the PAL setting). And, if you're using a widescreen TV, set Widescreen to On; otherwise, leave this setting in the Off position.

Now, when you begin playback, the audio/video signal will be sent over the connecting cable to your TV. Make sure your TV is set to the proper video or auxiliary input; then you should see the selected video in all its big-screen glory.

> **caution** Videos played on an iPod are lower resolution than standard television programming. This is especially noticeable if you're playing a file encoded at 320 x 240 resolution—about half the size of a standard 640 x 480 television program. (Since September 2006, all videos offered by the iTunes Store are offered at 640 x 480 resolution.)

Converting Other Videos to iPod Use

Apple's iTunes Store isn't the only source of videos for your iPod. You can convert any existing video you have stored on your computer (including your own home movies) to an iPod-compatible format—and you can find other sites on the Web that offer iPod-format videos.

Converting Existing Videos

Viewing your existing movies on your iPod is a bad news/good news proposition. The bad news is that your existing videos probably aren't in a format that can be viewed on your iPod. The good news is that it's relatively easy to convert those videos to an iPod-compatible format.

QuickTime 7 Pro

Perhaps the easiest way to convert your existing video files is to use Apple's **QuickTime 7 Pro** software. This is a more fully featured program than the free QuickTime player you probably already have installed; one of those features is the ability to convert almost any type of video to the iPod-compatible QuickTime format, using the H.264 video codec.

QuickTime 7 Pro can import video files in a variety of formats, including AVI and MPEG-2. The program costs $29.99 and can be downloaded from www.apple.com/quicktime/pro.

> **tip** You can convert just about any type of video to iPod format—including home movies, television programs recorded via a TV tuner card in your PC, and videos downloaded from the Internet.

To convert a video file with QuickTime 7 Pro, open the video you want to convert, and then select File > Export. When the next dialog box appears, click the Export button and select Movie to iPod (320 x 240) from the drop-down list. Click the Save button, and the converted file is saved to your hard disk. You can now drag and drop the converted file onto the Movies or TV Shows window in the iTunes software.

Videora

Another program you can use to convert your videos is **Videora iPod Converter**. It's a free program and downloadable from www.videora.com.

To use Videora iPod Converter, begin by clicking the Convert button and then selecting Transcode New Video. Then click Open and select the video you want to convert. Click the Start button, and the conversion process begins. When done, copy the converted file into the iTunes software.

PQ iPod Movie Video Converter

Here's another program that handles the video-to-iPod conversion process. The **PQ iPod Movie Video Converter** imports more video formats than competing programs, including RealMedia videos and Microsoft's WMV format. It can export videos using either the MPEG-4 or H.264 video codecs.

Unlike the other programs, Movie Video Converter offers some useful video editing functions, including cropping, aspect ratio adjustment, and video splitting. The program costs $29.95 and can be downloaded from www.pqdvd.com/ipod-video-converter.html.

Cucusoft iPod Movie/Video Converter

The **Cucusoft iPod Movie/Video Converter** is similar to the PQ program. Like the PQ product, this is a Windows program that converts from a variety of formats (including AVI, DivX, RealMedia, and WMV) to the MPEG-4 format for iPod use. Unlike the PQ product, the Cucusoft program is a free download, available from www.cucusoft.com/ipod-movie-video-converter.asp.

Wondershare Video to iPod Converter

This program is a lot like the previous two, but with some nice video editing features—trimming, splitting, and so forth. The **Wondershare Video to iPod Converter** supports both H.264 and MPEG-4 codecs and converts from AVI, MPEG, RealMedia, WMV, and other popular file types. You can purchase it for $29.95 from www.dvd-ripper-copy.com/video-to-iPod.html.

iSquint for the Mac

If you have a Mac, you can use **iSquint** to convert your videos to iPod format. It works like QuickTime 7 Pro and is both fast and free. (Download it from www.isquint.org.)

Converting a video file is as easy as opening the file, selecting iPod as the size, setting the video quality, and then clicking Start. iSquint can even convert Flash video, which QuickTime 7 Pro can't.

Converting Recorded TV Programs

If you own a digital video recorder (such as a TiVo or other DVR supplied by your television provider), you probably have a lot of recorded TV programs stored on your DVR's hard drive. Wouldn't it be great if you could transfer those programs to your iPod to watch while you're away from home?

TiVo Recordings

For TiVo owners, this dream is now a reality. All you have to do is subscribe to the **TiVoToGo** service (free) and install **TiVo Desktop Plus** software ($24.95) on your PC. This combination lets you copy recorded programming from your TiVo to your computer, and then to your iPod.

Before you begin, you have to configure the TiVo ToGo software to convert to iPod format. You do this by selecting File > Preferences > Portable Devices. Click the Convert to Portable Media Device Format list, and then select AVC/H.264.

note The TiVo software is only available for Windows computers; no Mac version is available as yet.

Once configured, the conversion process is relatively straightforward. Select a recording to transfer from your Now Playing list to your TiVo Desktop Account, and then click Transfer. This transfers the recorded program from your TiVo device to your PC. (Naturally, both your TiVo and your computer have to be connected to the same network.)

Once the recording has been transferred, the software automatically begins converting the video file. The converted file is placed in the My Documents > My TiVo Recordings for Portables > AVC/H.264 file. You can then load the converted program into your iTunes software (from within iTunes, select File > Import), and then sync it to your iPod.

tip For instructions on connecting your TiVo to your computer network, see the TiVo website (www.tivo.com).

Windows Media Center Recordings

If you have a Windows Media Center PC, you already know you can use Media Center to record television programming to your PC's hard disk. Well, you can also convert these recorded programs to an iPod-friendly format, to view on your iPod device.

To convert Windows Media Center recordings, use the **MyTV ToGo** program. You can convert selected programs manually, or you can use the ReadySync feature to convert shows as soon as they're recorded.

MyTV ToGo costs $29.99 and can be purchased and downloaded from www.mytvtogo.com.

caution The only issue with converting TiVo programming in this fashion is the time involved. It might take up to two minutes to transfer and convert every minute of TiVo programming—that is, two hours to convert a one-hour program. This is why TiVo recommends transferring and encoding as an overnight process.

tip MyTVToGo can also convert programs recorded on TiVo devices.

Converting DVD Movies

Watching DVDs on your iPod is a trickier proposition because DVD video is encoded in such a way as to discourage ripping and subsequent conversion and distribution. But it can be done; the process involves ripping the DVD to your computer's hard disk and then recoding the resulting video file into an iPod-friendly format.

PQ DVD to iPod Converter

One way to approach this process is to use the **PQ DVD to iPod Converter**. This software costs $29.95 and can be purchased and downloaded from www.pqdvd.com/dvd-to-ipod-converter.html.

The DVD to iPod Converter offers one-click ripping and conversion of DVD movies. Start by opening the DVD disc within the PQ DVD to iPod Converter program. Then click the Recording It button. You can then select the desired resolution of the output file, file output size, audio quality, and so forth. The program then rips and converts the DVD, using either the H.264 or MPEG-4 codecs. The converted file can then be added to your iTunes Movies library.

Cucusoft DVD to iPod Converter

Similar to the PQ product is the **Cucusoft DVD to iPod Converter**. It's a free program, downloadable from www.cucusoft.com/dvd-to-ipod.asp. It can output using either the H.264 or MPEG-4 codecs and supports audio track selection, subtitle selection, and video splitting by DVD chapters. Conversion is faster than real time.

Wondershare DVD to iPod Ripper

Here's another program that performs the entire DVD ripping and file conversion process. The **Wondershare DVD to iPod Ripper** supports both the H.264 and MPEG-4 codecs and offers video splitting and trimming. You can customize the video file size and output quality, and you adjust brightness, contrast, and so on. It can be purchased for $39.95 from www.dvd-ripper-copy.com/dvd-to-iPod.html.

Instant Handbrake on the Mac

If you have a Macintosh, **Instant Handbrake** is a program worth your consideration. It's a free program, downloadable from handbrake.m0k.org.

Instant Handbrake converts files using either the H.264 or MPEG-4 codecs. Just insert the DVD you want to transfer, and then select the file format, picture format (fullscreen or widescreen), preferred audio (typically English), and then click the Convert button. It takes about an hour to rip and convert a typical DVD movie.

Recording "Live" Programming to the iPod

There's another way to get television programming, DVDs, and existing videos onto your iPod. You can record the programming, in real time, from the source device to the iPod, using an external recording device, such as the **DVD Xpress DX2** ($129.99, www.adstech.com), **iRecord** ($199.99, www.irecord.com), or **iSee 360i** ($185, www.atollc.com).

For example, the iRecord is a small white box with audio/video inputs on one side and an iPod connector on the other. Connect your cable or satellite set-top box, DVD player, camcorder, or audio/video outputs from your TV to the input jacks on the iRecord; connect your iPod to the output jack. Press Play on your source device and the Record button on the iRecord; the audio/video from the source device will be converted to an H.264-comparible video file and stored on your iPod. The process takes place in real time, so it'll take two hours to transfer a two-hour movie.

The iRecord has inputs for both composite video and S-Video, along with normal right and left audio. It uses 1GB of storage on your iPod for three hours of video. Because it will record virtually any type of video programming—including commercial DVDs—it's a great solution for transferring video to your iPod.

Other Places to Find iPod-Friendly Videos

Beyond iTunes, beyond the videos already stored on your PC, beyond the DVDs you own, where else can you find videos to watch on your iPod? Actually, quite a few sites offer iPod-compatible videos. Read on to find out more.

Sites with iPod-Format Videos

Check out these sites that offer some or all of their videos in iPod-compatible format:

- **Google Video** (video.google.com). One of the busiest video sites on the Web, complete with both user-submitted and commercial videos—for free and for purchase. To download the iPod video file, select Video iPod/Sony PSP from the Download For list, and then click the Download button, as shown in Figure 11.12.

FIGURE 11.12

Downloading an iPod-compatible video from Google Video.

- **GUBA** (www.guba.com). Like Google Video, a megasite with lots of videos for free download or purchase. Click the iPod button above a video to download it in iPod-compatible format.

- **Channel Frederator** (www.channelfrederator.com). Offers a variety of short animation films. Click Download This to download any video in the iPod-compatible .M4V file format.

■ **Apple Movie Trailers** (www.apple.com/trailers). A great source for downloadable trailers for currently playing and upcoming movies. Many offer iPod-compatible downloads; look for the iPod link or button, like the one in Figure 11.13.

FIGURE 11.13
A movie trailer with iPod-compatible download.

Converting YouTube Videos with iTube

One of the most popular video sites on the Web is YouTube (www.youtube.com). You're probably used to viewing YouTube videos in your web browser, but it's also possible to download YouTube videos to watch on your iPod.

The key is the **iTube** program, downloadable for free from www.benjaminstrahs.com/ itube.php. As you can see in Figure 11.14, all you have to do is enter a URL for the YouTube video, which is found on the YouTube video page. iTube then finds the file, downloads it, converts it to MP4 format, and then imports it into the iTunes software. It's that easy.

caution If you search Google for "iPod movie downloads," you'll get a lot of matches for sites that purport to offer unlimited iPod downloads for a set monthly fee. (Some of the URLs include ipod-movies.net, ipodblender.com, ipoddownloadreview.com, myipodownloads.com, ipod-moviesunlimited.com, and youripodmovies.com.) Beware of these sites; they don't actually offer any files for downloading. Instead, they link you to a BitTorrent search engine, where you may be able to find illegally posted files via file-sharing services—which you don't want to download. It's a total scam!

11

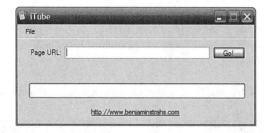

FIGURE 11.14

Downloading and converting YouTube files for your iPod, using the iTube program.

There are several other programs that perform similar YouTube-to-iPod conversion, including **Free YouTube to iPod Converter** (free, www.dvdvideosoft.com), **Ivy Video Converter** ($15, www.ipod-soft.com), and the Mac-only **TubeSock** ($15, www.stinkbot.com/Tubesock/). In

> **tip**
>
> iTube also converts videos from other video sharing sites, such as DailyMotion (www.dailymotion.com), Meta-cafe (www.metacafe.com), and so on.

addition, the vixy.net Online File Converter (www.vixy.net), shown in Figure 11.15, is a website that downloads and converts any YouTube video to iPod video format, no software necessary; the service is free.

FIGURE 11.15

Use the vixy.net Online File Converter to perform web-based YouTube to iPod conversions.

HOW POPULAR ARE IPOD VIDEOS?

As of the first quarter of 2006, Apple has sold more than 50 million videos from its iTunes Store. But according to one major survey, iPod users aren't spending a lot of time watching those videos.

Nielsen Media Research monitored a panel of 400 iPod users for a period of 30 days in October 2006. It found that of those users with video iPods, less than 2.2% of items played were videos. Even factoring in the length of programming, with 30-minute TV shows versus 3-minute music tracks, video watching comprised just 11% of the total time spent using video iPods.

In other words, even with video capability, most people use their iPods to listen to music.

What does this mean about a mass market for mobile video viewing via the iPod? It might be too early to tell; availability of appealing video programming is still spotty, at best. However, it might mean that not everyone wants to watch movies and TV shows on a tiny iPod screen. Perhaps bigger screens on future iPods will change this dynamic, as might greater availability of iPod-ready video programming. But for now, most people use their iPods for music, not for videos.

11

Games

What started as a single-purpose portable music player has evolved into an all-purpose multimedia entertainment device. And, as most of us know, a big part of entertainment today is game playing.

Thus the concept of iPod games. An iPod game, quite simply, is a videogame that you play on your iPod or iPod nano. (Not on your iPod shuffle, of course; you need a screen to play games.) This is a relatively new category for the iPod, but it's growing quickly—and it's a lot of fun!

Playing Built-In iPod Games

The fifth-generation iPod and second-generation iPod nano each come with four games preinstalled. You can find these games (and any other games you subsequently download) by selecting Extras > Games. The preinstalled games include the following:

- **Brick**, shown in Figure 12.1, is a Breakout-type game where you use the Click Wheel to move a paddle that hits a ball that (ideally) breaks through the row of bricks at the top of the screen.

- **Music Quiz**, shown in Figure 12.2, plays a snippet from a song in your Music library; you then have to guess which song that snippet is from. The faster you name that tune, the more points you rack up.

- **Parachute**, shown in Figure 12.3, allows you to use the Click Wheel to aim a gun and the center Select button to shoot down passing enemy planes and paratroopers.

- **Solitaire**, shown in Figure 12.4, is an iPod-friendly version of the classic card game; use the Click Wheel to select cards, and the center Select button to move cards and deal.

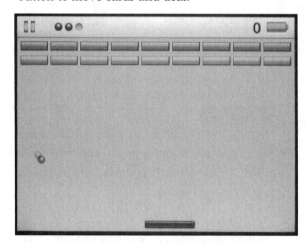

FIGURE 12.1
The Brick iPod game.

FIGURE 12.2
The Music Quiz iPod game.

FIGURE 12.3

The Parachute iPod game.

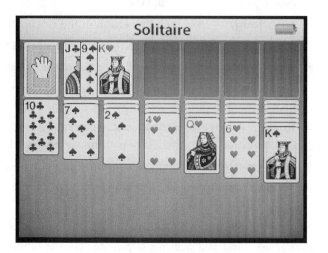

FIGURE 12.4

The Solitaire iPod game.

In all these games, you use a combination of Click Wheel scrolling and Select button pushing. Game play is fairly self-explanatory; press the Select button to both start and pause most games.

Purchasing and Downloading Games from the iTunes Store

Okay, let's be honest. The iPod's preinstalled games aren't all world class, and there aren't that many of them. Fortunately, more—and better—iPod games are available online, at the iTunes Store. The iTS offers a variety of popular games for the 5G iPod that you can purchase for $4.99 each.

caution Games from the iTunes Store are compatible with the fifth-generation iPod only, *not* with the iPod nano. If you have an iPod nano and download these games, they won't install on your nano—which means you'll be out the five bucks.

As of February 2007, the iTunes Store offered the following iPod games:

- **Bejeweled**, a puzzle game that requires you to line up different types of gems in a row
- **Cubis 2**, a 3D puzzle game in which you try to construct cubes while dealing with various obstacles
- **Mah Jong**, an iPod-friendly version of the classic tile game
- **Mini Golf**, a visually rich mini-version of real-world mini golf
- **Ms. Pac-Man**, an iPod-friendly version of the arcade classic
- **Pac-Man**, shown in Figure 12.5, a faithful re-creation of the classic arcade game
- **Royal Solitaire**, a more advanced version than the basic Solitaire game included with the iPod—with many more variations
- **Soduku**, a great-looking version of the popular word puzzle game
- **Tetris**, shown in Figure 12.6, which puts the popular block-building game on the iPod screen
- **Texas Hold'em**, which lets you play poker on your iPod
- **Vortex**, kind of a swirling 360-degree version of the Breakout brick-bashing game
- **Zuma**, a colorful, action-packed puzzle game—one of the best of the currently available iTunes games

FIGURE 12.5

Pac-Man on the iPod.

FIGURE 12.6

Tetris on the iPod.

To purchase these games, click iPod Games on the main page of the iTunes Store. Click any game to learn more, and then click the Buy Game button to make a purchase. The games you download are automatically transferred to your iPod the next time it's synced to your PC; the purchased games show up on the Games screen on your iPod.

EA GETS THE IPOD

Several of the initial games available in the iTunes Store come from the Electronic Arts company. It's not surprising that EA was one of the first game companies to jump on the iPod bandwagon; the company already does a big business in games for other mobile devices, such as cell phones and the Sony PSP.

iPod gaming is "very much a cousin to our existing mobile business," says Mitch Lansky, head of EA's mobile gaming initiatives. EA generated $393 million in mobile gaming revenue in its most recent fiscal year, or 14% of total revenues.

One of the nice things about designing games for the iPod is that it has a consistent design and interface. That's in contrast to designing games for mobile phones, where different versions have to be designed for different models.

That's not to say that iPod games are a walk in the park, design-wise. The iPod doesn't have near the graphics horsepower as does Sony's PSP or Nintendo's DS. In addition, the iPod's Click Wheel doesn't deliver the same speed or operational mobility as a standard game controller.

In spite of that, EA is having great success with its first batch of iPod games, of which Tetris is the best seller. Expect more to come.

Finding Other iPod Games Online

When you're looking for more games to play on your iPod, the first place to look is the iTunes Store. However, the iTS only offers so many titles. Where can you find even more games to play on your iPod?

Unfortunately, not a lot of games are available for the iPod—at least not yet. Most of what's available are text-based games that can be played on any iPod, not the graphically rich 5G iPod games you can download from the iTunes Store. Expect that to change, however, as major game developers recognize the iPod as a viable gaming platform.

That said, you might want to check out these sites that offer text-based iPod games:

- **iPod Arcade** (www.ipodarcade.com), offering a variety of freeware text-based trivia games for the iPod, including NFL Trivia, Lord of the Rings Trivia, Seinfeld Trivia, 007 James Bond Quiz, and so forth

■ **Malinche Entertainment**
(www.malinche.com/
ipodgames.html), which sells inter-
active fiction text-based games—
including the First Mile, Greystone,
and Pentari: First Light—for $9.95
each

tip Another way to get
games onto your iPod
(any model with a screen) is to
install the Linux operating system
and then download Linux games.
Learn more about installing Linux
for your iPod in Chapter 21, "iPod
Hacks."

12

PART

IV

Special Uses

13

Using Your iPod in the Living Room

The iPod is a terrific portable audio player—so terrific, in fact, that many people use their iPods to store their entire music collection.

Wouldn't it be great if you could play your iPod music collection in your living room so that others can listen with you? What you need is a way to pipe the output from your iPod to external speakers, or even to your existing home audio system.

When it comes to playing your iPod in your living, you have lots of options. Read on to learn the many ways to play your iPod in your living room—without earphones!

Connecting Your iPod to External Speakers

For many listeners, the easiest way to share your portable music collection is to connect your iPod to an external speaker of some sort. The simplest way to do this is to connect an external speaker (via some sort of adapter cable) to your iPod's earphone-out jack. A more sophisticated connection comes from those external speakers that connect to your iPod's docking connector; many of these devices also let you operate your iPod from the external speaker or remote control.

You can connect a ton of different types of external speakers to your iPod. There are tabletop speakers, speakers with built-in clock radios, portable speakers, even speakers that look like big jukeboxes. What type you choose depends on your intended use.

Connecting to Computer Speakers

First off, let's look at what exactly we mean when we say *external speaker*. For our purposes, an external speaker is one that is self-powered and has some sort of audio input connection. (The speaker has to be self-powered—that is, have its own built-in power amplifier—because it can't draw power from the iPod.)

What type of device fits this description? Computer speakers, of course. The speakers you connect to your computer are self-powered and connect to a source device via a mini-jack connection—the same type of mini-jack used for the Apple's earphone jack. Which means you can use your existing computer speakers (or any new speakers you purchase) with your iPod.

All you have to do is connect the mini-jack plug from the speaker system to the earphone jack on your iPod, as shown in Figure 13.1. Connect the speakers to a power outlet, turn them on, and then press Play on your iPod. You should now hear your iPod's music through the speakers; control the volume from your iPod or from the speakers' volume control.

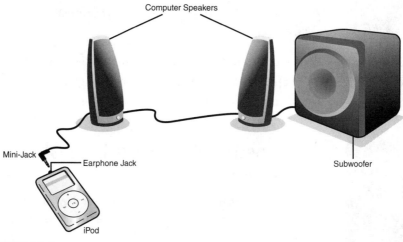

FIGURE 13.1

Connecting an iPod to a computer speaker system.

Although any computer speaker system can work with your iPod, a few models seem purposely designed for iPod use. For example, the JBL Creature II is a unique-looking three-piece speaker system (shown in Figure 13.2) that matches stylistically with Apple's white iPods. Although it's technically a computer speaker system, it connects directly to the iPod's earphone out jack and works just fine. The Creature II system retails for $99.95; learn more at www.jbl.com. (Also worth checking out: JBL's smaller Spot speaker system, priced at $129.95.)

> **note** Most computer speaker systems actually come with two or three speakers—left, right, and an optional subwoofer. In spite of the multiple speakers, there is typically only one input connector; the other speakers connect to the single main speaker, which then connects to your iPod.

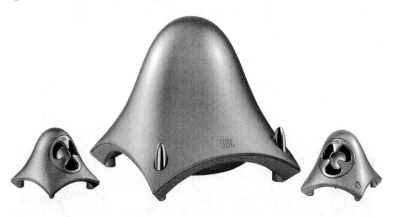

FIGURE 13.2
JBL's Creature II speaker system—computer speakers that work great with any iPod.

The advantage to using computer speakers with your iPod is that they're readily available and relatively low priced. The main disadvantage is placement; you have to position your iPod within a relatively short distance from the speakers, based on the length of the speaker connecting cable. In addition, connecting an iPod to a speaker via its earphone out jack means you still have to control playback via the iPod itself—which might not be that practical, depending on just how short the connecting cable is.

Connecting to a Tabletop Speaker

Okay, let's be honest. Oddities like the Creature II aside, most computer speakers are functional but not stylish; they just don't mesh well visually with the iPod. And, of course, you have the issue of control—or lack of it.

13

A better solution for many is to utilize a tabletop speaker or speaker system designed especially for iPod use. Most of these systems contain a dock of sorts in which you set the iPod; because the iPod connects via its docking connector, you can then (in many cases) control the iPod via the speaker system's controls or remote control. (The dock also recharges the iPod, in most cases.) Plus, of course, these little puppies look a lot more stylish than your typical computer speaker set.

The most common type of tabletop speaker is a box that contains one or more drivers and a dock for the iPod. This type of speaker is exemplified by Apple's own iPod Hi-Fi, shown in Figure 13.3. The iPod Hi-Fi incorporates three separate speakers (and two bass ports) for fairly good room-filling sound, and comes with a remote control that operates both the speaker system and the iPod, which fits into a dock at the top of the unit. The iPod Hi-Fi is a bit pricey, however; you can purchase it for $349 from www.apple.com/ipodhifi.

FIGURE 13.3

Apple's iPod Hi-Fi tabletop speaker system. (Photo courtesy Apple.)

Other popular iPod tabletop speaker systems include the following:

- Athena iVoice ($200, www.athenaspeakers.com)
- Bose SoundDock ($299, www.bose.com)
- Geneva Lab L ($599, www.genevalab.com)
- Griffin Amplifi ($150, www. griffintechnology.com/products/amplify)

- iLive ISPK2806 Amplified Speaker Docking System ($69.99, www.ilive.net)
- iLuv i888 ($49.95, www.i-luv.com)
- JBL On Stage II ($129.95, www.jbl.com)
- JBL Radial ($299.95, www.jbl.com)
- Kensington SX 3000R ($169.99, www.kensington.com)
- Klipsch iGroove HG ($199.99, www.klipsh.com)
- Logitech AudioStation ($299.99, www.logitech.com)
- mStation Orb ($149.95, www.mstationaudio.com)
- SpeckTone Retro ($149.95, www.specktone.com)
- XtremeMac Tango ($199.95, www.xtrememac.com)

note Also popular—but not necessarily in the living room—are iPod clock radios. These are tabletop iPod speaker systems with built-in digital clock and timer. Learn more about these types of units in Chapter 22, "iPod Accessories."

The chief advantages of an iPod tabletop speaker system are convenience and size. True to their name, most units are small enough to fit on an average tabletop and easily connect to your iPod, no extra cables required. The main disadvantage, however, is sound—or lack of it. That is, most of these units sound fine in small rooms but don't have the sonic oomph to fill larger rooms. For that, you need a more powerful type of system—which we discuss next.

Connecting to an iPod Bookshelf Audio System

You can get better sound than what's offered from a tabletop system if you have a more powerful amplifier and if you separate your speakers a little. To that end, check out the category of iPod bookshelf audio systems, which come with separate right and left speakers—and, in some cases, a freestanding subwoofer, for better bass. The advantage of this approach is that you get a slightly louder sound without distortion, and that you can position the speakers separately for optimal stereo separation.

For example, the iHome iH52 (shown in Figure 13.4) is a four-piece system that provides big enough sound for the average living room. The center piece of the system is the controller unit, which features an iPod dock, AM/FM radio, and three-line display. The dock connects to right and left speakers (each with dual drivers) and a separate 7.5-inch side-firing subwoofer. The

13

whole thing is operated via wireless remote control and serves up 32 watts of power. It sells for $199.99 at www.ihomeaudio.com.

FIGURE 13.4

The iHome iH52 iPod bookshelf audio system.

Other iPod bookshelf audio systems include the following:

- Griffin Evolve ($350, www.griffintechnology.com)
- iLive IHMD8816DT Home Docking System ($159.99, www.ilive.net)
- iLuv i9200 ($249.95, www.i-luv.com)
- JVC NX-PS1 ($249.95, www.jvc.com)
- Monitor Audio i-deck ($149.95, www.i-deckusa.com)

The advantages of using an iPod bookshelf audio system included improved sound quality, wider stereo soundfield (if you separate the left and right speakers, that is), a relatively compact footprint, and (in many cases) additional playback features, such as built-in AM/FM radio or CD player. The primary disadvantage is the higher price associated with most of these units, compared to the average iPod tabletop system.

Connecting Your iPod to Your Home Entertainment System

Of course, even a basic home audio system will sound better than the typical tabletop

tip If a bookshelf system isn't powerful enough for you, you might want to check out a slightly larger iPod speaker system. For example, the mStation Tower is a floor-standing system with two midrange drivers, two tweeters, and a built-in subwoofer, all attached to an iPod dock and wireless remote control. The system sells for $299.95 from www.mstationaudio.com.

13

or bookshelf system. And the best home audio systems are truly audiophile quality. So why wouldn't you want to play your iPod through your existing home system?

Well, you probably *do* want to, and you can—with the right connections. Read on to learn how to connect your iPod to an audio-only or audio/video home entertainment system.

Connecting for Audio via an Adapter Cable

If you only want to use your iPod for music (that is, you don't want to play your iPod videos through your home TV), the easiest and lowest-priced way to go requires nothing more than a simple cable connected to an audio system or receiver. This assumes, of course, that your audio system has a spare set of auxiliary input jacks—which most systems do. It doesn't matter how simple or how sophisticated your audio system; the most basic shelf system hooks up the same way as the most expensive hi-fi separates.

What you need is a way to connect from the single earphone mini-jack on your iPod to the right and left auxiliary audio input jacks on the back of your audio system or receiver. This is typically a Y cable, with a male mini-jack plug on one end and two male RCA plugs on the other. For example, Belkin's Stereo Link Cable for iPod cable ($19.99, www.belkin.com), shown in Figure 13.5, offers just this configuration, with 7 feet of cable between the two ends. You can find longer or shorter versions of this same basic adapter, and you can find cables priced higher or lower; alternatively, you can buy a Y adapter with *female* RCA jacks on the split end, and then connect those jacks to a standard R/L audio cable for connection to your audio system or receiver.

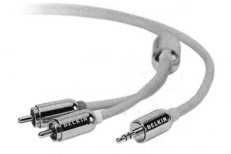

FIGURE 13.5

Belkin's Stereo Link Cable for iPod is a Y adapter that connects your iPod to your audio system or receiver.

The connection itself is shown in the diagram in Figure 13.6. The mini-jack end of the Y cable goes into the earphone jack on your iPod, and the right and left RCA plugs connect to the right and left audio auxiliary inputs on your audio system or receiver. Once connected, power on your iPod and your audio system, switch your system's input to Auxiliary, and whatever you're playing on your iPod will be heard through your home audio system. You still use your iPod to control playback, of course.

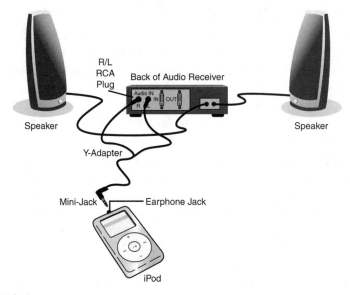

FIGURE 13.6

Connecting an iPod to a home audio system.

Connecting for Audio and Video

Connecting your iPod for both audio and video is a bit more complex. As first discussed in Chapter 11, "Videos," you need an adapter cable that not only splits for right and left audio, but also for video.

This type of cable connects to the dock connector on the bottom of your iPod, and then to the right/left audio inputs on your audio system or receiver and the composite video input on your television set. (Figure 13.7 illustrates this type of connection.)

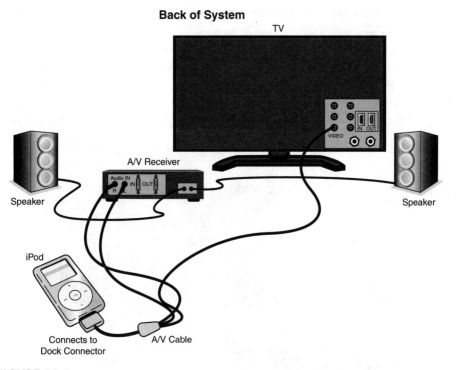

FIGURE 13.7
Connecting an iPod to a home audio/video system.

Popular audio/video iPod cables include the following:

- Apple iPod AV Cable ($19, store.apple.com)
- Belkin AV Cable for 4G/5G iPod ($19.99, www.belkin.com)
- Marware AV Cable for iPod Video and iPod Photo ($17.95, www.marware.com)
- Pacific Rim Technologies Retractable AV Cable for iPod ($9.99, www.pacrimtechnologies.com)

Connecting via an iPod Dock

A more versatile solution is to use an iPod dock to connect to your home entertainment system. With this approach, your iPod connects to the dock via its bottom-of-unit docking connector, which lets the dock itself (or the accompanying remote control) operate the iPod. The audio outputs on the dock then connect to the auxiliary inputs on your audio system or receiver, and the video output (when available) connects to the audio input on your TV.

For example, the DLO HomeDock Deluxe, shown in Figure 13.8, has the requisite iPod docking unit, with outputs for right/left RCA-jack audio and S-Video. It comes with an 18-function wireless remote, which can control your iPod from across the living room. When connected to your TV, the HomeDock Deluxe displays iPod song info and playlists (and iPod videos) on your TV screen. The whole thing costs $149.99 and is available from www.dlo.com.

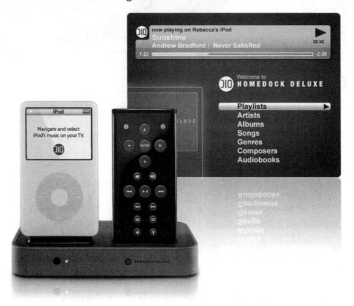

FIGURE 13.8
The DLO HomeDock Deluxe iPod dock.

Other similar iPod docks include the following:

- Apple AV Connection Kit (audio/video, $99, store.apple.com)
- Belkin TuneCommand AV (audio/video, $89.99, www.belkin.com)
- Belkin TuneSync (audio-only, $65.99, www.belkin.com)
- DLO HomeDock (audio-only, $99.99, www.dlo.com)
- Griffin TuneCenter (audio/video, $129.99, www.griffintechnology.com)
- Kensington Entertainment Dock (audio/video, $99.99, us.kensington.com)
- Kensington Stereo Dock (audio-only, $59.99, us.kensington.com)
- KeySpan AV Dock for iPod (audio/video, $79, www.keyspan.com)

Connecting Wirelessly

If you don't want to mess with stringing long runs of cables, consider a wireless connection solution. This involves connecting a wireless transmitter to the bottom of your iPod (to the dock connector) and a wireless receiver to the audio inputs on your audio system. The transmitter transmits audio and control information from your iPod; the receiver receives the audio and control info and feeds the audio to your audio system. This lets you use your iPod as a remote-control unit and play tunes from across the room, or even from another room.

One of the more popular wireless iPod systems is the Griffin BlueTrip LE, shown in Figure 13.9. The BlueTrip's transmitter connects to your iPod's dock connector, and then connects to the receiver unit via Bluetooth wireless technology. It works up to 33 feet away, with quite good sound quality. The BlueTrip LE sells for $99.99 from www.griffintechnology.com.

FIGURE 13.9

The Griffin BlueTrip LE wireless receiver.

A similar but more expensive solution is provided by the Scosche BlueLife System. Outfitted for home use, BlueLife consists of a Bluetooth transmitter that attaches to your iPod and a wireless receiver that connects to your home audio system. Scosche's iPod Receiver and Transmitter Kit costs $249.99 and is available from www.scosche.com. (Scosche also makes similar kits for wireless in-car iPod use.)

Then there's the Creative Xdock Wireless, shown in Figure 13.10. You dock your iPod into the base unit transmitter, which then connects wirelessly to up to four X-Fi Wireless Receiver units for whole-house audio. Each Xdock Receiver connects to a pair of powered speakers (or, via optical digital connection, to an audio/video receiver) and is controlled by its own wireless remote control. The Xdock Wireless bass unit sells for $299; each X-Fi Wireless Receiver sells for $149. Learn more at www.x-fi.com.

> **tip** Griffin's AirClick ($39.99, www.griffintechnology.com) takes a slightly different approach. You leave your iPod connected directly to your home entertainment system, but connect the AirClick receiver to the iPod's dock connector. You then control the iPod from across the room with the included remote-control unit. A similar approach is taken by the KeySpan TuneView ($179, www.keyspan.com), which includes a remote-control unit with color screen that mirrors the iPod display.

FIGURE 13.10
Creative's Xdock Wireless system for whole-house audio.

Connecting to iPod-Ready Receivers

Then there are those audio/video receivers that have iPod inputs. Many newer receivers are "iPod ready"—that is, they have dedicated iPod inputs. Some of these iPod-ready receivers simply have mini-jack inputs, others utilize a special iPod cable that connects to the iPod's dock connector, whereas others connect to a proprietary iPod dock. The last two options offer full iPod control and (in many cases) iPod display out to your television screen.

For example, many Onkyo receivers have inputs for the company's DS-A2 iPod Cradle, shown in Figure 13.11. All you have to do is connect the Cradle to your Onkyo receiver and then slide your iPod into the Cradle's dock. You can then control your iPod with your receiver's remote and view playlist and song information on your TV screen (providing you connect the video output on your receiver to the video input on your TV, of course). It's a relatively elegant solution. Purchase the DS-A2 for $99.95 from www.onkyousa.com.

FIGURE 13.11
The iPod Cradle for Onkyo-brand audio/video receivers.

iPod and iTunes for Audiophiles

Many people enjoy listening to their iPod or iTunes music over their home audio systems and think the music sounds just fine, thank you. Others think that iPod/iTunes music sounds markedly inferior to music played from CD. I find myself in the latter group.

The world of music lovers breaks down into two groups: the average listener and the audiophile. The average listener is satisfied with the compressed digital audio used by iTunes and the iPod; he can't hear the difference between the iPod version and the original. The audiophile, however, is a more critical listener; he hears the lower bit rate and the truncated frequency response, and is appalled.

Although audiophiles might (reluctantly) accept the compromises of compressed audio when listening via earbuds on an iPod, those compromises are unacceptable when listening on their home audio systems. These are people who invest thousands of dollars on high-end speakers, high-performance amplifiers, and low-noise pre-amplifiers, and they are unwilling to accept any sonic compromises. Unfortunately, compressed audio (in any format—AAC, MP3, or WMA) is a huge compromise and quite noticeable to the trained ear.

caution You may also run into volume level issues when connecting your iPod to your home audio system. The audio output level on the iPod is rather low compared to other audio components; this may require you to raise your receiver's volume level above what you're normally used to. Make sure you lower the volume on your receiver before switching back to CD, DVD, or television playback.

You will never see an audiophile connect an iPod directly to a home audio system. You will never see an audiophile play back compressed iTunes music over a home audio system. You will never see an audiophile replace his CD collection with digital music stored in iTunes.

So if you're an audiophile, what options do you have for listening to your iTunes library? Let me tell what I do.

First, I keep two separate libraries. My main library consists of my entire CD collection ripped to a large hard disk using lossless compression. (I happen to use the WMA Lossless format for playback via Windows Media Center, but you can also use the Apple Lossless format.) My subsidiary library, stored on a separate computer, consists of that subset of my CD collection I want to listen to on my iPod, stored in the default AAC (lossy compression) format.

It's a duplication, I know, but for now it's the only way to do it. I need lossless compression to preserve the original fidelity for playback on my home audio system, and I need lossy compression to store as many songs as possible on my iPod. Yes, I could listen to lossy files on my home audio system, but the sonic compromise is unacceptable to my ears; I could also use lossless compression on my iPod, but then I'd only be able to store about 10% of the songs I can store using lossy compression.

To maximize the benefits of both my home audio system and my iPod, I have to use these two different compression schemes—lossless compression for best

13

sonic fidelity and lossy compression for most storage. Unless and until Apple comes out with a 1-terabyte iPod (and that day may come), it's the only option available to audiophiles like me.

Using iTunes in Your Home Entertainment System

You don't have to connect your iPod to your home audio system to enjoy your digital music in your living room. Another approach is to connect your *computer* to your home audio system and play the music stored in your iTunes library. There are several ways to do this.

Connecting Your PC Directly to Your Home Audio System

Perhaps the easiest way to listen to your iTunes music on your home audio system is to connect your main computer directly to your audio system or receiver. This can be done simply or in a more sophisticated fashion.

The simple solution is to connect your PC to your receiver the same way you'd connect an iPod. That is, run a Y adapter from the mini-jack audio output on your computer to right and left RCA audio inputs on your audio system or receiver, as shown in Figure 13.12. You need a longish cable, of course, assuming you don't have your PC sitting right next to your audio system.

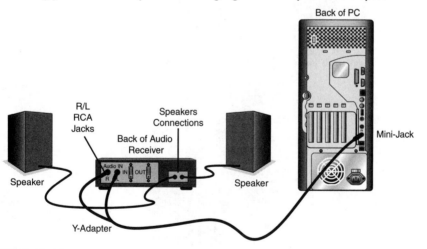

FIGURE 13.12

Connecting a computer to a home audio system.

Once connected, you control iTunes from your computer, and whatever music you select is heard via your home audio system. It's not the most elegant or the most versatile solution, but it is simple and cheap.

> **tip** When you're connecting your computer to your home audio system, consider purchasing a remote control for your PC, to operate iTunes from your living room. One such remote is the KeySpan Remote for iTunes, available for $39 from www.keyspan.com.

Connecting Wirelessly

Assuming that your computer isn't located in your living room, a different solution is called for. In this instance, you want to think about establishing a wireless connection between your computer and your home audio system.

Perhaps the most popular wireless solution uses Apple's AirPort Express, shown in Figure 13.13. The AirPort Express was designed specially for iTunes use. It sends digital music wirelessly from your computer to your home audio system, using 802.11b/g WiFi technology. Just plug the AirPort Express unit into a power outlet, and then connect it to your audio system or receiver using either an optical digital audio cable or right/left RCA analog audio cables. Once configured, the music you play in iTunes on your computer is then heard via your home audio system.

FIGURE 13.13

Apple's AirPort Express.

The AirPort Express works on both Windows and Macintosh computers. It sells for $99 from www.apple.com/airportexpress.

> **tip** The AirPort Express can also operate on a conventional Ethernet network.

Sharing Your Music Across Your Home Network

Here's something a lot of users don't know. You can listen to digital music stored on one computer with any other computer on your network that's also running iTunes. This would let you store your Music library on your main computer (a large desktop PC in your office, perhaps) and then play your music through another, smaller computer connected directly to your home entertainment system. Just make sure that both computers are connected to the same home network (either wirelessly or via Ethernet), and that iTunes is configured for network operation.

To configure iTunes for network operation, open iTunes on your main computer, select Edit > Preferences, and then select the Sharing tab, shown in Figure 13.14. Check the Share My Library on My Local Network option, and then select whether you want to Share Entire Library or Share Selected Playlists. If you select the latter option, you then check those playlists you want to share. Give your library a name, and check if you want to require a password for access. (You probably don't.) Click OK when done.

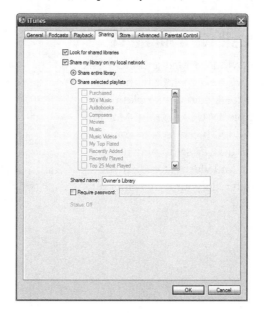

FIGURE 13.14

Sharing your Music library between PCs in iTunes.

Likewise, you have to configure iTunes on your remote (living room) computer to look for your shared Music library. Once again, select Edit > Preferences and select the Sharing tab. On this computer, check only the Look for Shared Libraries option. Now, the next time you start iTunes on your living room PC, it will search your network until it finds your shared Music library on your main PC. All the music on your main PC will appear in iTunes on the remote PC, under a Shared Music section in the Source pane. Just select the Shared Music section and the specific library you're sharing; playback should be transparent.

Listening to iTunes via Windows Media Center

If you have a PC running Windows Media Center, you can install a plug-in that lets you listen to your iTunes music from within Media Center, over your home network. The plug-in, called MCE Tunes Pro, is available for $29.99 from www.mcetunes.com.

You install the MCE Tunes Pro plug-in within Windows Media Center, so it's accessible from the Media Center menu system. You start by importing your iTunes music into MCE Tunes Pro—your entire library, or selected tracks or playlists. Once imported, you can play any iTunes track from within Media Center, as you would any WMA-format music.

Listening to Music with Apple TV

Speaking of Windows Media Center PCs, Apple now has a competitor to the Windows-based Media Center platform. The new Apple TV is like a mini-Mac for your living room. It connects to your home audio system and TV set to play back iTunes music and videos stored on your main computer via your home entertainment system.

note You need MCE Tunes Pro to play back DRM-protected music purchased from the iTunes Store. The lower-priced ($14.99) MCE Tunes application only plays back nonprotected music you've ripped from CD. MCE Tunes Pro also plays back videos you've purchased from the iTunes Store.

13

Specs and Connections

As you can see in Figure 13.15, the Apple TV unit is a computer that's just 7.7 inches square and 1.1 inches high. It runs an Intel processor (with either Mac OS X or Windows XP) and includes a 40GB hard drive for internal storage. It also connects to a home network (via built-in Ethernet or optional WiFi) to access media stored elsewhere on your home network. Operation is via a special iPod-like Apple Remote.

FIGURE 13.15

Apple TV—an iTunes computer for your living room. (Photo courtesy Apple.)

The Apple TV unit connects to your TV via HDMI or component video and to your audio system via optical digital or analog RCA audio connections. It supports all the audio, video, and photo formats supported by iTunes, and offers 480p, 576p, 720p, and 1080i resolution video.

Apple TV sells for $299 and is available from www.apple.com/appletv.

Using Apple TV

Once connected to your home network, Apple TV automatically syncs to any iTunes library stored on the network. You navigate through the onscreen menus to select music, movies, or photos for playback. Figure 13.16 shows the Apple TV main menu screen. Select Music to play your iTunes music, or select Movies or TV Shows to view videos downloaded from the iTunes Store.

13

FIGURE 13.16

The Apple TV main menu screen. (Photo courtesy Apple.)

When you select Music from the main menu, you're presented with a submenu that pretty much mirrors the iPod menu, with the following options: iTunes Top Music, iTunes Top Music Videos, Shuffle Songs, Music Videos, Playlists, Artists, Albums, Songs, Genres, and Composers. Make a selection to view available items or start playback. The track playback screen includes a large picture of the corresponding album cover, and a progress bar—very similar to what you see when playing music on your iPod. It's very elegant, and very easy to use.

> **note** The Apple TV interface is based on Apple's Front Row media player interface, found on newer Macintosh computers.

Compared to other similar living room solutions, Apple TV appears to priced on the high side. Still, when you consider that you're getting a mini-PC with 40GB of storage, along with network connection to your entire iTunes media library, it's not a bad deal—and the onscreen interface is to die for!

Apple TV vs. Windows Media Center

Apple TV is, in many ways, Apple's answer to Microsoft's Windows Media Center. An Apple TV unit performs many of the same functions as a Media Center PC, but with Apple's Front Row-like interface. It also integrates better with Apple's iTunes, including items purchased from the iTunes Store.

So which is the better deal—an Apple TV or a Windows Media Center PC? On this issue, I come down on the side of Windows Media Center, for several reasons.

First, a Media Center PC does a lot more than Apple TV does. Media Center isn't just a single-function device, as Apple TV kind of is; Media Center lets users play digital music, view digital photos, record television programming, play back recorded and downloaded videos, and even play DVDs and CDs. Apple TV is much more limited, pretty much just a digital music player, digital photo viewer, and downloaded video player. Apple TV has no facility for recording television programming and no built-in DVD or CD drive.

In addition, Media Center PCs are much more customizable. Media Center PCs can be configured with larger hard drives, more memory, multiple TV tuners, even CableCARD capability (to record cable programming without a set-top box). Not so Apple TV, which comes in only a single configuration.

And that configuration, although quite affordable, is extremely underpowered. How much music can you store on a 40GB hard drive? Not much at all—and don't even think about storing a lot of downloaded videos. The lack of a CD/DVD drive is also limiting, as is the lack of a TV tuner.

For $299, Apple TV is really nothing more than an iTunes-centric network media player, much like a Windows Media Center extender. By itself, Apple TV doesn't do much. For Apple TV to work, it must be connected (via your home network) to a more full-feature host computer.

In short, Apple TV does a lot less than a Media Center PC and nothing more than a lower-priced Media Center extender. If all you want to do is play back your iTunes music (already stored on another PC) on your living home entertainment system, Apple TV is fine, if a bit expensive. If you want a full-fledged digital media system, however, capable of storing and playing back all manner of music, movies, and TV shows, Apple TV (at least in its current incarnation) doesn't have what it takes to get the job done—despite the typically stylish Apple interface.

13

Using Your iPod in the Car

When you love your music, you want to listen to it everywhere—including and especially in your car. Although you *could* pop on your earphones to listen to your iPod while driving, that's not really safe and might even be illegal in your particular locale. A better solution is to somehow pipe the tunes from your iPod through your car's built-in audio system. How you do this depends on the features of your particular car (and car audio system) and how much trouble you want to go through.

Connecting to an iPod-Enabled Car

Some people have it good. These folks own cars that are iPod-compatible from the factory. Yes, it's true; a lot of today's new cars have built-in iPod connectivity.

If you own an iPod-compatible car, all you have to do is connect your iPod to the car stereo. How this works depends on the type of iPod integration.

Cars that offer full iPod compatibility provide a cable (often located in the car's glove compartment) or dashboard dock that connects to your iPod's dock connector. After you connect your iPod, you control it via the car's in-dash audio system, hear iPod playback over your car's speakers, and view track info on your system's in-dash display. As an added bonus, your iPod recharges when connected. (Figure 14.1 shows an iPod connected to a Volvo audio system.)

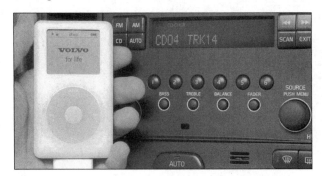

FIGURE 14.1

Connecting an iPod to a Volvo in-dash system.

Of course, not all iPod-compatible cars are this fancy. For example, GM's iPod "compatibility" consists of an auxiliary mini-jack input on the front of their factory-installed audio systems. You connect the earphone out jack on your iPod (or any MP3 player) to this auxiliary input, which means you're simply using your car audio system for audio playback; there's no in-dash display of track info or remote control of iPod operation. (Figure 14.2 shows an iPod connected to a GM audio system in this fashion.)

FIGURE 14.2

Connecting an iPod to a GM in-dash system.

Apple claims that more than two-thirds of all 2007-model cars sold in the United States offer some sort of iPod connectivity. Which brands offer iPod connectivity? Here's the current list:

- Acura
- Audi
- BMW
- Chrysler
- Dodge
- Ferrari
- Ford
- GM
- Honda
- Infiniti
- Jaguar
- Jeep
- Mazda
- Mercedes
- Mini
- Nissan
- Scion
- Suzuki
- Volkswagen
- Volvo

It goes without saying that not all makes and models from these brands offer iPod connectivity. In addition, iPod connectivity is often an option, not standard equipment—which means you'll pay a little extra for it. (For example, BMW's iPod Adapter costs $149 plus dealer installation.) But still, factory-installed iPod connectivity is definitely the easiest way to go; there's nothing for you to install, just connect your iPod and start listening, using your car radio's standard controls. If your current car isn't iPod compatible, make sure this feature is on your checklist when you're shopping for a new car.

note iPod connectivity is not limited to land vehicles. Many fishing and pleasure boats are now coming with iPod-ready sound systems, just like those offered by automobile manufacturers.

14

Installing an Aftermarket iPod-Ready Car Audio System

If your current car doesn't offer iPod connectivity, all hope is not lost. You can replace your current car audio system with a new one that does let you connect and control your iPod. And lots of options are available.

Many new aftermarket car audio systems offer connections to either the iPod docking connector or the iPod's earphone out jack. The docking connector option is the best way to go, because it lets you operate the iPod from the in-dash controls, display now-playing information on the in-dash display, and recharge the iPod while it's connected. An auxiliary connection to the iPod earphone jack offers none of these control or display options, it merely funnels the iPod's audio into the in-dash system.

For example, the Alpine CDA-9857, shown in Figure 14.3, has an iPod Direct Connection on its rear panel. Connect an optional Full Speed Connection cable between the back panel and your iPod's dock connector, and the in-dash unit controls all the iPod's operations. The in-dash display also shows artist, album, and track information. It's available for $349.99 from www.alpine.com.

FIGURE 14.3

Alpine's iPod-compatible CDA-9857 in-dash car stereo.

Which car stereo manufacturers offer iPod-compatible units? It's a long list, including the following:

- Alpine (www.alpine.com)
- Blaupunkt (www.blaupunkt.com)
- Clarion (www.clarion.com)
- Dual (www.dualav.com)
- Eclipse (www.eclipse-web.com)
- JVC (www.jvc.com)
- Kenwood (www.kenwoodusa.com)
- Panasonic (www.panasonic.com/consumer_electronics/caraudio)

■ Pioneer (www.pioneerelectronics.com)

■ Sony (www.xplodsony.com)

Prices on these units run from the sub-$100 range to more than $1,500. To my eye, you'll find the most options in the $200 to $400 range, including units that offer full iPod operability via the docking connector.

Installing a new car audio head unit is typically a job for a professional car audio installer, although many individuals choose to do it themselves. Make sure you choose a unit that fits in your particular dash; most car audio retailers offer charts or searchable databases that let you find the right systems for your car's specific make and model.

> **pick** Although I always recommend the services of local merchants, if you want to shop via mail order or the Web, Crutchfield (www.crutchfield.com) offers a wide selection and lots of useful online information.

Connecting to an Existing Car Audio System

What do you do if you want to play your iPod in your car but don't want to (or can't afford to) purchase a new car audio system? Again, you have several options.

The preferred option, in terms of sound quality, is to make a direct connection between your iPod and your car audio system. With a direct connection, you retain the full audio fidelity of your iPod; this is not the case if you connect via FM modulation (which we discuss later in this chapter).

You can make a direct connection between your iPod and your car audio system in many different ways. Some car connection kits are mere cables that run between your iPod (either the dock connector or the earphone out jack, depending) and the auxiliary input jacks found on the back of many OEM and aftermarket audio head units. Other kits feature adapters that utilize the CD changer port found on the back of many car radios. Some connection kits provide dock mounts for the iPod, whereas others offer auxiliary controllers and displays. As is the case with aftermarket audio systems, I recommend you have a professional installer help you decide which kits work best for your vehicle and perform the installation itself.

> **caution** iPod adapters that connect to the auxiliary input on your car radio do not receive power from your vehicle. You'll need to invest in a separate power adapter to connect your iPod to your car's cigarette lighter, or risk your iPod's battery running out in the middle of a long drive.

14

One of my favorite direct connection kits is the Harman Kardon Drive + Play, shown in Figure 14.4. The Drive + Play's "brain" is a small box that mounts in the glove box or under a front seat and connects to your existing radio's auxiliary input. Connected to the main unit is a backlit LCD display that displays iPod-style menus and track info, and a mushroom-shaped controller unit that works much like the iPod Click Wheel. You mount the display on your dashboard and the controller on your center console. The whole system sells for $149.99 and is available from www.harmankardon.com/drive-1.

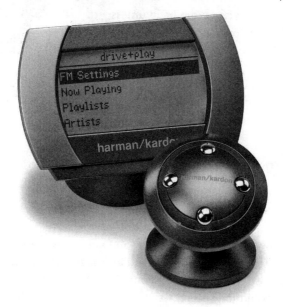

FIGURE 14.4

The Harman Kardon Drive + Play iPod direct connection kit.

Not all direct connection kits are quite this sophisticated, and not all kits work on all vehicles. In fact, some "kits" are nothing more than connecting cables, like the Neo iON kit from Mp3YourCar, shown in Figure 14.5. Check with the kit manufacturer to find the kit that works with your particular vehicle and audio system.

note If your existing car audio system doesn't have an auxiliary input, the Drive + Play can use FM modulation to play through your vehicle's FM radio.

FIGURE 14.5
The Neo iON direct connection kit.

Here are some of the more popular manufacturers of direct-connection iPod kits:

- Blitzsafe (www.blitzsafe.com)
- Mp3YourCar (www.mp3yourcar.com)
- PAC (www.pac-audio.com)
- Peripheral (www.peripheralelectronics.com)
- P.I.E. (www.pie.net)
- Smart Park iConnect (www.smartpark.net/iPod_iConnect.html)
- USA Spec (www.usaspec.com)
- VAIS Technology (www.vaistech.com/sli.html)
- Wire-Tunes (www.wire-tunes.com)

Expect to pay between $50 and $150 for these direct connection kits and cables.

Connecting via a Cassette Adapter

All the previous in-car solutions involve a bit of work. If you'd prefer not to pull your car radio out of the dash and fiddle with

tip There are lots of different ways to modify an existing car audio system for iPod use. For more information and ideas about in-car iPod installations, check out the iPod in Car blog (www.ipodincar.net).

14

this cable and that, you need a way to connect your iPod to the *front* of your car's audio system.

Naturally, if your audio system has an in-dash auxiliary input jack, you can connect a standard mini-jack cable between your iPod and this auxiliary input. Otherwise, you have to look for another solution.

If your car radio includes a cassette player (and some still do), a workable solution is to use a cassette adapter. These devices, like the Belkin Cassette Adapter shown in Figure 14.6, look like a cassette tape with a cable attached, but there's no tape inside. Instead, the adapter transfers the audio output signal from your iPod to the read head of your in-dash cassette deck. Just insert the adapter into your radio's cassette slot and connect the cable to the earphone out jack on your iPod. Switch your audio system to "cassette," press Play on your iPod, and you'll hear your iPod music over your car's speakers.

FIGURE 14.6

The Belkin Cassette Adapter lets you connect your iPod to your car's cassette player.

Cassette adapters don't sound quite as good as direct connections, but do sound noticeably superior to FM transmitters, which we discuss next. They're also lower priced than other options.

Some of the most popular cassette adapters include the following:

> **caution** Connecting your iPod to a cassette adapter does not provide power to your iPod. You'll need to invest in a separate power adapter to connect your iPod to your car's cigarette lighter.

- Belkin Cassette Adapter for iPod ($19.99, www.belkin.com)
- Griffin DirectDeck ($14.99, www.griffintechnology.com)
- Griffin SmartDeck ($29.99, www.griffintechnology.com)

■ iRock Car Cassette Adapter ($3.99, www.myirock.com)

■ Macally Cassette Tape Car Adapter ($14.99, www.macally.com)

■ Maxell CD-330 Cassette Adapter ($13.99, www.maxell-usa.com)

■ Sony DCC-E34CP Car Connecting Pack ($29.99, www.sonystyle.com)

Connecting via an FM Transmitter

The last type of iPod in-car connection we discuss is the most popular, but it's also the most problematic.

The technology is simple—a small FM transmitter connects to your iPod and transmits the iPod audio over an unused FM frequency to your car's FM radio. Although this type of system is simple to implement and use, the resulting sound quality often leaves a lot to be desired; the sound is noticeably lower fidelity than you get with any other connection method.

In addition, you often run into the issue of finding a free FM frequency, especially in large cities. And if you're on a long road trip, you must change frequencies as you drive from town to town, depending on which frequencies local FM stations are using. Even if you find an unused frequency, you might not also get good reception between your iPod and your FM radio. Like I said, this type of connection is problematic.

However, FM transmission is also very popular; unlike other connection methods, you can use FM transmission in virtually any vehicle that has an FM radio. It's also a portable solution, which is nice if you're using a rental car or move your iPod between multiple family vehicles. And, of course, it's a clean connection; there are no cables involved.

The typical FM transmitter attaches to the dock connector or earphone jack on your iPod and features some way to change and display FM frequencies. For example, the DLO TransDock, shown in Figure 14.7, connects to your iPod's dock connector, and then lets you scroll through the available FM frequencies. Set the frequency and then dial your car radio to the same frequency to hear what your iPod is playing. The TransDock is nice in that it also connects to your car's cigarette lighter, to power both the TransDock and your iPod; it also transmits video signals to an in-car video system, if you have a video iPod. You can purchase it for $99.99 from www.dlo.com.

tip When you're shopping for an iPod FM transmitter, look for a model that offers a large number of available frequencies. Some models only have a handful of preset frequencies; the more frequencies available, the more likely you'll find a free frequency to use for your iPod.

FIGURE 14.7

The DLO TransDock FM transmitter for iPod audio and video.

Other popular FM transmitters include the following:

- Arkon SF250 SoundFeeder FM Transmitter ($19.95, www.arkon.com)
- Belkin TuneBase FM ($79.99, www.belkin.com)
- Belkin TuneCast ($29.99, www.belkin.com)
- Belkin TuneCast II ($39.99, www.belkin.com)
- Belkin TuneCast 3 ($49.99, www.belkin.com)
- Belkin TuneCast Auto ($59.99, www.belkin.com)
- Belkin TuneFM ($49.99, www.belkin.com)
- DLO TransDock Micro ($69.99, www.dlo.com)
- DLO TransPod ($99.99, www.dlo.com)
- Griffin iTrip ($49.99, www.griffintechnology.com)
- Griffin iTrip Auto ($69.99, www.griffintechnology.com)
- Griffin RoadTrip ($89.99, www.griffintechnology.com)
- iRock 410FM ($19.99, www.myirock.com)
- iRock 440FM ($24.99, www.myirock.com)
- Macally FMCup ($59.99, www.macally.com)

- Macally FMTF ($49.99, www.macally.com)

- Macally IceFM ($29.99, www.macally.com)

- Maxell P-4A Digital FM Transmitter ($39.99, www.maxell-usa.com)

- Monster iCarPlay Wireless 200 ($99.95, www.monstercable.com)

- Monster iCarPlay Wireless Plus ($79.95, www.monstercable.com)

> **tip** The higher-priced FM transmitters tend to include an AC power adapter and plug into your car's cigarette lighter for power. Lower-priced models are either battery powered or derive their power from the iPod—which shortens your iPod's battery life.

As you can see from the wide variety of available models, this is a popular way to connect your iPod in the car.

CHOOSING THE RIGHT CONNECTION

I wish my 2004 Audi were iPod compatible, but it was manufactured before iPod connectivity became common. Like most of you, if I want to play my iPod in the car, I face a choice between installation convenience, sound quality, and everyday operation.

The one option I've tried and cannot personally recommend is that of FM transmission. Where I live, it's near impossible to find a free FM frequency; even the supposedly "empty" frequencies have too much background noise for most FM transmitters to overpower. I simply can't get an FM transmitter to work for me.

My car does have a cassette player (and I don't know why; I've never used it), so I could go the cassette adapter route. The sound is acceptable, but the mess isn't. That is, I really don't want a cable trailing out the front of the cassette deck to a hanging iPod. Too messy for me.

Because I also don't want to replace my factory audio system with an aftermarket model, I'm left with the option of installing a direct connection kit. It should be easy enough to find a kit that works with my Audi Symphony audio system, and this approach will give me the best possible sound quality—something that matters very much to my ears. The clean installation is also a good thing, with no cables trailing around the dash. It's not the cheapest way to go, but it offers the best results, at least for me.

14

Other iPod Car Accessories

Two other categories of iPod accessories make use in your car a bit easier. These include power adapters (so that you don't drain your iPod's battery) and car mounts (so that your iPod has someplace to sit while you're driving).

Power Adapters

If you're going to be driving for more than a few hours, it's a good idea to provide some auxiliary power for your iPod. Otherwise, you risk having your iPod's battery fizzle out in the middle of your trip, which is less than ideal.

The typical iPod power adapter, like the DLO Auto Charger shown in Figure 14.8, plugs into your car's cigarette lighter or power jack. A short cable connects the power adapter to the dock connector on the bottom of your iPod. The power adapter thus provides a steady stream of power for your iPod and recharges the iPod as you drive.

FIGURE 14.8

The DLO Auto Charger for the iPod and iPod nano.

Some of the most popular iPod car power adapter/chargers include the following:

- Arkon CA070 iPod Car Charger ($12.95, www.arkon.com)
- Belkin Auto Kit for iPod w/Dock Connector ($39.99, www.belkin.com)
- DLO Auto Charger ($19.99, www.dlo.com)
- Griffin TuneFlex ($49.99, www.griffintechnology.com)
- Griffin PowerJolt ($19.99, www.griffintechnology.com)
- iRock 12V DC Charger ($12.95, www.myirock.com)
- Macally USB Car Charger ($19.99, www.macally.com)
- Monster iCarCharger for iPod ($39.95, www.monstercable.com)
- Ten Technology flexibleDock ($49.95, www.tentechnology.com)

Car Mounts

Finally, there's the issue of where you put your iPod while you're driving. You could just lay it on the dashboard (until it slides off) or place it on the passenger seat (unless you have a passenger). A better solution, however, is to somehow mount it on your car's dash or windshield, where it's within eye sight and arm's reach—so that you can quickly and easily operate the Click Wheel while you're driving.

All manner of iPod car mounts are available. Some are vehicle specific, designed to mount to your car's dashboard or center console with bolts or adhesive tape, like the Pro.Fit miMount shown in Figure 14.9. Others are more portable, fitting into one of your car's cup holders, like the Griffin iSqueez shown in Figure 14.10. Still others attach to your windshield with suction cups, or fit into your car's cigarette lighter and do double-duty as power adapters. Which type of mount you choose depends on how attached you want it to be and where you want it positioned.

14

FIGURE 14.9

The Pro.Fit miMount iPod mount.

FIGURE 14.10

The Griffin iSqueez iPod cupholder mount.

That said, here are some of the more popular iPod car mounts:

- Arkon CM160-W Swivel Vent Mount ($19.95, www.arkon.com)
- Belkin TuneDok ($29.99, www.belkin.com)
- Gomadic Dash Car/Auto Mount ($34.95, www.gomadic.com)
- Gomadic Vent Car/Auto Mount ($34.95, www.gomadic.com)
- Gomadic Windshield Car/Auto Mount ($34.95, www.gomadic.com)
- Griffin iSqueez ($9.99, www.griffintechnology.com)
- Nyko Universal Car Mount ($39.99, www.nyko.com)
- Pro.Fit miMount ($29.95–$39.95, www.pro-fit-intl.com/mimount)
- ProClip Mounting System ($26.99–$59.99, www.proclipusa.com)
- Ten Technology iRide Glove Box Organizer ($79, www.tentechnology.com)

Using Your iPod as a Portable Storage Device

Your iPod is built around either a small hard disk drive or Flash memory—the same sorts of storage media used by your computer and other devices to store digital data. Why, then, can't you use your iPod to store computer data?

Well, you can. That's right, your iPod can be used as a portable storage device, much like a USB Flash drive or external hard disk drive. All you have to do is configure it for this type of use or install third-party software to do this management for you. Then you can move and copy any type of file to and from your iPod—which is great for taking data on the go.

Configuring and Using Your iPod for Data Storage

Yes, your iPod has a lot of storage space inside that sleek white (or black or blue or whatever) case. Even the basic iPod shuffle has 1GB of storage, which is as much as you get with most USB memory drives. The iPod nano has anywhere from 2GB to 8GB of storage, depending on your model, and the big iPod has either 30GB or a whopping 80GB of storage—more than you get with some notebook PCs. In other words, a lot of storage space is available if you want it (if it isn't already used for storing your digital music, of course).

Configuring Your iPod

This storage space, however, isn't immediately available for your use. To access your iPod's Flash memory or hard disk for data storage, you first have to configure your iPod as a storage disk—which you do from within the iTunes software.

To configure your iPod for data storage, follow these steps:

1. Connect your iPod to your computer, and then open the iTunes software (if it doesn't open automatically).
2. In the Source pane, select your iPod.
3. Select the Summary tab.
4. Check the Enable Disk Use option, as shown in Figure 15.1.
5. Click the Apply button.

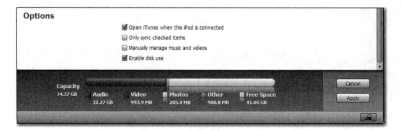

FIGURE 15.1
Configuring the iPod for disk use.

Managing Files

Once configured for disk use, your iPod now appears as a removable disk drive in My Computer, Windows Explorer, and the Mac Finder. (Figure 15.2 shows an iPod icon in My Computer.) You can now trans-

note If you're configuring an iPod shuffle, you also need to set the Storage Allocation slider to indicate the amount of memory you want used for data files.

fer files to and from your iPod using any of these file management tools, treating your iPod as you would any storage device.

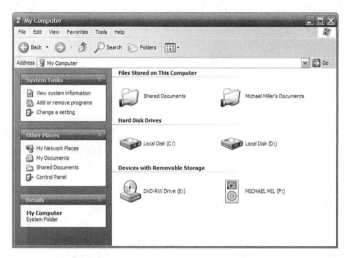

FIGURE 15.2
An iPod displayed as a storage device in My Computer.

Here's how to perform the most common file management functions from the My Computer, Windows Explorer, or Mac Finder windows:

■ To view the data files stored on your iPod, double-click the iPod icon.

■ To copy files to your iPod, open a second file window and drag the selected files onto the iPod icon or into the open iPod window.

■ To copy files from your iPod, do the reverse—drag files from the open iPod window onto another file window.

caution When you have your iPod configured for disk use, you can't just disconnect it from your computer like you're used to, even when it's done syncing with iTunes. Instead, you have to use the Eject iPod button at the bottom right of the iTunes window to manually "dismount" the iPod, and then disconnect the connecting cable.

note There's one type of file you won't see in the open iPod window: music files. To learn how to view and manage music files on your iPod, turn to the "Copying Music from Your iPod to a PC" section, later in this chapter.

15

■ To delete files from your iPod, select the file(s), and then press the Del button on your computer keyboard.

caution Any media files (music, video, or photo) you copy to your iPod via the data storage method are not playable on your iPod. Files transferred in this fashion are treated as pure data files, not as playable media files. To have media files accessible via your iPod, you need to transfer them using the iTunes software, as discussed in Chapter 5, "Using the iTunes Software."

SECURITY ISSUES

When you use your iPod as a portable data storage device, you run the risk of introducing file-borne computer viruses to any computer you connect to. That's an issue for corporate IT departments, as more and more employees bring their iPods (and other portable storage devices) to work.

There is the risk, however slight, that if you connect your iPod to your work PC (and have data storage enabled), a computer virus might be transferred from your iPod to your PC and then to other PCs connected to the corporate network. It's this prospect that has IT staff concerned.

In addition, some corporations are worried that sensitive documents stored on portable devices could fall into the wrong hands if that portable device is stolen. Given how easy it is to steal an iPod, you can see how this is an issue. All it takes is one worker copying customer files to his iPod, having that iPod stolen, and then having those personal files used by unscrupulous parties for massive identify theft. This is a potentially big security issue.

These—and other equally dire—scenarios have some IT staff threatening to ban all iPods and similar portable devices from the workplace. In fact, the Gartner consulting firm issued a report in 2004 titled "How to Tackle the Threat from Portable Storage Devices," in which it recommended just such a prohibition. Will you be able to bring your iPod to the office, even if it's just to listen to music? You probably can today, but a few major instances of iPod-related virus attack or identity theft might change this in the future.

Copying Music from Your iPod to a PC

The most common reason to access files on an iPod is to copy music files from the iPod to a PC, which is something you can't do in iTunes. As noted previously, however, when you enable your iPod for disk storage and then try to view its contents on your computer, the one thing you don't see are all your stored music tracks and playlists. So, how do you do it?

note Why does Apple configure all digital music files as "hidden?" Simple—to discourage illegal copying of copyrighted music.

First, let's examine why you can't see music files like you can other types of files. The reason is simple: These files are automatically configured as "hidden" files, and hidden files don't normally appear in My Computer, Windows Explorer, or the Mac Finder. If you can make these hidden files "unhidden," you can copy them.

But why would you want to copy files from your iPod to a PC? There are several reasons, including the following:

- Recover tunes accidentally deleted from your computer
- Restore tunes you've purposefully deleted from your computer, but still have stored on your iPod
- Restore tunes to a computer that's experienced a hard disk failure
- Copy tunes to a new computer you've just obtained
- Play the same tunes on your work PC that you do on your home PC
- Back up your music collection to a second computer

In any case, you need to transfer files from your iPod to that other computer—files that you can't normally see, and that iTunes won't let you transfer backward. Fortunately, there are several ways to copy music files from your iPod to a PC. Some, of course, are easier than others. We look at them all, next.

Copying Music the Windows Way

If you have a Windows computer, there's an easy way to make visible those previously hidden music files. Follow these steps:

1. With your iPod connected (and your iPod configured as a storage device), open My Computer.
2. Within My Computer, highlight the iPod icon.
3. Select Tools > Folder Options.

4. When the Folder Options dialog box appears, as shown in Figure 15.3, select the View tab.

5. Go to the Hidden Files and Folders item and select Show Hidden Files and Folders.

6. Click OK to close the dialog box.

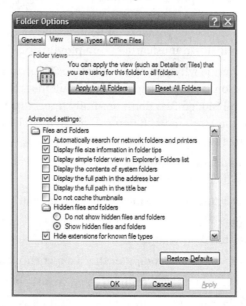

FIGURE 15.3

Configuring Windows to view hidden files.

With hidden files now visible, it's a relatively easy task to navigate to and copy or move your iPod's music files. Double-click the iPod icon in My Computer and navigate to the iPod Control > Music folder. What you see next is a series of subfolders, labeled F00, F01, F02, and so forth, as shown in Figure 15.4. This is the database that contains your iPod's Music library. Double-click any folder to see the individual audio tracks within, which you can then move, copy, or delete as you wish.

FIGURE 15.4

Hidden music folders on an iPod, as viewed from within Windows.

The problem with this approach, as you've no doubt noticed, is that your iPod doesn't label these folders and files in any usable fashion. How do you know which album is contained in the F00 folder, or which track is labeled ABGL? That's a puzzler and why this approach might not be the best one to take.

note There's a similar procedure to unhide hidden files on a Mac, but the same folder/file-naming problem persists—so why bother?

Copying Music with iPod File Management Programs

A better approach is to use a software program specifically designed to copy music and other files from your iPod to a computer (Mac or Windows). These iPod file management programs not only display all the hidden files on your iPod, they also decode your iPod's database information so that you know which albums, songs, and playlists you're looking at.

For example, Anapod Explorer, shown in Figure 15.5, displays the contents of your iPod in a tree-like list in Windows Explorer. To view all your songs, click the Audio Tracks item; to view your playlists, click Playlists; to view your albums, click Albums; and so forth. You can view the contents of your Music library by album, artist, or genre, and you can also use the program to view and manage your iPod's photos, videos, contacts, notes, and other files.

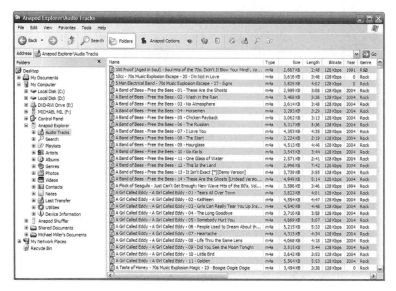

FIGURE 15.5
Viewing the contents of your iPod with Anapod Explorer.

To copy files or playlists from your iPod to your computer, just drag them from the Anapod Explorer list onto a drive and folder on your hard disk, either in the Explorer tree pane or another open My Computer window. To delete a file from your iPod, simply highlight it and click the Del key on your keyboard.

Anapod Explorer is just one of many third-party programs that let you manage music tracks and other files on your iPod. Table 15.1 provides details about the most popular of these iPod file management programs.

AUTHOR'S PICKS My favorite of these programs is Anapod Explorer, which looks and acts like Windows Explorer. Of the free programs, YamiPod is extremely versatile; it has an iTunes-like interface that not only lets you copy files, but also enables tag editing and other user operations.

15

Table 15.1   iPod File Management Programs

Program	Website	Platform	Price
Anapod Explorer	www.redchairsoftware.com/anapod	Windows, Mac	$20–$30[1]
Backstage	www.widgetfab.com/BackstagePage.html	Windows, Mac	$9.99
CopyPod	www.copypod.net	Windows	$19.90
El iPodo	www.funkelectric.com/products.html	Mac	Free
EphPod	www.ephpod.com	Windows	Free
Floola	www.floola.com	Windows, Mac	Free
iBack	www.raymondjavaxx.com	Windows	$10.99
iGadget	www.purpleghost.com	Windows	$19.99
iLinkPod	www.ilinkpod.com	Mac	Free
iPod Access	www.drewfindley.com/findleydesigns/ipodaccess	Windows, Mac	$19.99
iPod Music Liberator	www.zeleksoftware.com	Windows, Mac	$34.99
iPod.iTunes	www.crispsofties.com	Mac	$39
iPodCopy	www.wideanglesoftware.com/ipodcopy	Windows, Mac	$19.99
iPodDisk	ipoddisk.ourbiti.com	Mac	Free
iPodRip	www.thelittleappfactory.com	Windows, Mac	$14.95
Music Rescue	www.kennettnet.co.uk/musicrescue	Windows, Mac	$20
PodManager	www.podmanager.com	Mac	$7.95
Podworks	www.scifihifi.com/podworks	Mac	$8
Senuti	www.fadingred.org/senuti	Mac	Free
TransferMyMusic	www.shop.avanquest.com	Windows	$29.95
Tune Transfer for iPod	www.valusoft.com/products/tunetransfer.html	Windows, Mac	$19.99
TuneJack	www.purpleghost.com	Windows	$14.99
TunePlus	www.encoreusa.com	Windows	$19.99
vPod	www.vonnieda.org/vPod	Windows	Free
XPlay	www.mediafour.com/products/xplay	Windows	$29.95
YamiPod	www.yamipod.com	Windows, Mac	Free

[1] Price dependent on the type of iPod used; the shuffle edition is priced at $20, versions for other models are priced at $25, and a universal edition is priced at $30.

Copying Music the Apple Way

If you don't want to spring for one of these file management programs and all you need to do is move your Music library from one computer to another, version 7 of the iTunes software has a built-in backup feature that will do the job—with a bit of work on your part.

note iTunes also has a Transfer Purchases from iPod feature, but it only transfers songs purchased from the iTunes Store, not tracks you've ripped from CD or downloaded from other sources. For that reason, you want to use the backup feature, instead.

The iTunes backup feature can copy your entire library to a CD or DVD, or to your iPod—assuming your iPod has enough storage space to hold your entire library. You can then import the Backup library to another PC, and to that PC's copy of the iTunes software.

Backing up and then transferring your songs using your iPod is a multiple-step operation. Follow along carefully. It goes like this:

1. The first thing you want to do is configure your iPod as a data storage device and activate manual music management. To do this, connect your iPod to your first PC, select your iPod in the Source pane, go to the Summary tab, and check the Manually Manage Music option. (This also selects the Enable Disk Use option, which you also want selected.) Click the Apply button to apply these changes.

2. Next, you want to consolidate all the music in your iTunes library, for easier transfer. To do this, open iTunes, select Edit > Preferences, select the Advanced tab, then the General tab, and then check the Copy Files to iTunes Music Folder When Adding to Library option, as shown in Figure 15.6. Click OK to confirm (and close the dialog box), and then select Advanced > Consolidate Library. iTunes now copies all your music files to a new location on your computer's hard drive.

3. When the files are reorganized on your hard drive, it's time to copy all your music files to your iPod. With your iPod still connected to your PC, close the iTunes software and open My Computer, Windows Explorer, or the Mac Finder. Next, you want to locate and open your iTunes folder. On a Windows PC, it should be located in the folder C:\Documents and Settings*username*\My Documents\My Music. On a Mac, it should be located in the folder C:\Users*username*\Music. Open a second instance of My Computer, Windows Explorer (or the Mac Finder), and make sure the iPod icon is visible. Now drag the iTunes folder from the first window onto the iPod icon in the second window. Your computer will start copying all your music files from your computer to your iPod; this might take awhile.

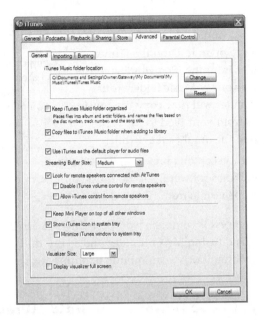

FIGURE 15.6

Using iTunes to consolidate your music files into a single location.

4. When the copying is complete, reopen the iTunes software, click the iPod icon in the Source pane, and then click the Eject iPod button in the lower-right corner of the window. When it's safe to do so, physically disconnect your iPod from your computer.

5. Now it's time to copy your music files from your iPod to your second computer. Make sure you have the iTunes software installed on the second PC, and then connect your iPod to this computer. (If the iTunes software launches at this point, close it.) Use My Computer, Windows Explorer (or the Mac Finder) to locate and open the Music or My Music folder on this PC. Now open a second instance of My Computer,

caution If you already have iTunes music stored on your second PC, you'll want to back it up before you copy music files from your iPod; otherwise, the new music will overwrite the old music library. To do this, open the iTunes software, select Edit > Preferences, select the Advanced tab, select the General tab, and then click the Reset button. Next, make sure the Copy Files to Music Folder When Adding to Library option is checked, and then click OK. Now select Advanced > Consolidate Library, and then close the iTunes software. Once you've copied music from your iPod to this PC, you can add the older music back to the library; open iTunes, select File > Add Folder to Library, select the iTunes folder, and then click OK.

15

Windows Explorer (or the Mac Finder) and double-click the iPod icon to open it. Drag the iTunes folder from the iPod window to the Music or My Music folder. Your computer will now copy the music files from your iPod to the computer; this might take awhile.

note You also want to authorize your second computer to play your purchased iTunes tracks. For instructions, see the "Authorizing Computers for Playback" section in Chapter 6, "Using the iTunes Store."

6. After the copying has completed, open the iTunes software. All the music that used to be on your old PC will now be visible from iTunes on the new PC.

When the process is complete, you probably want to delete the iTunes folder from your iPod (using My Computer and so on) and switch your iPod from manual updating back to automatic updating (using the iTunes software).

Different Ways to Use Your iPod for Data Storage

Now that you know *how* to use your iPod for data storage, it's time to ask *why* you might want to do so. Here are just a few of the ways you can use your iPod in this fashion.

Transferring Files from One PC to Another

You have a computer at work. You have another computer at home. You also have an iPod. Why not use your iPod to transfer files from one computer to another so that you can do your office work on your home PC (or vice versa)?

In this scenario, illustrated in Figure 15.7, you're using your iPod in much the same way you'd use a USB Flash memory drive, or (in the old days) a floppy disk. Assuming your iPod has ample free storage space, it's easy to copy files from your work PC to your iPod, and then from your iPod to your home PC, and then back again the next day.

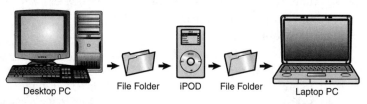

Desktop PC   File Folder   iPOD   File Folder   Laptop PC

FIGURE 15.7

Using your iPod to transfer files from one PC to another.

To do this, you first have to configure your iPod for data storage. Then, on your first PC, use My Computer, Windows Explorer (or the Mac finder) to copy the selected files from your computer's hard drive to your iPod. Take your iPod home, and then reverse the process by copying these same files from your iPod to your home PC. It's quite easy to do.

> **tip** If you intend to use your iPod to transfer files between Windows and Mac PCs, you have to format your iPod for Windows use. Macs can read both Mac and Windows drives, but Windows PCs can read only Windows drives. To format your iPod for Windows use, connect your iPod to your Windows computer, launch the iTunes software, select your iPod in the Source pane, select the Summary tab, and then click the Restore button.

Backing Up Important Data

Here's one that a lot of people don't think about. If you have a large-capacity iPod, you can use it to store back up copies of your important computer data, as illustrated in Figure 15.8. That way if your computer crashes, you can restore the data files from your iPod.

FIGURE 15.8

Using your iPod as a backup device.

This process is as easy as identifying the files you want to back up on your computer and then copying those files to your iPod, using My Computer or a similar utility. Remember to create new backup copies on a regular basis (once a day is probably safe), copying the new versions of these files over the old versions stored on your iPod. If you ever have to restore lost files, just copy them from your iPod back to your PC.

> **tip** The 30GB and 80GB iPods are recommended for backing up a lot of files. If you're only backing up a few files, any of the Flash-based iPods will do the job.

15

Storing Digital Photos on the Go

In addition to storing digital photos for on-the-go viewing, you can also use your iPod to transport photos you take while you're out and away. If you don't need to view these photos, but merely want to free up storage space on your digital camera, copy them to your iPod as data files.

The challenge to this scenario is getting the digital photos from your camera to your iPod. As discussed in Chapter 10, "Photos," you can use Apple's iPod Camera Connector or Belkin's Digital Camera Link to establish a direct connection between your camera and your iPod (as illustrated in Figure 15.9) or transfer files via memory card using Belkin's Media Reader accessory (as illustrated in Figure 15.10). Make sure your iPod is configured for data storage, and then copy the digital photo files into their own folder on your iPod; once copied, you can delete them from your camera's memory card, freeing up space for new photos. When you get back home, you can then copy these digital photos from your iPod to your home computer, using My Computer or a similar utility.

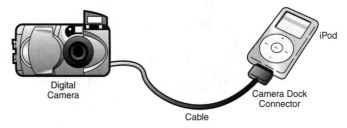

FIGURE 15.9

Copying photo files from a digital camera to an iPod using a connector cable.

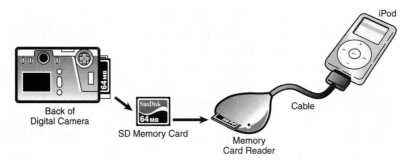

FIGURE 15.10

Copying photo files from a camera's memory card using a media reader accessory.

USING YOUR IPOD AS A VIRTUAL PC

If you have a Windows PC, you can take your favorite applications and settings with you, using your iPod as a transfer device. The MojoPac application essentially creates a virtual Windows desktop on your iPod. Connect your iPod to another PC, and it boots up just like your main PC. All your Windows settings (including desktop configuration) are applied to the second PC, as are the applications and files you selected to transfer. Even better, you don't leave any trace of your activities on the second computer; everything travels with you on your iPod.

To use MojoPac, you must have your iPod configured for data storage use. Launch MojoPac, and you're prompted to select which settings, files/folders, and such you want to carry with you on your iPod. You can then install copies of your favorite applications onto the iPod, using the MojoPac virtual Windows environment.

To access your virtual PC on another computer, all you have to do is connect your iPod. The MojoPac virtual desktop will automatically load onto this PC, enabling access to all the applications and files you've specified. It's really quite neat.

MojoPac costs $49.99 and can be purchased and downloaded from www.mojopac.com.

16

Using Your iPod to Record Audio and Podcasts

Back in the day, if you wanted to record an interview or a conversation, you used a portable cassette recorder. Technology evolves, of course, and the standard cassette recorder morphed into the microcassette recorder (using smaller tapes) and the digital audio recorder (using Flash memory for storage). Given that the iPod, in data storage mode, works similarly to a Flash memory storage device, why can't you use your iPod for voice recording?

The answer is, of course, that you can. With the right accessories, you can use your iPod to record conversations and interviews, and even to record and mix podcasts for broadcasting over the Internet. Read on to learn more.

Turning Your iPod into a Voice Recorder

The secret to turning your iPod (from the Flash-based nano to the bigger hard disk iPod) into a voice recorder is to somehow attach a microphone to the unit, and then input digital audio signals from the mic to the iPod's internal storage. Which is exactly what several accessory manufacturers have done.

How iPod Microphones Work

All iPod microphones work in a similar basic fashion. You connect the microphone to either the iPod's earphone jack or dock connector. When powered on, the microphone picks up the surround sound and sends it into the iPod for storage.

Using an iPod mic is as simple as turning it on, configuring the recording settings, and then pressing the Record button. While recording, elapsed recording time typically displays on the iPod's screen, and you can listen to what you're recording via the iPod's earphone jack.

The audio you record is automatically stored on your iPod, where it can later be retrieved by the data storage methods discussed in Chapter 15, "Using Your iPod as a Portable Storage Device." (Naturally, you can also play back your recordings on the iPod itself, as you would any audio file.) Once exported, you can edit your recorded file in any audio editing program, such as Apple's GarageBand.

Popular iPod Microphones

Most iPod microphones let you control the type (mono or stereo) and quality (bit rate and volume level) of the recording, and then save the recording as an audio file on the iPod's hard disk or in the unit's Flash memory. Some microphones are monophonic (containing a single mic), others are stereo (with two mics built into the unit), and still others feature jacks for connecting external microphones.

Let's look at some of the available models.

XtremeMac MicroMemo

One of the more unique iPod microphones is the XtremeMac MicroMemo. As you can see in Figure 16.1, the MicroMemo attaches to the dock connector on the bottom of the iPod or iPod nano, and features a flexible, removable microphone and a built-in speaker to listen to the recordings you make.

FIGURE 16.1

The XtremeMac MicroMemo iPod microphone.

The MicroMemo doesn't limit you to its attached microphone. You can connect any external microphone to the unit's 3.5mm mini-jack connector. (XtremeMac happens to sell a neat little lapel microphone, dubbed the MemoMic, that's a good fit with the MicroMemo.)

In terms of recording quality, the MicroMemo offers two different quality levels—Low and High. The Low level records 8-bit audio at a 22kHz sample rate. High level records 16-bit audio at a 44.1kHz sample rate. As you might expect, the two settings result in different file sizes. The Low level requires 2.6MB per minute of recording; the High level requires 10.3MB per minute. Use the High level for better-sounding recordings, but make sure you have enough storage space for longer recordings. All recordings are in WAV-format files.

Different versions of the MicroMemo are available for the fifth-generation iPod and the second-generation iPod nano. Both versions sell for $59.95 and are available from www.xtrememac.com.

Griffin iTalk Pro

Taking a slightly different design approach, the Griffin iTalk Pro also connects to the iPod's dock connector, but uses two miniature microphones built in to the unit's compact case to record in stereo. As you can see in Figure 16.2, the iTalk Pro is very discrete; it looks like a short extension to the bottom of the iPod.

FIGURE 16.2

The Griffin iTalk Pro add-on microphone.

As to sound quality, the iTalk Pro records 16-bit stereo audio at 44.1kHz or 16-bit mono at 22kHz. If the twin built-in mics are not good enough for you, you can connect any external mic to the 3.5mm mini-jack connector on the bottom of the unit.

The iTalk Pro sells for $49.99 and is available from www.griffintechnology.com.

Belkin TuneTalk Stereo

Another high-performance stereo microphone is the Belkin TuneTalk Stereo. It's compatible with the fifth-generation iPod and connects to the bottom dock connector.

As you can see in Figure 16.3, the TuneTalk Stereo contains two small microphones, mounted in the middle of the unit. You can also connect an external microphone via the 3.5mm mini-jack connector. Also nice is the ability to adjust recording levels in real time, using the iPod's Click Wheel controls; the screen displays a useful clipping indicator.

FIGURE 16.3
Belkin's TuneTalk Stereo, connected to a 5G iPod.

You can purchase the TuneTalk Stereo for $69.99 from www.belkin.com.

Belkin Voice Recorder for iPod

If you have a different or older iPod model, check out Belkin's Voice Recorder for iPod. As you can see in Figure 16.4, it's relatively universal in operation, in that it connects via the iPod's earphone jack. It's a mono unit with a built-in speaker for listening to playback of your recordings.

The Voice Recorder for iPod sells for $49.99 from www.belkin.com.

tip Any iPod voice recorder that has an input for an external microphone should also be able to connect to most telephone handsets to record phone conversations. Just use the appropriate connector cable to go from the earphone output jack on your phone to the mic input on the voice recorder accessory.

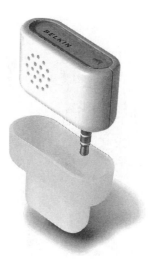

FIGURE 16.4

Belkin's Voice Recorder for iPod, a universal add-on microphone.

RECORDING QUALITY

On older iPod models (fourth generation and earlier), Apple limited audio recording quality to a 8kHz sample rate. This sample rate is barely acceptable for voice recording or dictation, and clearly unacceptable for recording music.

With the fifth-generation iPod, Apple opened up audio recording to a full 44.1kHz in WAV format, which is near CD quality. It certainly produces broadcast-quality voice recordings, and quite listenable music recordings. If you're serious about recording, you'll want to trade in your older iPod for a 5G model with this higher-quality recording capability.

Recording Podcasts on Your iPod

Many people use their iPods to record class lectures. Others use them professionally, to record interviews for broadcast or background. Still others use their iPods to surreptitiously record live music at concerts.

All this is great, but there's one more use for your iPod as an audio recorder. If you're at all into podcasts, you can use your iPod as a storage device for any podcasts you record.

Recording in the Field

One advantage to recording podcasts on your iPod is that if you use a compact iPod microphone, such as the MicroMemo or iTalk Pro, you can record your podcasts in the field; recording can take place anywhere you can carry your iPod. (Although, to be fair, you probably want to use a better-quality mic than the ones built in to the snap-on iPod microphones. Look for a good external mic with a mini-jack plug to connect to the snap-on mic accessories.)

When you have finished recording your podcast, just dock your iPod to your PC and transfer the audio files to your computer. Once loaded on your computer, the podcast files can be edited (if you like) and then uploaded to your podcast hosting site.

Recording with TuneStudio

Whether you're recording in the field or at home, you should check out Belkin's TuneStudio, an all-in-one podcast recording/editing workstation that uses the iPod as the host storage device. As you can see in Figure 16.5, you dock the iPod into the TuneStudio, connect your microphone(s), and then start mixing and recording. As a mixer, it's relatively small and lightweight; carry it with you or set it up in your home studio.

FIGURE 16.5

Belkin's TuneStudio, an all-in-one mixing/recording console.

The TuneStudio is a four-channel mixer. You can connect up to four microphones or instruments; two of the mics can use either 1/4-inch jacks or balanced XLR connectors (with phantom power for up to 60dB gain).

Each channel in the mixer has a three-band EQ and recording level and stereo pan controls. There's also a knob for on-the-fly audio compression, and LEDs to indicate master audio level, recoding peak, compression, and recording status.

The audio you mix is fed directly to the iPod for recording and storage. Recording is to a 16-bit, 44kHz-quality WAV file.

And here's something else neat about the TuneStudio. You can connect it to your computer via USB and have it function as an external sound card. This lets you feed the audio from the TuneStudio to your PC for hard disk recording—or the audio from your PC to the TuneStudio be mixed with other inputs.

The TuneStudio sells for a quite-affordable $179.99 from www.belkin.com. It comes bundled with Ableton Live Lite digital audio workstation software for your Windows or Mac computer.

Editing Podcasts on Your Computer

Whether you record your podcasts on your iPod or on your computer, chances are you'll want to do a little editing from time to time. Maybe you want to edit out hemming and hawing or dead space, or add some background music, or even combine two or more separate recordings into a single podcast. Fortunately, you can use just about any audio recording program to perform these editing tasks.

Although really serious podcasters use professional recording/mixing software—such as Cakewalk, Cubase, or even ProTools—this can be overkill when you're talking about low-fidelity voice recordings that will be distributed in compressed MP3 format. Anything too fancy gets lost in the mix.

That said, there are some affordable and easy-to-use audio-editing programs available:

- Audacity (free, audacity.sourceforge.net)
- ePodcast Creator ($89.95, www.industrialaudiosoftware.com/products), shown in Figure 16.6
- PodProducer (free, www.podproducer.net)
- Propaganda ($49.95, www.makepropandana.com)

■ WebPod Studio Standard ($89.95, www.lionhardt.ca/wps)

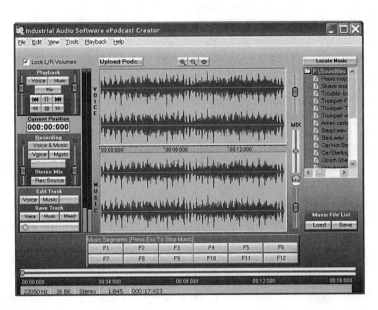

FIGURE 16.6
Editing podcasts with ePodcast Creator.

Any podcast you record on your iPod should be saved in uncompressed WAV format, at the highest possible sample rate, and you should stay in the WAV format throughout the editing process. However, you don't distribute your podcasts in WAV format. Instead, most podcasts are distributed in MP3 (or, for iTunes Store distribution, AAC) format. So after you have your podcast in its final form, you then export the file into MP3 or AAC format. If the podcast is voice only, which most are, a relatively low bit rate (32 or 64kbps) is fine. If the podcast has a lot of music, consider a higher bit rate, up to 128kbps. Make sure you add the appropriate meta tags for all the podcast info, and it's ready for distribution.

tip
If you're a Mac user, you can use Apple GarageBand to produce and edit your podcasts. GarageBand is part of the iLive program suite; buy it for $79 from www.apple.com/ilife/garageband.

Distributing Your Podcast via iTunes

After you've saved your podcast (in MP3 or AAC format), you have to get it out on the Internet. And the best place to publish your podcast is via Apple's iTunes Store.

note Learn more about podcasts in the iTunes Store in Chapter 8, "Podcasts."

The first step to distributing your podcast is to upload the podcast MP3 file to a server. If you have your own personal website, you can use that server to store your podcasts. You need a fair amount of storage space because audio files can get rather large, depending on the recording quality and length. For example, a 30-minute podcast saved at 64kbps will be about 8MB in size. Use a higher bit rate and the file size goes up accordingly.

If you don't have your own server, consider using an audio blog hosting service, such as Hipcast (www.hipcast.com), Liberated Syndication (www.libsyn.com), Podbus.com (www.podbus.com), or Podcast Spot (www.podcastspot.com). You'll typically pay $5 to $10 per month for file storage, and most of these sites will also help you with the RSS syndication of your podcasts.

Which leads us to the second step of the process, the RSS syndication. This is how you make people aware of your podcasts, and will typically be accomplished via your podcast hosting service. Most blogging software and services can also generate an RSS feed, or you can use FeedBurner (www.feedburner.com) to do the work for you (for free). If you use FeedBurner, you must create a link on your website to the FeedBurner file so that people can find the feed.

Finally, we come to the fun part: sharing your podcast with users of the iTunes Store. To do this, launch the iTunes software, go to the iTunes Store, go to the Podcasts page, scroll to the Learn More box at the bottom of the page, and then click Submit a Podcast. This opens the page shown in Figure 16.7.

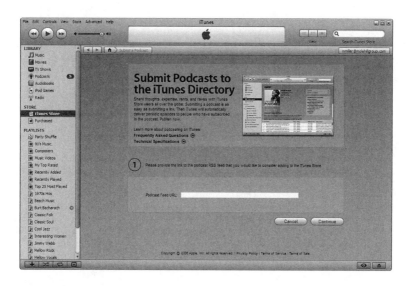

FIGURE 16.7

Submitting your podcast to the iTunes Store.

As prompted, enter the URL for your podcast's RSS feed. Click the Continue button and you'll be prompted to provide additional information about your podcast. Once submitted, Apple reviews your request and (assuming your podcast adheres to the site's rules and regulations) adds your podcast to the iTunes Podcast Directory.

And that's that. All you have to do now is wait for users to find your podcasts and subscribe to your feed—then your voice will be heard across the Web!

note To be included in the iTunes Podcast Directory, your podcast must have a title, description, subject, and other similar tags. If your podcast contains explicit language, it should be labeled with the "explicit material" tag. You can submit podcasts stored in either MP3 or AAC formats. Once submitted, your podcasts stay in the directory as long as the RSS feed remains available.

Using Your iPod for Running and Exercise

Listening to music on the go is particularly appealing for when you're running or exercising. Just pop your iPod in your pocket or into an armband, plug in your earbuds, and get ready to listen to your favorite tunes as you burn off the calories.

Exercising with your iPod can be that simple, or it can be infinitely more complex. It all depends on how fancy you want to go.

Choosing the Right iPod for Running and Exercise

The first choice you have to make when exercising with your iPod is choosing the right model for your needs. For reasons we discuss in a moment, the two preferred iPod models for exercise are the iPod nano and iPod shuffle—*not* the big color iPod.

Why might you not want to exercise with your hard disk iPod? The hard disk is the reason. A hard disk is a physical device that uses a series of rotating platters and moving arms to read the information (music tracks) stored within. As with all things physical, the iPod's hard drive doesn't respond well to bumping and jostling—the very types of motion that you'll subject it to while you're running or using the exercise equipment at your local gym. Bounce your iPod up and down, and the music is likely to start skipping.

This is why the iPod nano and iPod shuffle are more preferable in an active environment. Both of these models use electronic Flash memory for storage; there are no moving parts involved, thus nothing to skip. You can toss a nano or shuffle up and down and the music keeps on playing, no problems.

Choosing between the nano and shuffle is more of personal decision. The nano, of course, holds a lot more music and also offers more playback flexibility, thanks to its onscreen menus. The shuffle, however, is a lot smaller and lighter (as you can see in Figure 17.1), and can clip it onto your T-shirt or shorts without you even noticing it's there. If you don't think you'll be dialing up songs in the middle of a run (and you probably won't), it might be better to load up your favorite playlist onto an iPod shuffle and go with the smaller device.

FIGURE 17.1

Comparing the iPod shuffle with the iPod nano—a big difference in size.

That said, there are two other reasons why you might want to choose the nano over the shuffle. First, the nano offers stopwatch capability, which is nice if you're timing a run or a workout session. Second, the nano works with the Nike+iPod Sport Kit, which is a great way for runners and walkers to track their progress over time. We discuss both these options later in this chapter.

Carrying Your iPod While You Exercise

After you choose your iPod, you now have to figure out how to carry it with you when you run or exercise. Carrying the iPod shuffle is no big deal, thanks to its miniature size and built-in clip. But carrying an iPod nano is more problematic; it's a small device, yes, but not that small.

iPod Sports Cases and Armbands

To that end, a nice aftermarket in iPod sports cases and armbands has sprung up of late. You want a case that keeps the iPod secure while you're bounding about and also offers some degree of protection in case of tragic exercise accidents (flying off while biking, being dropped while lifting weights, and so forth).

Some of the most popular of these sports-oriented iPod cases include the following:

- ActiveSport Armband for iPod nano ($29.95, www.speckproducts.com/nano-activearm.html)
- Apple iPod nano Armband ($29, store.apple.com)
- Belkin Sports Sleeve for iPod nano ($14.99, www.belkin.com)
- Nike+ Sport Armband ($29, www.nike.com), shown in Figure 17.2
- Sport Grip for iPod nano ($9.95, www.marware.com)
- SportSuit Convertible for iPod nano ($29.95, www.marware.com)
- SportSuit Sprinter for iPod nano ($24.95, www.marware.com)
- TuneBelt iPod Armband Carrier ($12.95, www.tunebelt.com)
- XtremeMac SportWrap ($29.95, www.xtrememac.com)

17

FIGURE 17.2

The Nike+ Sport Armband in action.

Sports Earphones

You might also want to consider upgrading your standard iPod earbuds to a set of specialty sports earphones. These headphones and earbuds offer special features especially for use when exercising, running, or biking, such as wrap-around neckbands, sweat guards, and the like.

Some of the most popular of these sports earphones include the following:

- JVC HA-B17VS Backband Headphone ($14.95, www.jvc.com)
- JVC HA-EB50B Ear Clip Headphone ($8.95, www.jvc.com)
- Koss SportaPro ($29.99, www.koss.com)
- Logitech Curve Headphones ($29.99, www.logitech.com), shown in Figure 17.3

- Sennheiser MX 75 Sport twist-to-fit headphones ($49.99, www.style-your-sound.com)

- Sennheiser OMX 70 Sport clip-on headphones ($44.99, www.style-your-sound.com)

- Sennheiser PMX 70 Sport neckband headphones ($49.99, www.style-your-sound.com), shown in Figure 17.4

- Sony MDR-A35G S2 Sports Headphones ($19.99, www.sonystyle.com)

- Sony MDR-E827G Sports Series Fontopia Ear-Bud Stereo Headphones ($19.99, www.sonystyle.com)

- Sony MDR-G57G S2 Sports Street Style Headphones ($24.99, www.sonystyle.com)

17

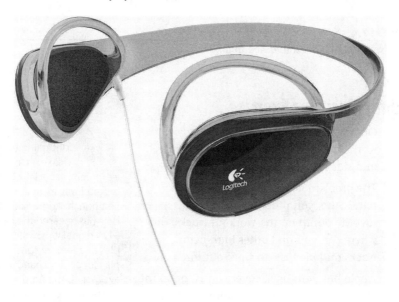

FIGURE 17.3

Logitech's Curve Headphones, with over-the-ear clips.

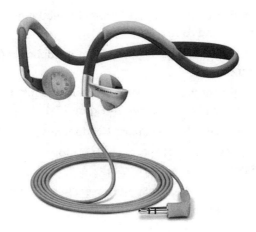

FIGURE 17.4

Sennheiser's PMX70 neckband headphones.

Finding Music for Exercise

Okay, you're all suited up and ready to work out. It's time to crank up the tunes and start to feel the burn!

The problem is, which tunes should you play? Sure, you probably have your favorite pump-up-the-workout tracks, but where can you find other high-octane tracks and playlists to work out to?

Apple has your back covered. Just go to the Music page in the iTunes Store, scroll to the More in Music box on the left, and then click the Nike Sport Music link. This displays the Sport Music page, shown in Figure 17.5, co-sponsored by Nike. (As you'll see, Nike has a very tight relationship with Apple, where music-powered workouts are concerned.)

tip Controlling your iPod while exercising can be a problem, especially if the iPod is tucked away in an armband or belt pouch. Addressing this issue, Nike has released the Flight+, a $129 digital wristwatch that doubles as a remote control and display for an iPod nano. Also available is the Amp+, a $79 wristwatch remote control sans display. See www.nikeplus.com for more details.

FIGURE 17.5
The Sport Music page in the iTunes Store.

From here you have access to all sorts of sports-related music, including the following:

- **Nike+ Workouts**—Workout albums and videos
- **Sport iMixes**—Workout-related playlists uploaded by other iPod users
- **Podcasts**—Sport-related podcasts, provided by Nike
- **Athlete Inspirations**—Favorite playlists submitted by top athletes (Figure 17.6 shows what Lance Armstrong listens to while he's biking)

FIGURE 17.6
Lance Armstrong's workout picks.

In other words, the Sport Music page is the place to find playlists, albums, and the like that will help pump up your workout. These are the tracks that your fellow exercisers and top athletes use to find inspiration; maybe they'll inspire you, too! (Naturally, you can purchase any and all tracks and playlists presented here.)

Even more iMixes, workout albums, and the like are available at the Nike+ website (www.nikeplus.com). Click the Sport Music icon to view what's available, such as the list of "power songs" (shown in Figure 17.7) that other users use to fire them up during the home stretch. (For some reason, Survivor's "Eye of the Tiger" ranks as number one.)

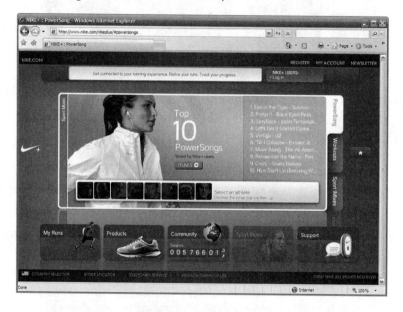

FIGURE 17.7
Power songs and more on the Nike+ website.

Using Your iPod as a Stopwatch

Now we get to the really fun stuff. Sure, you know that you can use your iPod to listen to tunes while you're working out. But did you also know that you can use your iPod to time your workouts? That's right, both the big iPod and the iPod nano have a built-in stopwatch you can use to time laps, runs, workouts, and the like. (Sadly, the iPod shuffle can't be used as a stopwatch—there's no display to read.)

To use your iPod or iPod nano as a stopwatch, select Extras > Stopwatch > Timer. This displays the Stopwatch screen, shown in Figure 17.8. To start timing your run or workout, select and click the Start button; the screen now displays your elapsed time, in minutes, seconds, and hundredths of a second.

FIGURE 17.8

Using the iPod as a stopwatch.

To pause the stopwatch, click the Pause button. If you have finished your workout, click Done, and your elapsed time is stored on the previous screen, as shown in Figure 17.9. Click a date/time to view the details of that session, as shown in Figure 17.10.

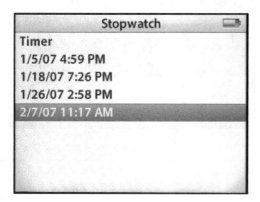

FIGURE 17.9

Viewing the times for your previous sessions.

FIGURE 17.10

Viewing the details for a previous workout or run.

You can also use the Stopwatch to time multiple laps. You do this by clicking the Lap button at the end of each lap; the screen now displays your elapsed time for each lap, as shown in Figure 17.11. Press Pause and then press Done when you've finished your final lap.

FIGURE 17.11

Timing multiple laps.

tip If you're serious about getting fit, you can use the Podfitness website to design your own custom audio workouts, which you then download to your iPod. The service costs $19.95 per month. Learn more at www.podfitness.com.

Training with the Nike+iPod Sport Kit

Timing laps isn't the only monitoring you can do with your iPod. If you invest in the Nike+iPod Sport Kit, you can use your iPod nano to track various details of your runs and walks, provide real-time feedback, and (of course) serve up your favorite playlists and tunes. The Sport Kit is one of the most impressive accessories for the iPod and a must-have for serious runners.

What's in the Kit?

The Nike+iPod Sport Kit consists of a small accelerometer/transmitter that fits in your shoe and a matching receiver that attaches to the dock connector of your iPod nano (both shown in Figure 17.12), and computer software designed to analyze and display the accumulated data. The transmitter, which is designed to fit selected Nike running shoes, collects data while you're running (how many steps you've taken, how far you've run, how long you've run, and so forth), and then transmits that data to the receiver unit. The data is then stored on the iPod nano, and later transferred to your computer when you sync your nano to your PC. Once stored on your PC, the data is imported into the Nike+ software, where it is analyzed and displayed. You can also upload your data to the Nike+ website for further analysis and comparison with other users.

FIGURE 17.12

The transmitter and receiver for the Nike+iPod Sport Kit.

The Nike+iPod Sport Kit sells for $29. Nike's Sport Kit–compatible running shoes are priced from $100 to $130. For more information, see www.nikeplus.com or www.apple.com/ipod/nike.

note The Nike+iPod Sport Kit works only with the iPod nano. Other iPod models, including the big iPod and iPod shuffle, are not supported.

Using the Sport Kit

To use the Sport Kit, you first have to fit the sensor into one of your running shoes. This is easy if you're using a Nike shoe specially designed with an insert for the sensor in the inside sole. Just place the sensor into the insert, as shown in Figure 17.13, and you're ready to go.

FIGURE 17.13

Inserting the Sport Kit transmitter into a Nike running shoe.

If you're not using Nike shoes, you can jury-rig the sensor into almost any pair of shoes with a bit of effort and imagination. You'll need to cut a hole in the center of the insole, insert the sensor, and then tape some foam padding over the inserted sensor. You could also try duct-taping or wrapping the sensor on the top of your shoe; this might not always provide accurate results, however.

Next, connect the receiver into the dock connector on the bottom of your iPod nano. Once connected, you see a new menu item for Nike+iPod on your nano. Click the Nike+iPod option to display the Workout screen shown in Figure 17.14.

tip Another option is to use the Marware Sport-suit Sensor+, which lets you attach the Sport Kit sensor to the tongue of any pair of running shoes. Buy it for $9.95 from www.marware.com.

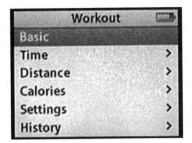

FIGURE 17.14

The new Workout screen on the iPod nano.

From here you can choose from four different types of workouts:

> **tip** To set a "power song" that you can trigger at any time during your run, select Settings > PowerSong. To trigger the power song, just hold down the nano's center Select button for several seconds until the song title appears in red on the screen.

- **Basic**—Open-ended time and distance

- **Time**—Set a time-based goal (*x* number of minutes)

- **Distance**—Set a distance-based goal (*x* number of miles)

- **Calories**—Set a calorie-based goal (burn *x* number of calories)

In addition, this menu lets you access the Nike+iPod settings and your workout history.

The screen on your iPod nano changes depending on the type of workout you've chosen. For example, the Basic workout displays the screen shown in Figure 17.15, with elapsed distance, pace, current song, and elapsed time (in large red numbers). In Distance mode, it's the elapsed distance that's shown in red. In Calories mode, calories burned display in red.

FIGURE 17.15

The Basic workout status screen.

While you're running, you'll occasionally hear spoken feedback from the Nike+iPod system. This feedback (in either a male or female voice; make your choice from the Settings menu) provides pacing information—how far you are into your run, how many feet or meters your have left, and so forth. This spoken feedback appears on top of your music so that your playlist isn't interrupted.

When you've finished, the nano displays statistics about your run. For example, Figure 17.16 shows the details of a Basic workout—distance, time, and pace (minutes per mile). Other types of workouts display similar types of stats.

FIGURE 17.16

The Basic workout statistics screen.

Analyzing Your Workout Data

The real fun starts when you've finished your run and connected your iPod nano to your computer. As it performs the normal sync process, it also transfers data about your workouts to your computer—and then, automatically to the Nike+ website.

You can view your workout data in a new tab in iTunes, but it's a rather plain presentation. The better approach is to access the Nike+ website (www.nikeplus.com), log in with your account info, and view information about your workouts in graphical form. Select the My Runs icon to display a screen like the one in Figure 17.17. Your run displays on a line graph, with key stats above the graph. You can also compare your workout history graphically, as shown in Figure 17.18. Mouse over any individual run to see that workout's key statistics. It's a neat and easy way to view your progress over time.

note The first time you sync your nano after using the Sport Kit, you are prompted to create a new account with Nike. This is free and necessary to use all the features on the Nike+ website.

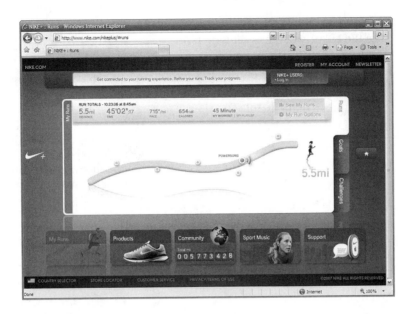

FIGURE 17.17
Viewing your workout stats online at the Nike+ website.

FIGURE 17.18
Comparing recent workouts online.

And that's not all you can do. You can also use the Nike+ website to set long-term workout goals, and to set up workout challenges among a group of friends. Check it out. If you're an active runner, this site should prove quite useful!

note Although the Nike+ website offers a wealth of activity analysis, even more analysis is available at Runometer (www.runometer.com). The Runometer site lets you upload your Nike+iPod data, and then maps your data to running routes uploaded from GPS data, downloaded from Google Earth, or sketched out on the site itself.

17

Using Your iPod as a Calendar/Scheduler

Among the many auxiliary features of the iPod are some that help it perform similarly to a personal digital assistant (PDA). In particular, you can sync your calendar appointments and contact information to your iPod, so that you'll always be aware of what you need to do and who you need to see. There's no need to carry both a PDA and your iPod; the iPod does double-duty just fine in this fashion.

That said, let it be known that one thing the iPod *doesn't* let you do is input new calendar or contact information; there's no keyboard on the iPod, after all. Instead, what you do is transfer existing calendars and contacts from Microsoft Outlook and similar applications, which you then view on your iPod while you're on the go.

Importing Calendars into Your iPod

The iPod and the iPod nano (but not the iPod shuffle) both let you import many different types of calendars. That's because most software-based and online calendars either export to or are compatible with the iCalendar and vCal calendar formats, both of which the iPod is also compatible with. Just convert your existing calendar to either iCalendar (file names ending in .ics) or vCal (filenames ending in .vcs) format, and then import it directly into your iPod.

Getting Your iPod Ready for Calendar Use

To use your iPod to view calendars, you first have to configure your iPod for disk storage. You learned how to do this in Chapter 15, "Using Your iPod as a Portable Storage Device." To recap, here's the quick version.

Start by connecting your iPod to your computer, and then open the iTunes software. In the Source pane, select your iPod, and then select the Summary tab. Check the Enable Disk Use option, and then click the Apply button.

You're now ready to start working with calendars and contacts.

Importing Calendars from Microsoft Outlook

Probably the most used Windows-based calendar application is Microsoft Outlook, which is compatible with the vCal format. Assuming you have Outlook 2003 or 2007 installed on your PC (and that you're running Windows Vista, Windows XP, or Windows 2000), syncing your Outlook calendar to your iPod is a relatively easy process. Just follow these steps:

1. Connect your iPod to your computer.
2. Open the iTunes software, if it doesn't open automatically.
3. Select your iPod in the Source pane.
4. Select the Contacts tab, shown in Figure 18.1.
5. In the Calendars section, select Sync Calendars from Microsoft Outlook, and then select either All Calendars or selected calendars from the list.
6. Click the Apply button.

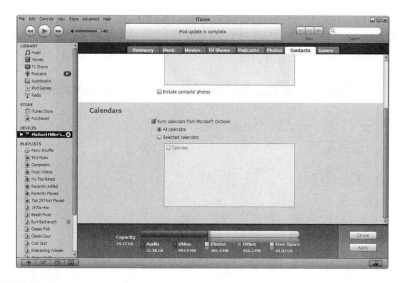

FIGURE 18.1

Syncing Outlook contacts in iTunes.

iTunes now grabs the selected calendars from Outlook and copies them to your iPod.

Importing Individual Calendar Items from Microsoft Outlook

Here's a trick that few users know about. Instead of importing entire Outlook calen-

caution iTunes doesn't always grab all appointments from Outlook calendars. If individual events don't automatically appear in your iPod calendar, you'll have to import individual calendar items manually, as described in the next section.

dars, you can import a select number of individual events. It's not quite as seamless as a full calendar import, but it's nice for when you don't want to carry a complete calendar around with you on your iPod.

The process of importing individual calendar items is a manual one:

1. Connect your iPod to your computer.

2. Open My Computer so that the iPod icon is visible.

3. In Microsoft Outlook, find the item you want to move to your iPod and double-click it to open it.

4. From the event's window, shown in Figure 18.2, select File > Save As.

5. In the Save As dialog box, pull down the Save As Type list and select iCalendar format.

6. Still in the Save As dialog box, pull down the Save In list (at the top of the window), select your iPod, and then select the Calendars folder.

7. Click the Save button.

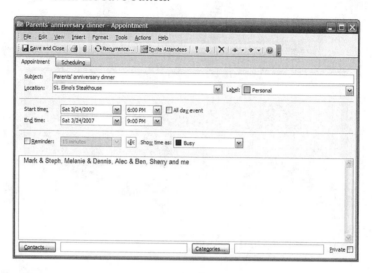

FIGURE 18.2

Exporting a calendar event from Microsoft Outlook.

The selected event is now saved to your iPod and should appear in your iPod calendar.

Importing Calendars from iCal

If you're a Mac user, you're probably using iCal to manage your calendars. Because iCal is synonymous with the iCalendar format, all your iCal calendars can be easily synced to your iPod.

If you're using Mac OS X version 10.4 or later, you sync your calendars to your iPod using the iTunes software. Follow these steps:

1. Connect your iPod to your computer.

2. Open the iTunes software, if it doesn't open automatically.

3. Select your iPod in the Source pane.

4. Select the Contacts tab.

5. In the Calendars section, select Sync iCal Calendars, and then select either All Calendars or selected calendars from the list.

6. Click the Apply button.

Importing Google Calendars

Many people create their calendars online, where they can be accessed from any computer. Online calendars are great for public organizations and events; multiple users can see what's coming up, just by using their web browsers.

One of the more popular online calendars is Google Calendar (calendar.google.com), shown in Figure 18.3. Unfortunately, it's no easy matter to export your Google calendars to iCalendar format, which is necessary to import to your iPod.

> **tip** The process is slightly more complex if you have an older Mac running a version of OS X older than 10.4; you must use the iSync application instead of iTunes. Just connect your iPod to your computer, open iSync, and choose Devices > Add Device. Next, select iPod and click Sync Now. Your calendar(s) will now be transferred.

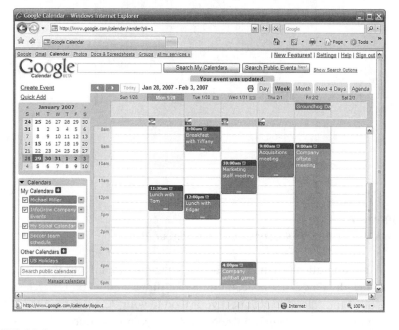

FIGURE 18.3

A Google calendar on the Web.

Although some long and tedious workarounds do exist, the best approach is to download the iPodCALsync program, which is available for free at ipodcal-sync.ueuo.com. Once installed, the program appears as an icon in the Windows system tray; click the icon and select Settings to configure the program.

What you have to configure, as shown in Figure 18.4, are the URLs for your Google calendars. You get the URL by opening the Google calendar page, clicking Settings, selecting the Calendars tab, clicking the link for the calendar, right-clicking the iCal button in the Calendar Address section, and then selecting Copy Shortcut. Now return to the iPodCALsync Settings dialog box, select the first open Calendar item, and click the Paste button. You can sync up to five Google calendars. Click Save Settings when done.

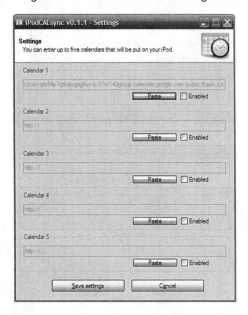

FIGURE 18.4

Use iPodCALsync to import Google calendars to your iPod.

To automatically sync your Google calendars when your iPod is connected, click the iPodCALsync icon and make sure Update iPod is checked. To manually sync calendars, connect your iPod to your PC, click the iPodCALsync icon, and then select Synchronize Now. When your calendars are synchronized, the program displays the confirmation message shown in Figure 18.5.

The calendars on your iPod have been updated.

FIGURE 18.5

Your Google calendars are synced!

Importing Yahoo! Calendars

Another popular web-based calendar site is Yahoo! Calendar
(calendar.yahoo.com), shown in Figure 18.6. Yahoo! Calendar lets you save its
calendars in .CSV format, which can then be converted to iCal format for
import to your iPod.

FIGURE 18.6

A Yahoo! calendar on the Web.

To begin the process, open your Yahoo! calendar, click Options, select
Import/Export, and when the Import/Export page appears (shown in Figure
18.7), scroll down to the Export to Outlook section and click the Export button.
When prompted, choose to save the yahoo.csv file—and remember where you
saved it.

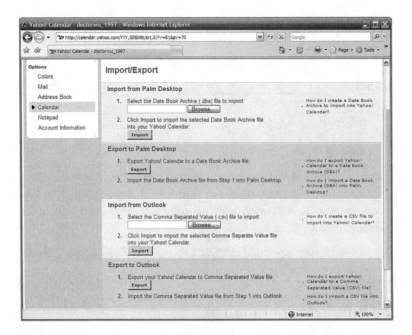

FIGURE 18.7
Exporting a Yahoo! calendar.

Now you need to convert the .CSV file to an iCal file. You do that at the Yahoo CSV to iPod Converter web page (www.manastungare.com/projects/yahoo2ical), shown in Figure 18.8. Click the Browse button in step 2 to locate and select the CSV file, and then click the Start the Conversion button. When prompted, choose to save the resulting ICS-format file to the Calendar folder on your iPod. (Your iPod must be connected to do this, of course.) The Yahoo! calendar will now appear on your iPod.

Using iPod Calendars

After you've synced your various calendars to your iPod, it's easy enough to view them with a spin of the Click Wheel. Here's how.

FIGURE 18.8

Converting a Yahoo! calendar to iCal format.

Viewing Calendars

To view a calendar on your iPod, select Extras > Calendar > All. The calendar now appears onscreen, as shown in Figure 18.9. Scroll to and click a day to view the events scheduled for that day.

> **tip**
> If you've imported more than one calendar, each calendar is listed separately on the Extras > Calendar screen.

FIGURE 18.9

Viewing a calendar on your iPod.

Setting an Alarm for Calendar Events

Here's something most users don't know. You can, with a little effort, configure any event to sound an alarm on your iPod when the event comes near.

The effort is all in your calendar program. All you have to do is configure the scheduled event with a notification alarm. Then export the event manually as an iCal file to your iPod, as described previously in this section. Assuming you have your iPod's Alarm feature activated (Extras > Calendar > Alarms > Beep), your iPod will beep when the event comes due.

Importing Your Contacts into Your iPod

Importing contacts into your iPod is similar to importing calendars. You can easily import contacts from Microsoft Outlook, Outlook Express, and your Mac.

Importing Contact Lists from Outlook and Outlook Express

Your iPod can import and display contacts stored in either Microsoft Outlook or Outlook Express (via the Windows Address Book application). The process is similar for both.

Probably the most used Windows-based calendar application is Microsoft Outlook, which is compatible with the vCal format. Assuming you have Outlook 2003 or 2007 installed on your PC (and that you're running Windows Vista, Windows XP, or Windows 2000), syncing your Outlook calendar to your iPod is a relatively easy process. Just follow these steps:

1. Connect your iPod to your computer.

2. Open the iTunes software, if it doesn't open automatically.

3. Select your iPod in the Source pane.

4. Select the Contacts tab, shown in Figure 18.10.

5. In the Contacts section, select Sync Contacts from Microsoft Outlook or Windows Address Book (if you're using Outlook Express), and then select either All Contacts or selected groups from the list.

6. Click the Apply button.

FIGURE 18.10
Syncing Outlook contacts in iTunes.

iTunes now grabs the selected contacts from Outlook and copies them to your iPod.

> **tip** If you want to import photos for your contacts (assuming you've assigned photos within your contact management program), check the Include Contacts' Photos option.

Importing Individual Contacts from Outlook and Outlook Express

Instead of importing your entire contact list or address book, iTunes lets you import only selected contacts. Follow these steps:

1. Connect your iPod to your computer.

2. Open My Computer, double-click the iPod icon, and then double-click the Contacts icon to open the Contacts folder.

3. Open Microsoft Outlook or the Windows Address Book, and then drag individual contacts from that application onto the iPod Contacts folder in My Computer.

> **tip** Outlook and Outlook Express aren't the only two Windows contact management programs you can sync to your iPod. The iPod is also compatible with Eudora, the Palm Desktop, and other similar programs, as long as you use the manual import process described here.

The contacts you dropped onto the iPod Contacts folder will now appear in your iPod contacts list.

Importing Contacts from Your Mac

Importing contacts from a Mac is similar to importing calendars. Follow these steps:

> **tip** If you have an older Mac running a version of OS X earlier than 10.4, use iSync to import contacts to your iPod. Just connect your iPod to your computer, open iSync, and choose Devices > Add Device. Next, select iPod and click Sync Now. Your contacts will now be transferred to your iPod.

1. Connect your iPod to your computer.
2. Open the iTunes software, if it doesn't open automatically.
3. Select your iPod in the Source pane.
4. Select the Contacts tab.
5. In the Calendars section, select Sync Address Book Contacts, and then select either All Contacts or selected groups from the list.
6. Click the Apply button.

Viewing Contacts on Your iPod

Viewing contacts on your iPod is a snap. Select Extras > Contacts to display the Contacts list, as shown in Figure 18.11. You then use the Click Wheel to scroll down the list and click the contact you want to view. (Figure 18.12 shows the information for a typical contact; whatever information was present in your host contact management program will appear on your iPod screen.)

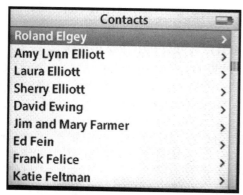

FIGURE 18.11

Viewing your contact list on your iPod.

FIGURE 18.12

Viewing individual contact information on your iPod.

> **tip** You can also sync Outlook to-do lists to your iPod. It's best to open individual items in your Outlook Task list, and then save them as ICS iCal files in your iPod's Calendar folder.

18

Using iTunes to Manage Your Music Purchases

Back in Chapter 6, "Using the iTunes Store," we discussed how to find, purchase, and download songs and other items from Apple's iTunes Store. But there's more to managing your purchases than just clicking the Buy button. The iTunes Store offers a variety of features that can help you control your purchases and monitor your spending—which is a great help for music lovers whose ears are bigger than their wallets.

Managing Your iTunes Purchases

When you first sign in to the iTunes Store, you're prompted to provide your credit or debit card number. That's so the iTS can charge your card whenever you click a Buy button. It's not surprising that Apple wants to make it as easy as possible to make purchases. It's also not surprising that this 1-Click ordering can result in out-of-control purchases and a high credit card bill if you don't watch what you're doing.

How, then, can you better get a grip on your iTunes Store purchases? There are a few things you can do.

note Does the term *1-Click* sound familiar to you? It should if you shop at Amazon.com—from which Apple licensed the 1-Click technology.

Use the Shopping Cart Instead of 1-Click

Perhaps the easiest way to slow down out-of-control 1-Click purchases is to turn off the iTunes 1-Click purchase feature. That's right, you don't have to use 1-Click purchasing. Without that 1-Click button, you have to work harder to make a purchase, which gives you the time to think twice before you buy.

tip To keep from buying duplicate songs, find out whether you already have a track in your Music library. Ctrl+Click (Mac: Option+Click) the arrow next to the track or artist name in the iTunes Store, and iTunes switches to display all songs by that artist stored on your computer's hard disk.

When you turn off 1-Click purchasing, the items you purchase go instead into the iTunes shopping cart (shown in Figure 19.1)—where they stay until you manually and deliberately check out. At that point in time (and at any time before), you can delete items from your shopping cart, which is one of the best defenses against irresponsible impulse buying.

FIGURE 19.1

The iTunes Store shopping cart.

To turn off 1-Click purchasing, open the iTunes application, select Edit > Preferences, and then select the Store tab, shown in Figure 19.2. Check the Buy Using a Shopping Cart option, and then click OK.

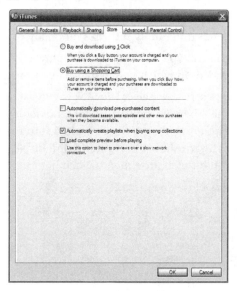

FIGURE 19.2

Turning off 1-Click purchasing.

As you can see in Figure 19.3, all the Buy Now buttons in the iTunes Store are now changed to Add Song or Add Album buttons. Click an Add button to add an item to your shopping cart.

FIGURE 19.3

Adding an album to your shopping cart.

To view your shopping cart, click the Shopping Cart item in the Store section of the iTunes Source pane. To finalize the purchase of any item in your shopping cart, click the Buy button next to that item—or, to buy all the items at once, click the Buy Now button at the lower right of the iTunes window. This will bill your credit card and start the download process.

> **tip** To remove an item from your shopping cart, click the X next to the Buy button for that item.

Use Wish Lists Instead of Buying

Here's another way to slow down your out-of-control iTunes purchases. Instead of purchasing an item, add it to your wish list. Then you can return to your wish list at a later date and make any purchases you want—or forward your wish list to friends and family if there's a holiday or birthday coming up.

To create a wish list, you actually create a playlist of the music previews for the tracks or videos in which you're interested. Here's how it works.

From the iTunes software, select File > New Playlist, and then give the new playlist a name. Then, in the iTunes Store, navigate to a track or video you want and drag that item onto the new playlist in the Source pane. When you select this playlist, as shown in Figure 19.4, it displays all the items you've wished for, with a Buy button next to each item.

FIGURE 19.4
A wish list playlist.

You can now listen to or view individual track previews or buy individual items. You can also share your wish list with friends and family by publishing it as an iMix and sending the iMix link to whomever you want.

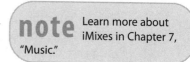

note Learn more about iMixes in Chapter 7, "Music."

Keep Track of Your Purchase History

There's one more thing you can do to better manage your iTunes purchases, and that's to keep track of all the purchases you've made. You can do this by going to the iTunes Store, clicking the Account link in the Quick Links box, and then clicking the Purchase History button. This displays the Purchase History page, shown in Figure 19.5, which lists your most recent iTunes purchases.

FIGURE 19.5

Reviewing your iTunes purchase history.

If you see something on this Purchase History list that you didn't actually purchase, click the Report a Problem button. When prompted, select Inadvertently Purchased This Item and enter any notes explaining the situation. iTunes support personnel will review your request and get back to you within 72 hours.

tip To view all your previous purchases, click the right arrow next to each invoice listed in the Previous Purchases section.

Managing Your Children's iTunes Purchases

The iPod is big with kids of all ages, from 2 to 92. To purchase from the iTunes Store, however, you have to have a credit card in your name—which most kids high school age and younger simply don't have. Short of giving your children free use of your credit card, how do you let them purchase music and videos from the iTunes Store?

Give Your Kids an iTunes Allowance

Aside from giving your child an iTunes gift card (which we discuss later in this chapter), the easiest way to let them purchase from the iTunes Store is to create an allowance for them within the store. Essentially, you provide your credit card information to the iTS, and then specify a dollar amount that your child can charge to your card in any given month.

For example, if you want your son or daughter to be able to purchase up to $20 of tunes a month, you establish an iTunes allowance of $20 for that child. It's quite easy to do.

Start by going to the iTunes Store home page. Then click the Buy iTunes Gifts link in the Quick Links box. When the iTunes Gifts page appears, scroll down to the Allowances section at bottom of the page and click Set Up an Allowance Now.

On the Set Up an iTunes Allowance page, shown in Figure 19.6, enter your name and your child's name. Then click the Money Allowance button to select an allowance amount, from $10 to $200 per month. You then have to specify an iTunes account for your child, either an existing one or a new one you can set up now. Click Continue to verify the information and set up the allowance.

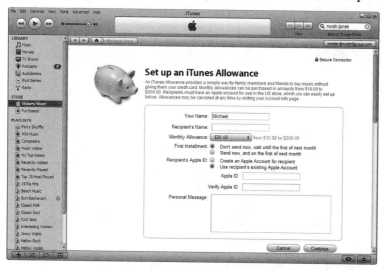

FIGURE 19.6

Setting up an iTunes allowance.

Now, when your child accesses the iTunes Store using the account number you specified, he or she can buy tunes and videos up to the allowance amount each month. It's that simple.

Deauthorize Your Childrens' Computers

If you'd rather your children not purchase from iTunes at all, you can deauthorize their computer to keep them from buying on your iTunes account. This will also keep them from playing any music previously purchased from the iTunes Store.

To deauthorize a computer, launch the iTunes software on that computer, and then select Store > Deauthorize Computer. From this point on, no one can use this computer to purchase music from the iTS on your iTunes account.

Keep Your Kids from Buying Explicit Content

Here's one more thing you might want to consider if your kids are visiting the iTunes Store. There are probably some tunes you don't want them to listen to, based on explicit content. Fortunately, Apple lets you block your kids from listening to and purchasing explicit tracks.

To restrict your children's purchases, launch the iTunes software, select Edit > Preferences, and then select the Parental Control tab, shown in Figure 19.7. To restrict access to explicit content in the iTunes Store, check any or all of the following options: Restrict Explicit Content, Restrict Movies to *Rating*, or Restrict TV Shows to *Rating*. (Use the pull-down lists to select the restricted rating level.)

caution Just because a track isn't labeled as Explicit doesn't necessarily mean that it doesn't contain explicit content. Not all tracks are examined and labeled in this manner, so there's lots of explicit content on iTunes not labeled as such.

19

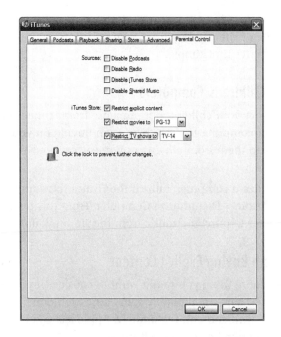

FIGURE 19.7

Configuring iTunes' parental control options.

After you've made your choices, click the lock icon in the dialog box, and then enter a username and password. This keeps your children from undoing the changes you just made. Click OK, and your kids won't be able to access or download things they shouldn't.

tip To block all access to the iTunes Store, check the Disable iTunes Store option.

Giving the Gift of Music

Another way to let your children (and others) purchase from the iTunes Store without needing a credit card is to give an iTunes gift card or gift certificate. You can also give individual songs and albums to others. iTunes makes giving easy!

Giving Gift Cards and Gift Certificates

Gift cards are big business, and they're especially nice for those friends and family who love music. They can "spend" the card on whatever music they want. You don't have to guess what they do or don't like, or do or don't already have in their library.

To give an iTunes gift, go the main iTunes Store page and click the Buy iTunes Gifts link in the Quick Links box. When the iTunes Gifts page appears, as shown in Figure 19.8, choose the type of gift you'd like to give—a physical gift card, a printable gift certificate, or an email gift certificate (great for recipients who you might not see in person).

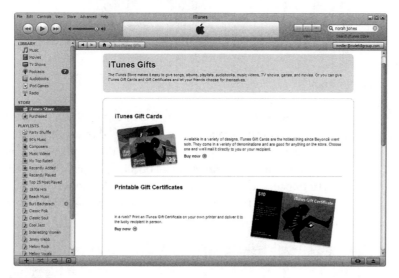

FIGURE 19.8

Choosing an iTunes gift.

The process for giving a gift is similar no matter which type of gift you give. Click the Buy Now link, and then enter the necessary information—your name, the recipient's name, amount of the gift, and so forth. (Figure 19.9 shows the form you fill out to give an email gift certificate.) Click the Continue button to confirm your gift and arrange payment.

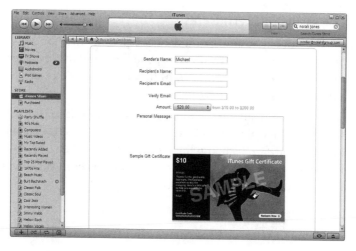

FIGURE 19.9

Giving an iTunes email gift certificate.

When someone receives an iTunes gift card or gift certificate, he doesn't even need an iTunes account to redeem the gift. Instead of logging in to the iTunes Store with an account name, you instead go to the iTunes Store home page and click the Redeem link in the Quick Links box. When the screen shown in Figure 19.10 appears, enter the redemption code found on the gift card or certificate, and then click the Redeem button. You can then make purchases up to the amount of the gift.

FIGURE 19.10

Redeeming an iTunes gift.

Giving Songs, Albums, and Playlists

There's another way to give the gift of iTunes music. The iTunes Store lets you give individual songs, albums, and playlists. Just make the purchase and send a download link to the gift recipient.

The easiest way to gift a piece of music is to search or browse for the music you want to give and then click the Gift This Music link, like the one shown in Figure 19.11. When the Give a Gift screen appears, as shown in Figure 19.12, click the Gift Album or Gift Song button. You're now prompted for the recipient's name and email information, as shown in Figure 19.13. Fill in the blanks, click the Continue button, and verify your purchase. The recipient will now receive an email message notifying her of the gift, with a link she can click to download the song or album.

FIGURE 19.11

Click the Gift This Music link to give the gift of music.

FIGURE 19.12

Giving an album or individual tracks as a gift.

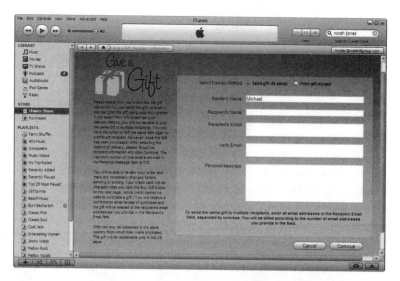

FIGURE 19.13

Fill in the blanks to purchase and send the gift.

You can also give complete playlists as gifts. Just assemble a playlist in iTunes and click the right arrow next to the playlist name in the Source pane. You'll now see the dialog box shown in Figure 19.14. Click the Give Playlist button.

FIGURE 19.14

Giving a playlist as a gift.

iTunes now processes your playlist, accesses the iTunes Store, and determines which songs on your playlist are available for purchase. You'll now see a screen like the one in Figure 19.15, which lists the tracks available for giving. Enter the necessary information. Then click the Continue button to purchase and give all the available songs on the playlist to the recipient.

FIGURE 19.15

Finalizing the playlist gift.

Secrets

20

iPod Tips and Tricks

Want to do more with your iPod or iTunes than just listen to one song after another? To become a power iPod user, you need to learn the tips and tricks that turn your iPod into something more than just a simple portable music player.

For example, did you know you can record FM radio for playback on your iPod? Or use your iPod to give business presentations? Or view email? Did you know that you can use iTunes to separate hidden CD tracks? Or view PDF files?

All this—and more—is easily doable, if you know the tricks.

iPod Tricks

We'll start with tips and tricks for your iPod. Most of these tricks work on all late-model iPods (including the nano and, in some instances, the shuffle).

Extend Your iPod's Battery Life

One of the bigger beefs with all iPod models is the battery. No matter how long the battery life is, it's never enough—especially when your iPod dies in the middle of your favorite song.

How can you get longer life on each battery charge? Here are a few tips:

- If you're not listening to your iPod, pause it. Otherwise the unit keeps playing, which keeps draining the battery.

- Minimize use of the backlight—or turn it off completely. Use the Settings > Backlight Timer setting to change the amount of time you want the backlight to remain lit. Because the backlight uses additional power, the less you use it, the less drain you put on your iPod's battery.

- Turn off the equalizer (Settings > EQ > Off). Believe it or not, the equalizer uses additional power and drains the battery faster than playing your music "flat."

- Minimize track hopping. The more you manually change tracks, the more work the iPod's hard disk has to do—which uses more power. When you play a playlist or album straight through, the iPod caches the next few tracks in advance, which minimizes hard disk use. Manually change tracks and you don't get the benefits of caching.

- Store your music in compressed format (AAC or MP3 formats) rather than in uncompressed WAV or AIFF formats. The iPod can cache more compressed music than it can uncompressed tracks, which minimizes hard disk use.

- The iPod's battery is most efficient at room temperature. Try not to place the unit in conditions under 32° or above 95° Fahrenheit; exceeding the normal range will reduce the current battery charge and weaken the battery's long-term life.

- If your iPod's been out in the cold, let it warm up to room temperature before you turn it on. If the ambient temperature is too low (think overnight in a car in the dead of winter), the iPod's low-battery icon may appear, and the unit won't wake up from sleep. Let it warm up to return to normal operation.

- To keep from accidentally turning on your iPod when you're not using it, use the Hold switch on the top of the unit. This prevents accidental Click Wheel presses from turning on the unit.

- Make sure you unplug your earphones when you're done listening. When you leave your earphones plugged in, your iPod won't automatically turn off after a period of disuse; unplug them, and your iPod will shut off after a few minutes on pause.

20

Then there's the issue of long-term battery life—that is, how long the battery itself will last before it stops holding a charge. The iPod uses a lithium-ion battery that's rated for a minimum of 500 charging cycles. If you recharge your iPod's battery every day, those 500 charges will last you about 18 months. Recharge every other day, and the battery should be good for about three years. In other words, the less frequently you recharge your battery, the longer it will last.

note A charging cycle is a full discharge—that is, you run the battery all the way down and then follow that with a full recharge.

note The iPod fast-charges its battery to the 80% level in just an hour. It takes longer to charge the remaining 20%, however—up to 4 hours to complete a full recharge.

Knowing that, we come to our first tip for extending the life of your iPod battery—don't recharge it every day! Instead of "topping off" the charge nightly, let the battery run further down before you recharge.

That said, you might not want to let your battery die completely before recharging. And you should do a somewhat regular charge, to keep the battery from fully draining. Look to recharge your iPod at least once every two weeks or so, for maximum battery performance. (That's because, at normal room temperature, the iPod's battery will discharge itself in 14 to 28 days of disuse.)

Recharge Your iPod—Without a PC

If you have a later-model iPod, the only cable you have is the one that connects your iPod to your PC's USB port. This cable not only serves to sync your iPod, it also serves to recharge it.

What if you need to recharge your iPod but don't have a computer handy? Then you need a third-party iPod AC adapter or USB power adapter, such as the Griffin PowerBlock, $29.99, shown in Figure 20.1(www.griffintechnology.com). These devices connect to your iPod's dock connector and then to any power outlet, so you can power and recharge your iPod directly, no computer necessary.

20

FIGURE 20.1

Recharge your PC from any wall outlet with the Griffin PowerBlock.

Get Extra Life with an External Battery

Sometimes you don't even have a wall outlet handy. For those times when you're on the go and your iPod's battery goes out, use an external battery to give your iPod a new lease on life. Just connect the external battery to your iPod's dock connector, and you get several more hours of listening pleasure. Figure 20.2 shows one of the more popular external batteries, Griffin's TuneJuice 2 ($29.99, www.griffintechnology.com), which provides up to 14 hours of additional use.

FIGURE 20.2

Get additional power on the go with Griffin's TuneJuice 2 external battery.

Rate a Song

The song rating feature is one of the most underused features of iPod/iTunes. That might be because most people don't know how to rate a song that they're listening to on their iPod.

Rating a song is actually quite easy. While the song is playing, press the center Select button three times, and then scroll the Click Wheel to add or subtract stars, as shown in Figure 20.3. Press the Select button again when you're done.

FIGURE 20.3

Rating a song on the iPod.

This not only changes the rating of the song on your iPod, but also the rating in iTunes—when you next sync your iPod, that is.

Use Your iPod as an Alarm Clock

Assuming you have your iPod connected to an external speaker (or that you wear earphones while you sleep—which is probably unlikely), you can use your iPod as an alarm clock. All you have to do is set the iPod's internal alarm and choose the playlist you want to hear when you wake.

To set the iPod's alarm, select Extras > Clock > Alarm Clock > Alarm > On. Scroll to Time to set the wake time, and then scroll to Sound to select a wake-up playlist (or annoying beep). When the wake-up time comes, your iPod wakes up and starts playing.

Use Your iPod as a Laser Pointer—or a Flashlight

You know, of course, that your iPod contains an internal battery; that's how it obtains the power to play all your tunes. What you might not know is that

20

you can use that internal battery to power other add-ons and devices. Which leads us to our next trick.

When you connect Griffin's iBeams to your iPod, you can use your iPod as a fancy-dancy laser pointer, perfect for highlighting items during presentations. As you can see in Figure 20.4, the iBeams also functions as a conventional flashlight, which lets you use your iPod to shine the way in dark rooms. Kind of an unconventional use for the old iPod, but kind of cool nonetheless.

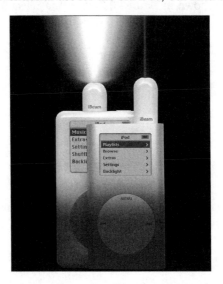

FIGURE 20.4

Use your iPod to light up the room with Griffin's iBeams.

The iBeams is compatible with older (pre-5G) iPods and the iPod mini. It sells for $19.99 from www.griffintechnology.com.

Use Your iPod for Presentations

Speaking of presentations, did you know you can use your iPod to give presentations? That's right, you don't have to haul your notebook PC around the country anymore. Just load your presentation to your iPod, connect the iPod to a projector, and start presenting.

The key is to convert the slides in your presentation into a series of JPG images. That is, each slide becomes a separate JPG file. You should be able to do this from within your presentation program, or by using a separate screen capture program and capturing each slide as a JPG file. Store the resulting JPG files in a single folder on your PC's hard disk, and then sync that photo folder to your iPod.

Even better, use the iPresent It utility to automatically convert your PowerPoint and PDF presentations into iPod slideshows. The program lets you create slideshows using drag-and-drop operations. Buy it for $17.95 from www.zapptek.com.

To play your presentation, start by connecting your iPod to some sort of video projector, using the Apple iPod AV Cable ($19, store.apple.com) or something similar. Then select Photos > Photo Library to select the presentation folder, press Play to start playing a slideshow, and use the iPod's Click Wheel to move from slide to slide. Of course, make sure you enable manual advance rather than automatic advance (Photos > Slideshow Settings > Time Per Slide > Manual) and turn off the shuffle function (Photos > Slideshow Settings > Shuffle Photos > Off).

Record FM Radio for iPod Playback

Even when you have your iPod packed full with your favorite songs, there's still more music out there. If you happen to have a decent local FM station, you can record FM radio programming for later playback on your iPod.

The easiest way to do this is with Griffin's radio SHARK 2 ($49.99, www. griffintechnology.com), shown in Figure 20.5. This shark fin–shaped device receives AM and FM radio signals and lets you record them on your computer. Just connect the radio SHARK 2 to your PC, use the included software to record programming from a given station, and then transfer that recording to your iPod for future listening.

20

FIGURE 20.5

Use Griffin's radio SHARK 2 to record AM or FM radio for playback on your iPod.

Record Internet Radio for iPod Playback

When terrestrial radio sucks, turn to Internet radio for lots more variety. And, because you receive Internet radio over your PC, you can record that programming for later playback on your iPod.

To record Internet radio, use the Replay A/V program ($49.95, www.replay-video.com). Just tune in your desired Internet radio station, configure the program to save the Internet radio stream to MP3 format, import the MP3 file into iTunes, and then sync it to your iPod. It's that simple.

Store Cocktail Recipes on Your iPod

You can take all sorts of information with you on your iPod—including cocktail recipes! The iBar program ($29.95, www.talkingpanda.com) contains instructions for mixing more than 450 different drinks. As you can see in Figure 20.6, you access the recipes as you would tracks in a playlist on the iPod screen. Most recipes are text based, although some come with audio instructions.

FIGURE 20.6

A bartender's best friend—Talking Panda's iBar program.

Teach Yourself Foreign Languages on Your iPod

Talking Panda also distributes several other interesting iPod software programs, including the iLingo line of foreign language instruction. Download a specific iLingo package and start learning to speak French, German, Italian, Spanish, Portuguese, Russian, Cantonese, Mandarin Chinese, Japanese, or Korean. As you can see in Figure 20.7, words and phrases are shown onscreen, along with audio examples. Multilanguage packs are available for $39.95 (AsiaPack) or $49.95 (Euro Pack) from www.talkingpanda.com.

20

FIGURE 20.7

Learn foreign languages with Talking Panda's iLingo packs.

View Subway Maps on Your iPod

Here's something else you can view on your iPod: subway maps. Go to iSubwayMaps.com (www.isubwaymaps.com) to find downloadable iPod-compatible maps of most major metro subways systems—including Boston, Chicago, New York, San Francisco, even London and Paris.

As you can see in Figure 20.8, the maps are quite detailed. All maps are free and easily downloaded to your 5G iPod. Just unzip the downloaded ZIP file and place all resulting images into a single folder on your hard drive. Load the images to your iPod as you would any photo folder.

FIGURE 20.8

A New York subway map, for viewing on your iPod.

View Google or Yahoo! Maps on Your iPod

Subway maps are nice, but what about other more general maps? Well, no program or site currently available offers iPod-compatible map images—but there is a way to manually create maps for your iPod.

This little trick works with any map site, including both Google Maps and Yahoo! Maps. The trick is to save a screen capture of the map you want to use, and then copy that image file to your 5G iPod for viewing as a photo.

20

Start by creating the map you want on the mapping site. Next, minimize the size of the map as much as possible; too large an image is overkill on the iPod's smallish screen.

Now comes the fun part. You need to capture the map image. If you have a screen capture program, such as Full Shot, you can use that. If not, you can use the built-in "print screen" feature in Windows or on your Mac. In Windows, press the PrtScr or PrintScreen button on your keyboard. On a Mac, press Option+Shift+3. Either approach captures your entire computer screen into your computer's clipboard.

Next, you need to paste that captured screen into an image editing program. For example, if you're using Adobe Photoshop Elements, select File > New > Image from Clipboard. (Other programs have a similar function.) The entire screen you captured should now appear in an editing window. Use your program's crop control to crop the image so that only the map itself is visible. Now save the cropped file into the folder you use to house your iPod photos.

When you next sync your iPod, the map image will be transferred automatically. As you can see in Figure 20.9, you can now display the map on your iPod's screen, as you would any image file.

FIGURE 20.9
Viewing a Google map on the iPod screen.

Read Your Email on Your iPod

Although you can't use your iPod to send or receive email, you can use it read email. All you have to do is use the k-pod program (free, k-deep.com/k-pod.htm) to transfer messages from your email program's inbox to your iPod. Messages are automatically copied when you sync your iPod to your PC. You then use your iPod Notes feature (Extras > Notes) to read the individual messages.

Listen to Your Email on Your iPod

Maybe you like the idea of reading your email on your iPod, but don't like the way it looks on the iPod's smallish screen. Fortunately, MagneticTime offers the MT1 application that converts text-based email messages into spoken-word audio files, so you can listen to your email instead of reading it.

tip Note that k-pod is a Windows-only application. Mac users can get similar functionality with the Mac-only PodMail program (free, www.podmail.org).

Once installed, MT1 puts a new toolbar in Microsoft Outlook and Outlook Express. Click the toolbar to convert selected email messages (or any text-based file) into MP3 format, which you can then play on your iPod. (Your emails appear in a new playlist called MagneticTime Emails.) Order MT1 for $39.99 from www.magnetictime.com.

View Web Pages on Your iPod

Email isn't the only Internet content you can view on your iPod. The iPodulator website (www.theplaceforitall.com/ipodulator), shown in Figure 20.10, lets you easily convert the text content of any web page into a text file, which you can then copy to your iPod. Just enter the URL of the web page and click the iPodinate button.

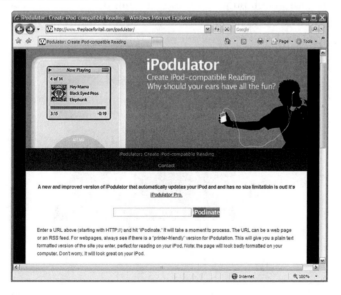

FIGURE 20.10

Converting web content to an iPod-friendly text file.

When the results appear in your browser, use your browser's Page > Save As function to save the text page to the Notes folder on your iPod. (Obviously, your iPod must be connected to do this.) To view the content on your iPod, select Extras > Notes and select the appropriate file. The file is now displayed onscreen, as shown in Figure 20.11.

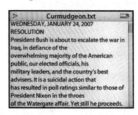

FIGURE 20.11

Viewing text-based web content on your iPod.

The only problem with this approach is that your iPod can't handle really big text files. If a file is larger than 4KB, your iPod only displays the first 4,096 characters in the file.

To work around this limitation, download the iPodulator Pro 2 software (free, www.ipodulatorpro.theplaceforitall.com), shown in Figure 20.12. iPodulator Pro 2 does everything that the web-based iPodulator does, and more—and it breaks large web pages into smaller notes files that your iPod can easily read. The software also handles RSS feeds, automatically downloading new content to your iPod as it appears online.

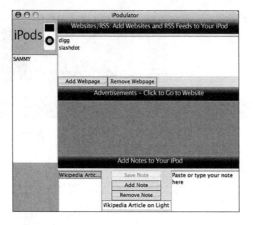

FIGURE 20.12

Converting web content with iPodulator Pro 2.

Find Out How Much Free Space You Have Left

Okay, this next trick is just a little one, but still might prove useful. When you want to see how much free space is left on your iPod, you could connect your iPod to your PC and view the space indicator at the bottom of the Summary tab. Or you could skip all that hassle and just select Settings > About on your iPod. As you can see in Figure 20.13, this screen displays all sorts of neat information, including your iPod's name, the number of videos and photos stored, the total storage capacity, and the amount of storage still available.

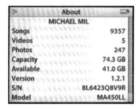

FIGURE 20.13

Viewing information about your iPod.

Rename Your iPod

Don't like the name that was originally assigned to your iPod? Change it. Connect your iPod to your PC and click the iPod item in the iTunes Source pane. As you can see in Figure 20.14, this opens the name for editing. Enter a new name, press Enter, and you're good to go.

FIGURE 20.14

Changing your iPod's name in iTunes.

Customize Your iPod's Main Menu

Here's something even cooler. Don't like the way things are presented on your iPod's main menu? You're in luck, because the main menu is fully customizable, from the iPod itself.

20

All you have to do is select Settings > Main Menu. This displays the Main Menu screen (not to be confused with the Main menu itself), shown in Figure 20.15. Click any item to switch it from On (displayed on the main menu) or Off (not displayed).

FIGURE 20.15

Customizing the iPod's main menu.

Mod Your iPod

Maybe it's the *outside* of your iPod that you want to customize. If so, you're in luck. Many third-party iPod repair sites will install new backs and (sometimes) fronts for your iPod.

> **tip**
>
> To reset the iPod's main menu to its factory default settings, scroll to the bottom of the Main Menu screen and select Reset Main Menu.

For example, iPodMods (www.ipodmods.com) not only offers iPod repair services but also installs color cases, color screens (for older iPods), and the like. (I particularly like their iVue Crystal Clear Panels, shown in Figure 20.16.) Similar colored cases and skins are offered by ColorWare (www.colorwarepc.com) and Skinpod.it (www.skinpod.it). Contact each company for prices.

FIGURE 20.16
The iVue clear iPod case from iPodMods.

Use Cheat Codes for iPod Games

For our final iPod-related trick, we present some insider cheat codes for two of Apple's most popular iPod games: Texas Hold'em and Vortex.

Texas Hold'em

To use cheat codes in Texas Hold'em, go to the Options menu, select New Player, and then enter the cheat code as a new player name. After the cheat code has been entered, the game jumps to the checkmark character. When you see this, hold down the center Select button until the code activates, at which point you'll see the word *Secret* appear onscreen.

Table 20.1 details some of the more popular cheat codes for this game.

20

Table 20.1   Texas Hold'em cheat codes

To Do This	Use This Cheat Code
Access a secret menu with options to unlock all tournaments; start with $100,000 in cash; show tells; show down cards; and adjust the artificial intelligence to fold normally, often, or never	YOUCHEAT
See secret characters	ALLCHARS
Play the hidden iTunes Bar tournament	BARTUNES
Play the hidden Stonehenge tournament, shown in Figure 20.17	BIGROCKS
Play the hidden Dogs tournament	PLAYDOGS
Play the hidden Futuristic tournament	SPACEACE
Play the hidden Apple Conference Room tournament	THREEAMI

FIGURE 20.17

Use cheat codes to play the hidden Stonehenge Texas Hold'em tournament.

Vortex

To enter a cheat code in Vortex, bring up the Main menu without a game in progress. Select the Personal Info option, select Rename, and then enter the cheat code. Hold down the center Select button until the code activates.

Table 20.2 details some of the more popular cheat codes for this game.

Table 20.2   Vortex Cheat Codes

To Do This	Use This Cheat Code
Activate the laser power-up (burns through bricks in a straight line)	ME PAZ
Activates the gun power-up (destroys bricks one at a time)	I GUNZ
Get a powerball (shatters multiple bricks at a time)	PWR B (space-PWR-space-B)
Get 24 lives	FORSIX
Unlocks special backgrounds	NO ID (NO-space-ID-space)

iTunes Tricks

These iPod tricks aren't the only tricks you can use to enhance your iPod-related enjoyment. You can also apply tricks to the iTunes software that you might find fun and useful.

Search Smarter

When you're looking for music in the iTunes Store, it's easy to get overwhelmed by the sheer number of choices available. That's why I recommend searching over browsing, but even then it's sometimes difficult to find exactly what you're looking for.

With that in mind, here are some tips for smarter searching in the iTunes Store:

- **Use Power Search.** While you can do some smart searching from the basic search box, there are a lot more options available when you click the Power Search link in the Quick Links box on the iTunes home page, as you can see in Figure 20.18.

20

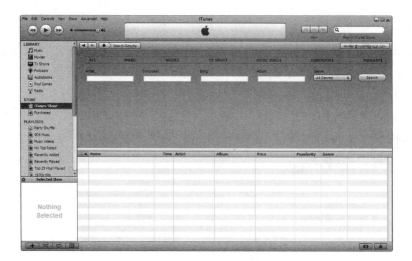

FIGURE 20.18

Use the iTunes Power Search functions to search by artist, composer, song, album, or genre.

- **Search by artist.** Probably the most common way to Power Search is to search by artist. Interested in everything put on disc by Fountains of Wayne? Just enter **Fountains of Wayne** into the Power Search Artist field and click the Search button; iTunes returns a list of all the albums and individual tracks available.

- **Search by composer.** Sometimes it's the song's composer that you're interested in. For example, if you're a big Burt Bacharach fan, you can generate a list of all Bacharach-penned tunes in the iTunes Store by entering **Burt Bacharach** into the Power Search Composer field.

- **Search for an individual song.** If you know a song title—or even part of a title—just enter what you know into the Power Search Song field. Entering a partial song name will return a list of all songs that include these particular keywords.

- **Search by genre.** Are you a big folk fan? Then pull down the Power Search Genre list, select Folk, then click the Search button. iTunes will now return a comprehensive list of all albums, tracks, and artists within the selected genre.

- **Combine your searches.** The search boxes on the Power Search page don't have to operate independent of each other. That is, you can fine-tune a search by entering keywords into more than one field. Let's say, for example, you want to search for all Burt Bacharach tunes sung by Dionne Warkwick, enter **Dionne Warwick** into the Artist field and

Burt Bacharach into the Composer field. Likewise, if you want to see all of Joni Mitchell's folk tunes, enter **Joni Mitchell** into the Artist field and then select Folk from the Genre list. Be as creative as you want!

Request a Tune

If a search doesn't return any matching tracks, you can request that iTunes add the song(s) you want. Just click the Request link on the Search Results page; this opens your web browser to the Request Music page shown in Figure 20.19. (You can go to this page directly by entering this URL: www.apple.com/feedback/itunes.html.)

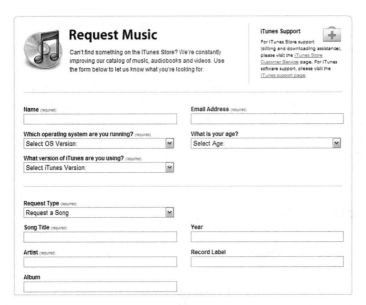

FIGURE 20.19
Request any music that iTunes doesn't offer.

Enter your name and email address, then pull down the Request Type list and select what you want—a song, artist, album, podcast, and so on. Enter the name of the song, artist, or whatever into the appropriate boxes, and any other comments into the Comments box. Click the Send Feedback button to send Apple your request; if and when iTunes adds what you're looking for, you'll get an email letting you know.

Use iTunes Hotkeys

If you use iTunes a lot, you'll appreciate the fact that you can access most of the software's functions using just your keyboard, without need of the mouse. (For many users, keyboarding is faster than mousing.) What shortcut keys are available? See Table 20.3 for the list.

Table 20.3   iTunes Shortcut Keys

To Do This	Use This Hotkey
Pause or unpause a track	Spacebar
Advance to next track	Right arrow
Return to previous track	Left arrow
Raise volume	Ctrl+up arrow (Mac: Command+up arrow)
Lower volume	Ctrl+down arrow (Mac: Command+down arrow)

In addition, when you press a letter key on your keyboard, it will go to the first item starting with that letter in the highlighted column. For example, if you have the Artist column highlighted and you press the B key, you should go to the first track by B. B. King (or whomever your first *B* artist is.) Likewise if the cursor is in the Source pane, pressing a letter key takes you to the first playlist that starts with that letter.

Customize the Visualizer

There are even more hotkeys in iTunes, but they apply to the visualizer. (You remember the Visualizer—activate it by selecting View > Show Visualizer or pressing Ctrl+T.)

There are actually lots of visualizer settings that you can control, but only via hotkeys. Table 20.4 provides the details; obviously, the visualizer has to be running to activate the effect.

20

Table 20.4   Visualizer Hotkeys

Effect	Hotkey
Display track information	I
Display visualization information	C
Display visualizer help	H
Switch between normal or high-contrast colors	N
Cycle through visualization shapes	Q and W
Cycle through visualization effects	A and S
Cycle through colors	Z and X
Display random effect	R
Cycle through random, user, and freeze modes	M
Change the frame-rate display	F
Change the frame-rate capping	T
Reset to default visualization	D
Save current effect configuration	Shift+0 *through* Shift+9
Recall saved configuration	0 *through* 9

Add New Visualizations

The visualizations built in to iTunes are fun, but you might get bored with them after a time. When you want new and exciting visualizations, turn to the following websites:

- Eyephendrine (Mac only, www.giofx.net/GioFX/Eyephedrine.html), shown in Figure 20.20
- iGoom (Mac-only, www.ios-software.com/?page=projet&quoi=1)
- Jumping Steve (www.memention.com/js)
- SoundSpectrum (www.soundspectrum.com)
- Steel Skies (www.steelskies.com)
- Ultragroovalicious iTunes Visualizer (Mac only, www.groovyvis.com)

20

FIGURE 20.20
The Eyphendrine iTunes visualizer.

Back Up Your Purchased Music

When you purchase music from the iTunes Store, that music is stored on your computer's hard disk (and, eventually, synced to your iPod). But what do you do if your hard disk crashes?

Using the techniques discussed in Chapter 15, "Using Your iPod as a Portable Storage Device," you could copy the songs back from your iPod to a new hard disk. You could also authorize a new computer within iTunes (assuming you're not up to your authorization limit) and redownload your purchased music.

A better solution, however, is to create a backup of all your saved music. iTunes 7 offers just such a backup option. For most users, backing up to a data DVD or multiple CDs is probably the best approach.

To back up your iTunes Music library, select File > Back Up to Disc. When the iTunes Backup dialog box appears, as shown in Figure 20.21, choose to back up your entire library or only iTunes Store purchases. You can also choose to do an incremental backup, copying only those files that are new or changed since your last backup. Click the Back Up button and you're prompted to insert a blank CD or DVD into your computer's drive. Do so and then follow the onscreen instructions to complete the backup. (You'll be prompted to insert additional discs if your library is too big for a single disc.)

FIGURE 20.21
Backing up your iTunes library to CD or DVD.

Enhance Your Audio

The equalizer built in to iTunes is functional, but it probably isn't full-featured enough for true audiophiles. For even more audio control and enhancement, check out the Volume Logic plug-in ($19.95, www.volumelogic.com). The Volume Logic plug-in digitally remasters your music in real time, adding a variety of digital signal processing effects.

As you can see in Figure 20.22, the Volume Logic window offers a variety of sound presets. Select the preset that matches the type of music you're listening to and listen to the DSP kick in. You can also adjust various parameters, such as bass boost, volume level, and so forth.

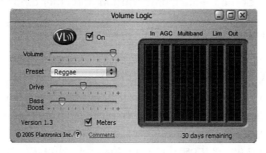

FIGURE 20.22
Advanced digital signal processing with Volume Logic.

20

Create Multiple iTunes Libraries

These days, the single-iPod family is rare. What do you do if you have multiple iPods synced to a single PC?

iTunes 7 lets you create multiple libraries on a single PC. This means you can create different libraries for different iPods, or even different libraries for a single user with varying tastes. For example, you might want one library of videos to watch when you're on the road, and another library of music for listening around the house. Or you might create one library for your private use, and another to share over your home or work network.

Unfortunately, this multiple-library feature is fairly well hidden. Here's the trick on how to find and use it.

First, if you have the iTunes software open, close it. Now hold down the Shift key (Mac: Option) and double-click any iTunes icon to open the program. Instead of the program starting right up, you instead see the dialog box shown in Figure 20.23.

FIGURE 20.23

Creating multiple libraries in iTunes.

If you've already created a second library, click the Choose Library button and select the library file from the next dialog box. If you want to create a new library, click the Create Library button and enter a name for the library when prompted. iTunes now launches, completely devoid of content. This is the empty library you just created. Fill it up as you see fit.

Delete Duplicate Tracks from Your Library

After you've used iTunes for awhile, you're bound to end up with at least a few duplicate tracks—songs you've burned or downloaded more than once. Because storage space is valuable, it pays to periodically go through your library and delete those duplicate tracks, freeing up space for newer music.

Fortunately, iTunes has an easy way to identify duplicate tracks in your library. All you have to do is select View > Show Duplicates. This lists all tracks that share the same name, in alphabetic order. Examine each of the duplicate tracks, and delete one or more instances as necessary.

Find Out Which Playlists Contain a Certain Song

Here's a way to find duplicates of another sort. Ever wonder what playlists contain a given song? That is, do you have "*Something*" in more than one playlist?

All you have to do is select the song in question (anywhere in iTunes), right-click it, and select the Show in Playlist option. This expands the pop-up menu to show all the playlists that contain that song, as shown in Figure 20.24. Neat!

> **caution** Not all tracks with the same name are actually the same track. Sometimes there is more than one song with the same title. Other times, it might be the same song performed by a different artist, or even performed by the same artist on a different album. (Comparing song timings is a good way to weed out false duplicates.) Make sure a track is truly a duplicate before you permanently delete it.

FIGURE 20.24
Viewing all the playlists for a given song.

Convert Multiple Tracks in a Batch

One neat feature of iTunes is that it lets you convert digital audio files from one format to another. So, for example, if you have an MP3 file, you can use iTunes to convert it to AAC format—or vice versa.

Even better, you can use iTunes to convert multiple files in a single batch. Here's how you do it.

Start by configuring iTunes for the proper conversion. Select Edit > Preferences, select the Advanced tab, and then select the Importing tab. Pull down the

Import Using list to select the final file format you want, and then use the Setting list to determine the desired audio quality. Click OK when done.

Now it's time to do the batch conversion. Open your Music library and select the tracks you want to convert. Select Advanced > Convert Selection to; iTunes creates a new copy of all your selected songs, in the file format you specified. (The original files will remain on your hard disk; iTunes doesn't delete anything during this process.)

Rip a CD Directly to a Playlist

Here's a bit of a time saver. If you have a new CD that you want to rip to hard disk and also add to a preexisting playlist, you can do the ripping and adding in a single step. Just insert the CD into your PC's CD drive, select all the songs on the CD within iTunes, and then drag the songs to the desired playlist in the Source pane. When you start the rip, the CD tracks will be automatically added to your library *and* to the selected playlist, all in a single step.

Correct Ripping Errors

When you rip a lot of music from CDs, you'll occasionally end up with a track or two that has a slight click in the audio. That clicking noise is an error introduced when there is some sort of defect on the CD—a speck of dust perhaps, or maybe a slight scratch, something that causes a dropout in the digital audio.

To correct against this sort of error, iTunes includes error-correcting circuitry. Unfortunately, this error correction is not enabled by default.

To turn on error correction, select Edit > Preferences, select the Advanced tab, select the Importing tab, and then check the Use Error Correction When Reading Audio CDs option. This should do the trick.

Remove Copy Protection from a Track—and Use Your Music Any Way You Want

As you're by now aware, you don't really purchase music from the iTunes Store—you rent it. That's because every track you download includes Apple's FairPlay digital rights management (DRM) technology, a kind of copy protection scheme that limits how you can use the downloaded music. For example, you're limited as to how many computers can play the downloaded track (5) and how

caution Because checking for errors takes time, enabling error correction will result in longer rip times.

the track can be burned to CD (especially when included within a playlist).

If you want to free your tracks from the chains of DRM, you have two options. First,

you can burn a DRM'd track to CD, then re-rip the track from CD back to your hard disk. The process of burning-and-ripping removes the DRM wrapper and creates a new track without any playback or burning restrictions.

Given that this process is a bit of a bother, the second approach is to use a DRM remover program, such as QTFairUse (www.hymn-project.org/download.php). This program removes the DRM wrapping from iTunes-purchased music files, and lets you play and burn them any way you wish.

Split a Hidden Track into Its Own Track

As you're probably aware, some CDs come with "hidden" tracks. These are typically songs tacked on to the end of the CD's final track, so that the final track actually contains two songs—the listed song and the hidden song.

If you want to list the hidden track separately in your iTunes library, you can use iTunes to split the two songs into two tracks—that is, split the hidden track into its own track.

The first step is to make a duplicate copy of the track you want to split. The easiest way to do this is to drag the track from the iTunes window onto your computer desktop. Rename the track on your desktop to the name you want for the hidden track, and then drag it back onto the iTunes window.

You now have two copies of the same track, but with two different names. Start playing the track with the original name and note the times where the first song ends and the second one begins. Right-click this track and select Get Info. When the next dialog box appears, as shown in Figure 20.25, select the Options tab. Now enter the new end time into the Stop Time box, check the Stop Time option, and click OK. The resulting track now contains only the original song.

20

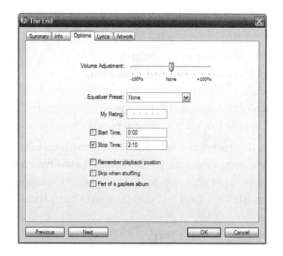

FIGURE 20.25
Trimming a hidden track from the original track.

Now right-click the track with the new name, select Get Info, and select the Options tab. Enter the new start time (as previously determined) into Start Time box, check the Start Time option, and then click OK. The resulting track now contains only the previously hidden song.

Group Compilation Albums

By default, iTunes has a little trouble handling compilation albums—those CDs that contain tracks by multiple artists. In particular, iTunes tends to spread the tracks of a compilation album across the width and breadth of the library, by artist.

If you'd rather see all the tracks of your compilation albums together, you have to configure iTunes appropriately. Select Edit > Preferences, select the General tab, and then check the Group Compilations When Browsing option. With this option selected, all the tracks from a single compilation album will be grouped together in the library.

Use Groupings to Create Sophisticated Playlists

As you learned in Chapter 7, "Music," you can use iTunes' Smart Playlists feature to create very sophisticated playlists based on specific criteria you select. However, you're limited to basing your criteria on existing fields—song title, composer, genre, and the like. Or are you?

20

iTunes has one more field that, although seldom used, can be used to create even smarter smart playlists. This is the Grouping field, a field that is typically left empty (and that most users—me included—have no idea what it's really designed for).

The key to this trick is to enter your own defining criteria into a track's Grouping field. Then you can create a smart playlist based on that Grouping field.

For example, suppose you want to create a playlist of all tunes that remind you of summer vacation. Assuming you've entered **Summer** into the Grouping field of those tunes, it's easy enough to select File > New Smart Playlist and create a rule for Grouping > Contains > Summer, as shown in Figure 20.26.

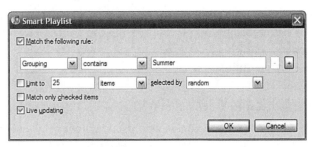

FIGURE 20.26
Creating a smart playlist based on a Grouping criteria.

To enter a term (or terms) into the Grouping field, just right-click a track, select Get Info, select the Info tab (shown in Figure 20.27), and enter the defining term into the Grouping box.

FIGURE 20.27
Defining a Grouping term.

And here's an additional tip—you can enter more than one term into the Grouping box, using periods to separate each term. For example, to define a track as Summer, Dance, and Beach, enter **.summer.dance.beach**. That way you can define separate smart playlist rules for **summer**, **dance**, and **beach**, and have this track appear on all three playlists.

Improve Preview Playback on a Dial-Up Connection

If you're on a slow dial-up Internet connection, you know just how annoying it is, especially when trying to listen to or watch song or video previews in the iTunes Store. A slow connection often results in stuttery playback as you wait for the rest of the preview to download and play.

To prevent playback stuttering, you can configure iTunes to load the entire preview before beginning playback. From the iTunes software, select Edit > Preferences, select the Store tab, and then check the Load Complete Preview Before Playing option.

Download Free Music and Videos via Podcast Subscriptions

The del.icio.us website (URL: del.icio.us) is a great source of free music and videos. People use the site to tag or bookmark their favorite picks. If you want to keep track of all new MP3 and video files bookmarked on the site, you can use the iTunes podcast subscription feature to do the job.

Start by selecting Advanced > Subscribe to Podcast in iTunes. When the Subscribe to Podcast dialog box appears, enter the URL for the type of del.icio.us media you want to track:

- **Music**: http://del.icio.us/rss/tag/system:filetype:mp3
- **Popular music**: http://del.icio.us/rss/popular/system:media:music
- **Mashup MP3s**: http://del.icio.us/rss/tag/system:filetype:mp3+mashups
- **Videos**: http://del.icio.us/rss/tag/system:media:video
- **Popular videos**: http://del.icio.us/rss/popular/system:media:video
- **Screencast videos**: http://del.icio.us/rss/tag/system:media:video+screencast

When iTunes grabs the selected feed(s), you can peruse the list of items and click the Get button to download specific songs and

note Learn more about iTunes podcast subscriptions in Chapter 8, "Podcasts."

videos. When you find a song or video you want to keep, drag it into your iTunes library (in the Source pane).

View PDF Files in iTunes

We'll end with a very unusual and little-known feature of iTunes: the ability to store and display PDF documents. This PDF capability exists to facilitate the display of liner notes that come with some albums available in the iTunes Store, but you can use it to read any PDF document from within iTunes. For example, you can create (or scan) your own album notes for any CD, and then store those notes as a PDF file in your iTunes library.

To add a PDF file to your library, just drag and drop it onto the Library item in the iTunes Source pane or onto a specific playlist. As you can see in Figure 20.28, the item appears in the library list by name only, with a little booklet icon next to the name. Double-click the item to open the document in a separate Acrobat Reader window.

FIGURE 20.28

A PDF file in the iTunes library.

And here's a final tip within a tip: To organize all your PDF files together, create a smart playlist with the rule Kind > Contains > PDF. Neat!

20

iPod Hacks

The tricks presented in the preceding chapter are easy enough for anyone to attempt. However, you can customize your iPod even more—if you have the technical expertise. These advanced tricks, more appropriately known as *hacks*, require getting inside your iPod, so to speak, and modifying the device's firmware or operating system—the software that controls your iPod's operation.

What kinds of hacks are we talking about? The most common iPod hacks let you customize the display—the fonts, the graphics, the icons, the screen background, you name it. Other hacks let you run additional applications on your iPod, above and beyond the official iPod applications currently on the market.

In short, you hack your iPod because you can—and because you want to turn it into something different from the stock device that everybody else has.

Hacking Your iPod with iPodWizard

For most hackers, the easiest way to hack the iPod display is with a program called iPodWizard. This Windows-only freeware program, available from www.ipodwizard.net, lets you customize

> **caution** Modifying your iPod using the methods described in this chapter will void your iPod's warranty. Do so with care.

everything about the way your iPod looks—fonts, graphics, colors, you name it.

As with most hacker tools, however, iPodWizard is a bit of a tweaky program, which means it's not for the faint of heart or for those utterly devoid of technical skills. Still, if you're willing to take the leap, it'll let you make a lot of cool changes to your iPod's display.

As you can see in Figure 21.1, the iPodWizard interface is a tad imposing to the uninitiated. There are a lot of settings to deal with, and they're not necessarily intuitive. A thorough explanation of everything the program can do is beyond the scope of this chapter, but instructions are available on the iPodWizard website. Read them carefully—there's a lot you can change for any model iPod.

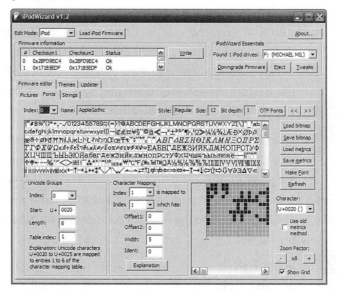

FIGURE 21.1

Customizing your iPod display with iPodWizard.

iPodWizard works by modifying either the iPod's built-in firmware or Apple's iPod Software Update utility (which then modifies the firmware). Perhaps the easiest way to change the look and feel of your iPod is to apply a complete theme; this changes fonts and graphics in tandem, much the way you apply new themes to your computer desktop. (Figures 21.2 and 21.3 show two such iPodWizard themes; note the different fonts and graphics on each.) Numerous user-created themes are available for download from the iPodWizard site.

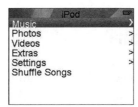

FIGURE 21.2

The Aqua Blue iPodWizard theme.

FIGURE 21.3

The iVista iPodWizard theme.

In addition, you can use iPodWizard to modify specific sections of the iPod firmware. These modifications are made on the following subtabs in the iPodWizard software, under the Firmware Editor tab:

- **Pictures**—Change any onscreen graphic, from icons to background pictures

- **Fonts**—Change the size and type of font used in the iPod's menus

- **Strings**—Modify text strings displayed on the iPod's menus

> **note** Firmware is the underlying software built in to the iPod that enables it to perform basic hardware operations.

21

To edit any of these settings, you need to know which codes to change. These codes differ for different-model iPods and are far too involved to cover here. Consult the instructions and the forums on the iPodWizard site for the information you need.

Hacking Your iPod with Rockbox

Another approach to hacking the iPod interface is to replace that interface—that is, use a different firmware in place of the standard iPod firmware. Rockbox is such a replacement firmware, designed for use on iPods and competing MP3 players. Rockbox is freeware, available from www.rockbox.org.

caution If you don't know what you're doing, it's possible to totally muck up your iPod with iPodWizard. Fortunately, you can easily reset your iPod to its factory-default display—just connect your iPod to your PC, select your iPod in the iTunes Source pane, and then click the Restore button on the Summary tab.

note At present, Rockbox supports third-, fourth-, and some fifth-generation iPods (the 30GB and 60GB models—but not the 80GB model) and the iPod mini and first-generation iPod nano.

As you can see in Figure 21.4, the default Rockbox screen isn't quite as pretty as the normal iPod screen, although it provides the same library navigation as the regular firmware does. What Rockbox does offer, however, is customization. To change the interface on your Rockbox-enabled iPod, simply select a new theme.

FIGURE 21.4
The default Rockbox file browser interface.

Figures 21.5 and 21.6 illustrate two different themes available with Rockbox. The first theme emulates the Windows Media Player interface; the second emulates the WinAmp program. Both are worlds away from the standard iPod interface.

FIGURE 21.5
The jBlackGlass Rockbox theme.

FIGURE 21.6
The RockAmp Rockbox theme.

Changing themes with Rockbox is extremely easy—just go to the main menu and select Browse Themes. Rockbox ships with a number of predesigned themes built in. Additional themes are available on the Rockbox website.

Hacking Your iPod with iPodLinux

There's another way to customize your iPod display and add extra functionality. This approach involves installing a version of the Linux operating system on your unit, to coexist with the normal iPod operating system. Linux lets you run a lot more applications than you can run normally.

> **tip**
> Rockbox themes can include both visual and audio elements. For example, you might have one theme with volume and equalization set for earphone listening, and another for listening in your car.

21

The version of Linux designed especially for iPods is called (naturally) iPodLinux. It's freeware that you can download from www.ipodlinux.org. As with the iPodWizard hack, modifying your iPod with iPodLinux is recommended only for the technically astute. That said, the installation of iPodLinux is well beyond the

note iPodLinux is compatible with first-, second-, and third-generation iPods only. It does not currently work with newer generations of iPod, nor with the iPod mini, nano, or shuffle.

scope of this chapter. If you're technically inclined, you can find all the information you need at the iPodLinux site.

When you install iPodLinux on your iPod, you essentially hack the iPod's firmware so that it dual boots between the normal iPod operating system and the Linux operating system. As with all firmware hacks, you can undo the hack by connecting your iPod to your PC, selecting your iPod in the iTunes Source pane, and then clicking the Restore button on the Summary tab.

Once installed, you boot in to Linux by holding down the Menu and Play buttons until you see the Apple logo. Then press and hold the Rewind button until the iPodLinux logo appears, as shown in Figure 21.7. To boot back in to the normal iPod operating system, select Reboot iPod > Absolutely from the Linux menu. (The iPod will always boot in to the standard iPod operating system by default.)

FIGURE 21.7

The iPodLinux boot screen.

Changing Your iPod's Interface

The interface you see when you boot in to iPodLinux is called podzilla. As you can see in Figure 21.8, this interface looks very much like the standard iPod menu system. Know, however, that podzilla is a customizable interface. You can install different podzilla *schemes*, which are like the themes used in iPodWizard and Rockbox.

FIGURE 21.8
The default podzilla interface.

For example, Figure 21.9 shows a scheme based on the popular *Family Guy* cartoon, and Figure 21.10 shows a stylish silver-and-black theme.

tip   You can find a list of all available podzilla schemes at www.ipodlinux.org/Special:Scheme.

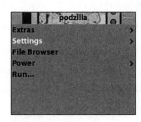

FIGURE 21.9
The Family Guy podzilla scheme.

FIGURE 21.10
The Impressions podzilla scheme.

Adding Functionality to Your iPod

You add functionality to your Linux-enabled iPod via the use of *modules*. A module is a Linux version of an application or utility. For example, if you want to play the Linux version of Pong on your iPod, you download and install the Pong module into podzilla.

21

What applications are available for iPodLinux? Table 21.1 details some of the more popular iPodLinux modules.

Table 21.1   Popular iPodLinux Modules

Module	Description	URL
BrickMania	Breakout-clone game, shown in Figure 21.11	www.ipodlinux.org/Special:Module/brickm
Calculator	Simple four-function calculator	www.ipodlinux.org/Special:Module/calc
Calendar	vCal-compatible calendar viewer	www.ipodlinux.org/Special:Module/calendar
Clocks	Various clock faces	www.ipodlinux.org/Special:Module/clocks
Contacts	vCard-compatible contact viewer	www.ipodlinux.org/Special:Module/contacts
Dialer	Touchtone dialer (hold earphone to telephone to dial numbers)	www.ipodlinux.org/Special:Module/dialer
Encyclopodia	Read Wikipedia on iPod	www.ipodlinux.org/Special:Module/encyclopodia
File Browser	Browses files on iPod	www.ipodlinux.org/Special:Module/browser
Guitar Tab Reader	Displays chord tabs for guitar	www.ipodlinux.org/Special:Module/chrd
Icon UI	Icon-based replacement iPod interface, shown in Figure 21.12	www.ipodlinux.org/Special:Module/iconui
iDeal or No Deal	iPod version of Deal or No Deal game	www.ipodlinux.org/Special:Module/ideal
iDoom	Doom game	www.ipodlinux.org/Special:Module/idoom
Invaders	Space Invaders game, shown in Figure 21.13	www.ipodlinux.org/Special:Module/invaders
iPod MIDI Player	Plays MIDI files	www.ipodlinux.org/Special:Module/midihelper
iWeather	Weather forecasts	www.ipodlinux.org/Special:Module/iweather
Metronome	Lets iPod function as musical metronome	www.ipodlinux.org/Special:Module/metronome
Pacman	Pac-Man game	www.ipodlinux.org/Special:Module/pacman
Periodic Table	Displays periodic table of elements	www.ipodlinux.org/Special:Module/periodic
Photos	Digital photo viewer	www.ipodlinux.org/Special:Module/photos
PodPaint	Painting program	www.ipodlinux.org/Special:Module/podpaint
PodPoker	Texas Hold'em poker game, shown in Figure 21.14	www.ipodlinux.org/Special:Module/podpoker
PodRead	Text reader	www.ipodlinux.org/Special:Module/podread
PodWrite	Plain-text word processor	www.ipodlinux.org/Special:Module/podwrite
Pong	Pong game	www.ipodlinux.org/Special:Module/pong

Table 21.1   Popular iPodLinux Modules

Module	Description	URL
Recording	Enables recording and playback of WAV files	www.ipodlinux.org/Special:Module/recording
Steroids	Asteroids-like game	www.ipodlinux.org/Special:Module/steroids
Sudoku	Sudoku puzzle game	www.ipodlinux.org/Special:Module/sudoku
Tip Calculator	Calculates restaurant tips	www.ipodlinux.org/Special:Module/tip
TuxChess	Chess game	www.ipodlinux.org/Special:Module/tuxchess
Vortex	Tempest-like game	www.ipodlinux.org/Special:Module/vortex
World Map	Displays world maps and weather, shown in Figure 21.15	www.ipodlinux.org/Special:Module/wmap

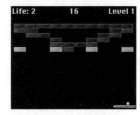

FIGURE 21.11
The BrickMania Breakout–style game.

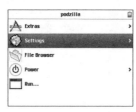

FIGURE 21.12
The Icon UI replacement interface.

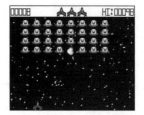

FIGURE 21.13
The Invaders game.

FIGURE 21.14
The Texas Hold'em game.

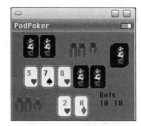

FIGURE 21.15
The World Map module.

That's just a partial list of the iPodLinux modules available. You can find a complete list at www.ipodlinux.org/Special:Module.

tip If you're really into games, consider installing the iPodMAME module into iPodLinux. This game emulator lets you play virtually any Linux game on your iPod. Download it at www.ipodliniux.org/ipodmame.

WHY HACK YOUR IPOD?

Earlier-generation iPods didn't do anything more than play music. Whereas that was enough for most users, some adventuresome types saw the potential of using their iPods to store calendar and contact information, display photos, play videos, play games, and so on. Because the basic iPod software didn't allow for these functions, the art of iPod hacking was born.

Some hackers took the approach of modifying the built-in firmware, although this approach was somewhat limited; about all you could hack was the iPod's interface and display. Other hackers realized that if you could install the Linux operating system beside the normal iPod operating system, you could add all sorts of functionality not present on those earlier models.

Hence you had 3G and 4G iPods hacked for video playback long before the 5G video iPod, and all sorts of games available well before the official launch of the iTunes 5G iPod games. In other words, hacking an earlier-generation iPod gave it much the same features as today's current-generation models.

This begs the question, of course, of why one might want to hack a current-generation iPod. After all, the 5G iPod does just about everything a hacked earlier-generation iPod can do. What more could you ask for?

Beyond the obvious answer of customizing the iPod interface, that's a fair question. And, in fact, most of the hacks available are for older-generation iPods only. You can't, for example, install iPodLinux on a 5G iPod. Not that you'd necessarily need to, in any case.

The moral of the story, of course, is that good things come for those who wait—and for those to learn to hack.

Hacking iTunes

It's not just the iPod you can hack; you can also hack the iTunes application. More precisely, you can use *scripts* to automate certain functions within iTunes. Read on to learn more.

note A script is a set of instructions in a simple programming language, used to control aspects of an application.

21

Hacking iTunes on the Mac

Automating iTunes is a big thing on the Mac, due to the use of the AppleScript programming language. AppleScripts written for iTunes are used to automate otherwise time-consuming operations.

> **tip** Learn more about AppleScript programming in the book *Teach Yourself AppleScript in 24 Hours* (Jesse Feiler, Sams Publishing, 2003).

For example, the following script tells iTunes to play track 10 of a specific playlist:

```
tell application "iTunes"
    play track 10 of user playlist "Oldies"
end tell
```

The first line identifies the application (iTunes) to which the script applies. The second line issues the instruction to play track 10 of the Oldies playlist. And the final line ends the script.

Not all scripts are this simple, of course. Although this isn't the place for a complete AppleScript tutorial, rest assured that you can use AppleScript to automate almost all aspects of iTunes operations, including the following:

- Manage tracks
- Edit track info
- Manage track artwork
- Create and manage playlists
- Export information
- Convert file formats
- Manage audio files
- Control playback

And on and on.

For a comprehensive list of iTunes scripts, check out the website Doug's AppleScripts for iTunes (www.dougscripts.com). This site hosts more than 400 user-submitted scripts, all ready to download and run on your own Mac.

Hacking iTunes on Windows

AppleScript is a Macintosh-only scripting language, which means that any AppleScript-based scripts won't run on a Windows PC. There are ways to create similar automation in Windows, however—even though the methods are a bit more complex.

21

First, you can use the JavaScript and VBScript scripting languages to create simple iTunes scripts. These scripting languages are more complex than AppleScript, but can still do what you need them to do. You can find ready-made Windows scripts online at ottodestruct.com/blog/2005/10/20/itunes-javascripts, projects.nateweiss.com/nwdc/itunes/scripts, and www.maximized.com/freeware/scriptsforitunes.

More-advanced developers will want to check out the iTunes COM for Windows Software Development Kit (SDK). This official kit from Apple provides documentation, header files, and sample JavaScript files that provide control of iTunes from JavaScript, Visual Basic, C++, and C#. Download the SDK from developer.apple.com/sdk/#iTunesCOM.

21

PART

VI

Support

iPod Accessories

In addition to the market for the iPod itself, the iPod phenomenon has created an entire economy for third-party accessories. Whether it's high-quality earphones, protective cases, or external speakers, iPod owners are spending a lot of money to accessorize their portable music players.

Although it's virtually impossible to detail a complete list of all available accessories, this chapter presents an overview of the various types of accessories available and highlights the best and most popular products within each category.

Cases

We start our examination of the iPod accessories market with perhaps the most popular type of accessory, the iPod case. Dozens of companies offer hundreds of different protective cases, in all manner of shape, size, and style.

When choosing an iPod case, you first need to determine why you need a case. If it's for carrying convenience, you don't need a super-durable case, just something that either fits in your pocket or clips on your belt. If it's for protection, judge how much protection you need. A leather or rubber case will protect your iPod from

note For many of the accessories detailed in this chapter, we list the manufacturer's suggested retail price— even though you might be able to find the item at a lower price at some retailers.

scratches, but a hard-body case will protect it from more substantial damage. If it's purely for style, go wild—a lot of cool and stylish cases are available.

That said, here's a short list of some of the most popular iPod cases, sorted by manufacturer:

- **a.b. sutton** (www.absutton.com), offering a variety of leather cases for all iPod models.
- **Agent18** (www.agent18.com), offering clear cases and stands for all iPod models. Particularly interesting is the **VideoShield Kit**, a combination case and stand in clear polycarbonate plastic for the 5G iPod.
- **Apple** (store.apple.com), offering a basic **Armband** for the iPod nano.
- **AVA** (www.avashowcase.com), offering leather cases for the traditional iPod and the ABS plastic **Smooth E** hard-shell case (with rubberized exterior) for the iPod nano.
- **B2** (www.b2stuf.com), offering a line of **mi Lites** flashing electronic cases.
- **Belkin** (www.belkin.com), offering a **Sports Sleeve** for the iPod nano.
- **Better Energy Systems** (www.solio.com), offering **Tread** cases made from recycled Colombian truck tires.
- **carrie.scott** (www.carriescott.com), offering the unique **JAMBAND** sport wristband for the iPod nano.
- **Contour Design** (www.countourcase.com), offering the **iSee** clear and **Showcase** rubber iPod cases.
- **Core Cases** (www.corecases.com), offering stylish aircraft-grade aluminum iPod cases in a variety of colors.
- **Griffin** (www.griffintechnology.com), offering the **CenterStage** stand for the 5G iPod, the **iClear** clear polycarbonate case, and the **Disko** polycarbonate case with colored LED lights, shown in Figure 22.1.
- **H2O Audio** (www.h20audio.com), offering waterproof housings for all iPod models.
- **ifrogz** (www.ifrogz.com), offering custom iPod cases that you can design from their various component parts.

22

FIGURE 22.1

The Griffin Disko iPod case.

- **iPodMods** (www.ipodmods.com), offering custom iPod modifications, including the see-through **iVue Crystal Clear** cases.

- **iSkin** (www.iskin.com), offering a variety of popular iPod cases, including the rubberized **eVo3** with belt clip, shown in Figure 22.2.

- **Macally** (www.macally.com), offering the **Icesuit** protective sleeve and the **MPOUCH** leather pouch.

- **Marware** (www.marware.com), offering a variety of iPod cases, including the formfitting **Sportsuit** and the innovative **Sidewinder**, shown in Figure 22.3, with pull-out slide for earphone storage.

FIGURE 22.2

The iSkin eVo3 iPod case.

FIGURE 22.3

The Marware Sidewinder iPod case.

- **Miniot** (www.miniot.com), offering monogrammed **iWood** wooden iPod cases. (That's right, cases made from *wood*.)
- **Mophie** (www.mophie.com), offering the **Wraptor** case for the 2G iPod shuffle.
- **Nike** (www.nike.com), offering a **Sport Armband** as part of its Nike+ line.
- **Noreve** (www.noreve.com), offering leather **Tradition** cases for the iPod and iPod nano.
- **Orbino** (www.orbino.com), offering leather **Cambio** cases for the iPod, iPod nano, and first-generation iPod shuffle.
- **OtterBox** (www.ottterbox.com), offering rugged waterproof cases for the iPod, iPod nano, and first-generation iPod shuffle.
- **Pacific Design** (www.pacificdesign.com), offering a variety of molded leather flip cases for the iPod, iPod mini, and iPod nano.
- **Podstar** (www.thepodstar.com), offering a variety of cases with wild colors and designs, including the **Diablo Spectrum** for the 2G nano.
- **Power Support** (www.powersupportusa.com), offering a variety of iPod cases and stands, including the tear-resistant **Silicone Jacket**, transparent **Crystal Jacket**, and leather **Kimono**.
- **Proporta** (www.proporta.com), offering aluminum, leather, and silicone iPod cases.
- **Sena** (www.senacases.com), offering a variety of magnetic flip cases, including the all-leather iPod video **PremiumStand**.
- **ShieldZone** (www.shieldzone.com), offering the **invisibleSHIELD** iPod screen protector.
- **Spawntek** (www.spawntek.com), offering the **ITECTOR** all-aluminum case for the iPod and iPod nano.

■ **Speck Products** (www.
speckproducts.com), offering a variety of iPod cases, including the
sneaker-inspired **CanvasSport**, the
rugged **ToughSkin**, the rubberized
SkinTight, and the **ActiveSport**
armband, shown in Figure 22.4.

> **AUTHOR'S
> PICKS** I recommend the
> iSkin eVo3 case,
> which is extremely durable yet
> retains full iPod functionality. I
> have a black version to match my
> black 5G iPod.

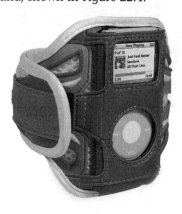

FIGURE 22.4

The ActiveSport armband from Speck Products.

■ **Radtech** (www.radtech.us), offering the **Cocoon** clamshell case.

■ **Sumo Cases** (www.sumocases.com), offering a variety of iPod flip cases.

■ **TuneBelt** (www.tunebelt.com), offering its namesake iPod Armband
Carrier.

■ **Vaja** (www.vajacases.com), offering a variety of colorful leather
i-volution cases.

■ **XtremeMac** (www.xtrememac.com), offering the **SportWrap** armband and **Iconz** cases with a variety of character logos, from Homer
Simpson to Speed Racer to Superman.

Backpacks and Bags

If you're a student, your backpack is seldom far from reach. Why not get a backpack specially designed to hold your iPod? Here's a sampling of what's available:

■ **Delapod** (www.delapod.net), offering a variety of purses and bags
with integrated iPod compartments.

■ **G-Tech** (www.g-techworld.com), offering a wide variety of iPod-enabled
backpacks, like those shown in Figure 22.5. All let you carry your iPod
inside the pack, and then operate it via a five-button control in the
back strap.

■ **JanSport** (www.jansport.com), offering a variety of backpacks wired for remote iPod use. Some models also include built-in Bluetooth capability.

FIGURE 22.5

iPod-enabled backpacks from G-Tech.

Earphones

Second in popularity to iPod cases and bags are replacement earphones. That's because many users quickly become dissatisfied with Apple's default earphones and upgrade for better sound. You'd be surprised at the difference a good set of earphones can make.

When it comes to listening to your iPod, you can choose from earbuds or traditional headphones. Earbuds, of course, are like headphones without the phones. Instead of bulky foam cups that enclose your entire ear, earbuds are tiny earphones that fit inside your ear. The advantage of in-ear devices is that they they're small and light, perfect for portable use. Headphones, although bigger and bulkier, often do a better job of blocking ambient noise.

Whether you opt for a set of headphones or earbuds, you need to evaluate two things: sound and comfort. Look for a unit that delivers a clear sound with no distortion; a deep and controlled bass without a lot of boominess; a smooth, even frequency response without bright or tinny highs; and good positioning of the

tip The very best earbuds are called *ear canal headphones*, because the rubber tips insert into your ear canal. This provides a much better seal than the typical earbud, and delivers impressive isolation and full sonic fidelity. The most popular of these in-ear phones include models from Etymotic, the Shure E-series, and Ultimate Ears super.fi models.

AUTHOR'S PICKS If you want a very quiet noise-canceling headphone, I recommend the Bose QuietComfort 3. It's lighter weight than the venerable QuietComfort 2 and features an on-ear design, which makes it ideal for on-the-go use.

22

sound image between the right and left channels. And be sure you like the way the phones or buds fit and feel. Imagine using the earphones for a couple of hours and determine how you'll like them after that kind of use. If the phones or buds start to feel a little uncomfortable in the store, think how much you'll hate them after a few hours of steady use!

With this advice in mind, here are some of the most popular earbuds and headphones for iPod use:

- **Altec Lansing inMotion iM716** noise-isolation earbuds ($129.95, www.alteclansing.com)
- **Bose In-Hear Headphones** earbuds ($99, www.bose.com)
- **Bose QuietComfort 2** noise-canceling headphones ($299, www.bose.com)
- **Bose QuietComfort 3** noise-canceling headphones ($349, www.bose.com), shown in Figure 22.6
- **Etymotic ER-6i Isolator** earbuds ($149, www.etymotic.com), shown in Figure 22.7

FIGURE 22.6

Bose's noise-canceling QuietComfort 3 headphones.

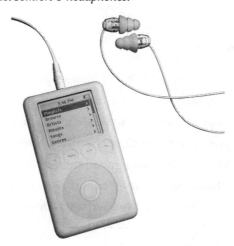

FIGURE 22.7

Etymotic ER-6i Isolator earbuds.

- **Etymotic ety8** Bluetooth wireless earbuds ($299 with iPod adapter, www.etymotic.com)
- **Grado iGrado** headphones ($49, www.gradolabs.com)
- **Grado SR60** headphones ($69, www.gradolabs.com)
- **Griffin TuneBuds** earbuds ($29.99, www.griffintechnology.com)
- **H2O Audio Waterproof Headphones** ($39.95, www.h2oaudio.com)
- **iSkin Cerulean XLR** earbuds ($29.99, www.iskin.com)
- **JVC HA-B17VS** headphones ($14.95, www.jvc.com)
- **JVC HA-EB50B** earbuds ($8.95, www.jvc.com)
- **Koss PortaPro** headphones ($49.99, www.koss.com), shown in Figure 22.8

FIGURE 22.8

Koss PortaPro headphones.

- **Koss SportaPro** headphones ($29.99, www.koss.com)
- **Logitech Curve** headphones ($29.99, www.logitech.com)
- **Logitech FreePulse** wireless headphones ($99.99, www.logitech.com)
- **Logitech Noise Canceling Headphones** ($149.99, www.logitech.com)
- **Macally IceBud** lanyard earbuds ($19.99, www.macally.com)
- **Philips SHE9501** earbuds ($19.99, www.consumer.philips.com)
- **Scosche Sport Bluetooth Headphone Kit** wireless headphones ($174.95, www.scosche.com)
- **Sennheiser CX300** earbuds ($89.85, www.sennheiser.com)
- **Sennheiser MX 70 Sport** earbuds ($34.95, www.style-your-sound.com)
- **Sennheiser OMX 70 Sport** earbuds ($44.95, www.style-your-sound.com), shown in Figure 22.9

- **Sennheiser PMX 70 Sport** earbuds ($49.95, www.style-your-sound.com)

- **Sennheiser PX100** headphones ($59.95, www.sennheiser.com)

- **Shure E2c** sound-isolating earbuds ($109, www.shure.com)

> **AUTHOR'S PICKS** I'm not a big fan of low-end earbuds. For better fidelity, I recommend the Shure E4c ear canal headphones, which deliver near-audiophile quality sound.

22

- **Shure E4c** sound-isolating earbuds ($319, www.shure.com), shown in Figure 22.10

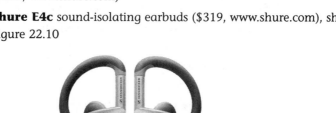

FIGURE 22.9
Sennheiser OMX 70 Sport over-the-ear earbuds.

FIGURE 22.10
Shure's audiophile-quality E4c sound isolating earbuds.

22

- **Shure E5c** sound-isolating earbuds ($549, www.shure.com)
- **Sony MDR-A35G S2 Sports** headphones ($19.99, www.sonystyle.com)
- **Sony MDR-E827G Sports Fontopia** earbuds ($19.99, www.sonystyle.com)
- **Sony MDR-EX81** earbuds ($49.99, www.sonystyle.com)
- **Sony MDR-G57G S2 Sports Street Style** headphones ($24.99, www.sonystyle.com)
- **Stanton DJ Pro 3000** headphones ($199, www.stantondj.com)
- **Ultimate Ears super.fi 3 Studio** earbuds ($99.99, www.ultimateears.com)
- **Ultimate Ears super.fi 5 EB** earbuds ($199.99, www.ultimateears.com)
- **Ultimate Ears super.fi 5 Pro** earbuds ($249.99, www.ultimateears.com)
- **Ultimate Ears triple.fi 10 Pro** earbuds ($399.99, www.ultimateears.com)
- **v-moda Remix M-Class** earbuds ($50, www.v-moda.com)
- **Westone UM1** earbuds ($109, www.westone.com)
- **Westone UM2** earbuds ($299, www.westone.com)
- **XtremeMac FS1** earbuds ($149.95, www.xtrememac.com)

Earphone Splitters

What do you do when you want to share your iPod music with a friend? Well, you could connect your iPod to an external speaker (which we discuss in a moment), or you could just split the output to run to two different sets of earphones. That's right, the easiest way to share your music is to use a low-priced earphone splitter. Connect two sets of earbuds or headphones, and you have your own private little party:

- **Belkin Speaker and Headphone Splitter** ($9.99, www.belkin.com)
- **Griffin SmartShare** ($14.99, www.griffintechnology.com)
- **iLuv i101** ($9.99, www.i-luv.com)
- **Macally Iceduo** ($9.95, www.macally.com)
- **Monster Cable iSplitter** ($9.95, www.monstercable.com)
- **Monster Cable iSplitter 200** ($19.95, www.monstercable.com)

Portable Speakers

When you want to listen to your iPod's music publicly, you need to connect to a speaker rather than to earphones. There are several types of iPod speakers on the market today; the first type we'll look at is the *portable* speaker. This type of speaker is typically small and lightweight, operating (in most cases) on either battery or AC power. This is the type of speaker you can stuff into your backpack, suitcase, or attaché case and carry with you from place to place. (I use mine to provide music in my hotel rooms when I travel.)

The sound quality of these speakers differ wildly. Some models provide barely adequate sound, but in a small package. Others, although not quite audiophile quality, at least can fill up a good-sized room with plenty of bass. And still others are designed in the boom box mold, often with additional audio functions (such as AM/FM radio). If at all possible, audition the speaker before you make your choice.

Now, on to the choices:

- **Altec Lansing inMotion iM7** ($249.95, www.alteclansing.com), shown in Figure 22.11

FIGURE 22.11

Altec Lansing's iM7 boom box-like portable iPod speaker.

- **Altec Lansing inMotion iM9** ($199.95, www.alteclansing.com)
- **DLO iBoom Black** ($79.99, www.dlo.com)
- **DLO iBoom Travel** ($89.99, www.dlo.com)
- **EGO Waterproof Sound Case** ($179.99, www.lovemyego.com)
- **Griffin Journi** ($130, www.griffintechnology.com), shown in Figure 22.12

FIGURE 22.12
The Griffin Journi foldable portable speaker system.

- **iHome iH26** portable travel alarm clock ($99.99, www.ihomeaudio.com)
- **iHome iH31** boom box ($129.99, www.ihomeaudio.com)
- **iLive IBCD3816DT Portable Docking Station** ($129.95, www.ilive.net)
- **iLive IBR2807DP Portable Docking Station** ($69.95, www.ilive.net)
- **iLuv i552** ($99.95, www.i-luv.com), shown in Figure 22.13

FIGURE 22.13
The iLuv i552 boom box speaker with AM/FM radio.

- **Kensington FX 300 Speaker to Go** ($29.99, www.kensington.com)
- **Logic3 i-Station 7** ($99.99, www.logic3usa.com)
- **Logitech mm28** ($59.99, www.logitech.com)
- **Logitech mm32** ($79.99, www.logitech.com)
- **Logitech mm50** ($149.95, www.logitech.com), shown in Figure 22.14

FIGURE 22.14
The Logitech mm50 portable speaker.

- **Macally IP-A111** plug-in speaker ($29.99, www.macally.com)
- **Macally IP-N1112** iPod nano speaker ($39.99, www.macally.com)
- **MTX Audio iThunder** boom box ($179.95, www.mtx.com/ithunder)
- **Pacific Rim Cube Travel Speaker** ($19.99, www.pacificrimtechnologies.com)
- **Sonic Impact i-P22 Portable** ($89.99, www.si5.com)
- **Tivoli Audio iPAL** ($149.99, www.tivoliaudio.com), shown in Figure 22.15
- **Tivoli Audio iSongBook** ($299.99, www.tivoliaudio.com)

AUTHOR'S PICKS For use on the road, I use and recommend the Logitech mm50 portable speaker system. The sound quality is the best of all the portable speakers I've auditioned, it's small enough to pack in my suitcase, and I like the remote-control operation of both unit volume and the iPod's controls.

FIGURE 22.15

Tivoli Audio's iPal portable speaker.

Bookshelf Speakers

Portable iPod speakers need to be smallish and easy to carry; sound quality, although important, is secondary. Tabletop or bookshelf iPod speakers, however, have no such size limitation, and can thus deliver much better sound than you find in portable models.

As you can see, there are a huge number and variety of bookshelf iPod speaker systems on the market. Look for the one that delivers the best sound for the price, and any other additional features you might be interested in— such as built-in iPod charging, remote-control operation, and the like:

- **Altec Lansing inMotion iM3c** ($129.95, www.alteclansing.com)
- **Altec Lansing inMotion iM500** for iPod nano ($129.95, www.alteclansing.com)
- **Altec Lansing M602** ($199.95, www.alteclansing.com)
- **Apple iPod Hi-Fi** ($349, www.apple.com/ipodhifi/)
- **Athena iVoice** ($200, www.athenaspeakers.com)
- **Bose SoundDock** ($299, www.bose.com), shown in Figure 22.16

FIGURE 22.16

The Bose SoundDock—one of the most popular iPod speaker systems.

- **Geneva Lab L** ($599, www.genevalab.com)
- **Geneva Lab XL** ($1,075, www.genevalab.com)
- **Griffin AmpliFi** ($150, www.griffintechnology.com), shown in Figure 22.17

FIGURE 22.17

The Griffin AmpliFi speaker system—complete with a big freakin' knob.

- **Griffin Evolve** ($350, www.griffintechnology.com)
- **iHome iH52** ($199.99, www.ihomeaudio.com)
- **iLive IHMD8816DT Home Docking System** ($159.99, www.ilive.net)
- **iLive ISPK2806 Amplified Speaker Docking System** ($69.99, www.ilive.net)
- **iLuv i888** ($49.95, www.i-luv.com)
- **iLuv i7500** ($149.95, www.i-luv.com)
- **iLuv i9200** ($249.95, www.i-luv.com)
- **iWoofer** ($119, www.raindesigninc.com/iwoofer.html)
- **Jamo i300** ($400, www.jamo.com), shown in Figure 22.18

FIGURE 22.18

Jamo's award-winning i300 iPod speaker system.

- **JBL On Stage II** ($129.95, www.jbl.com)
- **JBL On Stage Micro** ($99.95, www.jbl.com)
- **JBL Radial** ($299.95, www.jbl.com), shown in Figure 22.19

FIGURE 22.19
JBL's uniquely styled Radial iPod speaker.

- ■ **JVC NX-PS1** ($249.95, www.jvc.com)

- ■ **Kensington SX 3000R** ($169.99, www.kensington.com)

- ■ **Klipsch iFi** ($399.95, www.klipsch.com), shown in Figure 22.20

AUTHOR'S PICKS There are many good iPod bookshelf speaker systems. My favorites include the Griffin AmpliFi (great sound and a really cool, really big volume knob) and the Klipsch iFi (separate speakers for terrific separation and true hi-fidelity sound).

FIGURE 22.20
The Klipsch iFi multiple-speaker iPod audio system.

- **Klipsch iGroove** ($199.99, www.klipsh.com)
- **Logitech AudioStation** ($299.99, www.logitech.com)
- **Macally IceTune** ($59.99, www.macally.com)
- **Monitor Audio i-deck** ($149.95, www.i-deckusa.com)
- **mStation Orb** ($149.95, www.mstationaudio.com)
- **mStation Tower** ($299.95, www.mstationaudio.com)
- **Nyko Speaker Dock 2** ($79.95, www.nyko.com)
- **Saffire JukeBox Station** ($599.99, www.saffire-usa.com/jukebox.htm)
- **Sony CPF-iP001 Cradle Audio System for iPod** ($249.99, www.sonystyle.com), shown in Figure 22.21
- **SpeckTone Retro** ($149.95, www.specktone.com)
- **XtremeMac Tango** ($199.95, www.xtrememac.com)

FIGURE 22.21
Sony's Cradle Audio System—main speakers plus subwoofer.

Alarm Clocks

Within the bookshelf/tabletop speaker category is the subcategory of iPod alarm clocks—iPod speakers with built-in digital clocks and timers. Many of these units also come with AM/FM radios, for a full-featured morning wake-up experience:

- **George Wireless** ($549, www.chillsound.com)

- **iHome iH36** under-the-cabinet audio system ($99.99, www.ihomeaudio.com), shown in Figure 22.22

> **tip** If you want the best possible sound, consider investing in an audiophile tabletop radio that offers an auxiliary audio input, such as the Tivoli Model One ($119.99, www.tivoliaudio.com) or the Sangean WR-2 ($169, www.sangean.com). Even though these units are not iPod-specific units per se, connecting your iPod via the auxiliary input takes full advantage of the radio's full-spectrum audio reproduction.

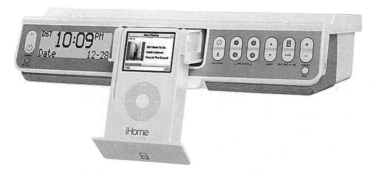

FIGURE 22.22

The iHome iH35 under-the-cabinet iPod clock radio.

- **iHome iH5** ($99.99, www.ihomeaudio.com)
- **i-Luv i277** ($149.99, www.i-luv.com)
- **i-Luv i777** ($99.95, www.i-luv.com)
- **i-Luv i999** ($249.99, www.i-luv.com)
- **JBL On Time** ($249.95, www.jbl.com)
- **Memorex iWake** ($79.99, www.memorexelectronics.com)
- **XtremeMac Luna** ($149.95, www.xtrememac.com), shown in Figure 22.23

FIGURE 22.23

The XtremeMac Luna iPod clock radio.

A/V Docks and Connecting Kits

Want even better sound? Then connect your iPod to your home audio system with one of these docking kits. Most kits connect via audio or audio/video cables; some are wireless. (The audio/video kits also connect to your television set, for both iPod menu display/control and video playback, if you have a 5G iPod.) Choose the model that offers the functionality you need for your particular system:

- **Apple AirPort Express** wireless network connection ($99, www.apple.com/airportexpress)
- **Apple AV Connection Kit** ($99, store.apple.com)
- **Belkin TuneCommand AV** ($89.99, www.belkin.com)
- **Belkin TuneSync** ($65.99, www.belkin.com)
- **DLO HomeDock** ($99.99, www.dlo.com)
- **DLO HomeDock Deluxe** ($149.99, www.dlo.com)
- **Griffin BlueTrip** wireless Bluetooth audio ($99.99, www.griffintechnology.com)
- **Griffin TuneCenter** ($129.99, www.griffintechnology.com)
- **Kensington Entertainment Dock 500** ($99.99, us.kensington.com)

- **Kensington Stereo Dock** ($59.99, us.kensington.com)
- **KeySpan AV Dock for iPod** ($79, www.keyspan.com)
- **KeySpan TuneView for iPod** ($179, www.keyspan.com), shown in Figure 22.24
- **Onkyo DS-A2** ($109, www.onky-ousa.com)
- **Scosche BlueLife** wireless Bluetooth system ($249.99)

> **AUTHOR'S PICKS** For a simple wired A/V connection solution, I like the KeySpan TuneView, which comes with a two-way remote-control complete with color LCD screen. For a wireless solution, both the Apple Airport Express and Griffin BlueTrip do a good job in most installations.

FIGURE 22.24
KeySpan's TuneView A/V dock and two-way remote control.

Audio/Video Cables

You don't necessarily need a fancy dock to connect your iPod to your audio/video system—a simple set of cables will do the same job. (Without recharging or remote-control operation, of course.) Here are some of the most popular iPod audio and audio/video cables you can use for this task:

- **Apple iPod AV Cable** ($19, store.apple.com)
- **Belkin AV Cable for 4G/5G iPod** ($19.99, www.belkin.com)

- **Marware AV Cable for iPod Video and iPod Photo** ($17.95, www.marware.com)
- **Pacific Rim Technologies Retractable AV Cable for iPod** ($9.99, www.pacrimtechnologies.com)
- **SendStation PocketDock Line Out USB** ($29.95, www.sendstation.com)

Remote Controls

If you do connect your iPod to your audio/video system, you don't necessarily want to walk across the room to change tracks. What's useful in this instance is a remote control for your iPod, so you can sit in your easy chair and control all your tunes. These remotes are also good for operating your iPod in your car—especially if you keep your iPod tucked away in the glove compartment or mounted way up on your dash. And some are designed especially for sport or exercise use; tuck your iPod away on an armband or on your belt, and control the iPod from the handy remote:

- **Belkin SportCommand** armband remote control ($79.99, www.belkin.com)
- **DLO iDirect** ($10.99, www.dlo.com)
- **Griffin AirClick** ($39.99, www.griffintechnology.com)
- **iJet Two-Way LCD Remote** ($129.99, www.ijetwireless.com), shown in Figure 22.25

FIGURE 22.25

The iJet Two-Way LCD Remote, complete with remote display of track information.

- **iJet Wireless Remote** ($52.99, www.ijetwireless.com)
- **iJet Wireless Remote V1** ($39.99, www.ijetwireless.com)
- **Monster iEZClick** ($69.95, www.monstercable.com)
- **Scosche iPod Video RF Remote** ($79.95, www.scosche.com)
- **Scosche Wireless RF Remote Sport Watch** ($79.95, www.scosche.com)
- **TEN Technology naviPod eX** ($49.95, www.tentechnology.com), shown in Figure 22.26

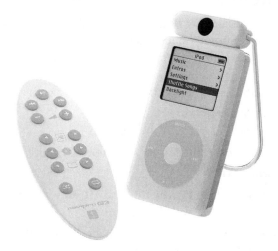

FIGURE 22.26
The naviPod eX wireless iPod remote control.

Recharging Docks

Although it's easy enough to connect your iPod to your PC for syncing and recharging, Apple's supplied connecting cable is a little less than elegant. Many users prefer a more sturdy dock connector, which can stay connected to your PC (via USB) and in-place on your desktop even when your iPod is away. Even better, some of these docks offer additional functionality—such as a built-in memory card reader:

> **AUTHOR'S PICKS** For a basic iPod remote, I like both the iJet Wireless Remote and the naviPod EX. My personal pick, however, is the higher-priced iJet Two-Way LCD Remote, which includes an LCD screen that displays information about the currently playing track.

- **AFT iDuo** combination iPod dock/memory card reader ($59.95 www.atechflash.com/products-iduo.html)

22

- **AFT iDuo Keyboard + Dock** combination iPod dock/keyboard ($59.95, www.atechflash.com/products-iduokeyboard.html)
- **EDGE Dock & Multi Flash Card Reader** ($24.95, www.edgetechcorp.com)
- **Griffin AirDock** charging dock with remote ($79.99, www.griffintechnology.com)

Power and Battery Kits

When your iPod's battery runs low, you need auxiliary power, and you don't always have a computer handy to provide that power. Lots of power solutions are available for your iPod, from simple USB-to-AC adapters to in-car cigarette lighter adapters to fancy external battery packs. Take a look to see which power solution meets your particular needs:

- **ABT PowerJet** auto charger ($19.95, www.ijetwireless.com/PowerJet.htm)
- **Apple iPod USB Power Adapter** ($29, store.apple.com)
- **Arkon CA070** iPod car charger ($12.95, www.arkon.com)
- **Belkin Mobile Power Cord for iPod w/Dock Connector** car adapter ($19.99, www.belkin.com)
- **Belkin TunePower** rechargeable external battery pack ($79.99, www.belkin.com), shown in Figure 22.27

FIGURE 22.27
Belkin TunePower external battery pack.

- **BTI IP-V01** external battery ($108, www.batterytech.com)
- **DLO Auto Charger** car adapter ($19.99, www.dlo.com)
- **Griffin PowerBlock** AC charger/adapter ($29.99, www.griffintechnology.com)
- **Griffin PowerDuo** car/home charging kit ($39.99, www.griffintechnology.com), shown in Figure 22.28

FIGURE 22.28
Griffin PowerDuo universal power kit.

- **Griffin PowerJolt** car charger ($19.99, www.griffintechnology.com)
- **Griffin TuneJuice II** external battery pack ($29.99, www.griffintechnology.com)
- **iLuv i108** USB power adapter ($34.99, www.i-luv.com)
- **iLuv i109** car adapter ($14.99, www.i-luv.com)
- **iLuv i604** clip-on external battery ($64.99, www.i-luv.com)
- **iLuv i605** external battery pack ($54.99, www.i-luv.com)
- **iRock 12V DC Charger** car charger ($12.95, www.myirock.com)
- **Kensington 4-in-1 Car Charger** ($29.99, www.kensington.com)
- **Kensington Travel Plug Adapter** worldwide USB AC adapter ($29.99, www.kensington.com)

22

■ **Macally USB AC Charger**
($19.99, www.macally.com)

■ **Macally USB Car Charger**
($19.99, www.macally.com)

■ **Monster iAirPlay** car charger
($29.95, www.monstercable.com)

■ **Monster iCarCharger** car charger
($39.95, www.monstercable.com)

■ **Monster iSlimCharger** AC adapter ($29.95, www.monstercable.com)

■ **SendStation smartCharge** car charger ($24.95,
www.sendstation.com/us/products/smartcharge)

■ **Solio** solar-powered battery charger ($99.95, www.solio.com)

■ **Sonnet USB Power Adapter for iPod** ($19.95,
www.sonnettech.com/product/ipod_usb_adptr.html)

■ **Sonnet Volta** external battery ($69.95, www.sonnettech.com/
product/volta.html)

■ **Tekkeon myPower for iPod** rechargeable battery ($69.99,
www.tekkeon.com/site/products-mypower.php)

■ **XtremeMac InCharge Traveler** AC/car adapter ($69.95,
www.xtrememac.com)

■ **XtremeMac MicroPack** external battery/recharger/adapater
($79.95, www.xtrememac.com)

Car Kits, Transmitters, and Mounts

Using your iPod in your car can be a somewhat complicated endeavor. How do you get the sound from your iPod to your car audio system? Where do you mount your iPod? How do you provide power to your iPod while driving?

The answers to these questions come in the form of the many and varied iPod car kits available today. Some kits provide the complete solution (typically connecting your iPod to your car radio via FM transmission), some only a single part. Which type of kit you buy depends on your needs, how much trouble you want to go to, and how picky you are about sound quality and looks:

■ **Arkon CM160-W** swivel vent mount ($19.95, www.arkon.com)

■ **Arkon SF250 SoundFeeder** FM transmitter ($19.95, www.arkon.com)

- **Belkin Auto Kit for iPod w/Dock Connector** AC charger/audio output amplifier ($39.99, www.belkin.com)
- **Belkin Cassette Adapter for iPod** ($19.99, www.belkin.com)
- **Belkin TuneBase FM** transmitter/car charger ($79.99, www.belkin.com), shown in Figure 22.29

FIGURE 22.29

Belkin's TuneBase FM—a combination power adapter/charger, FM transmitter, and iPod gooseneck mount.

- **Belkin TuneCast** FM transmitter ($29.99, www.belkin.com)
- **Belkin TuneCast 3** FM transmitter ($49.99, www.belkin.com)
- **Belkin TuneCast Auto** FM transmitter ($59.99, www.belkin.com)
- **Belkin TuneCast II** FM transmitter ($39.99, www.belkin.com)
- **Belkin TuneDeck for iPod nano** cassette adapter/mount ($49.99, www.belkin.com)
- **Belkin TuneDok** cupholder cradle ($29.99, www.belkin.com)
- **Belkin TuneFM** FM transmitter/car charger ($49.99, www.belkin.com)
- **DLO TransDock** FM transmitter/car charger ($99.99, www.dlo.com)

- **DLO TransDock Micro** FM transmitter/car charger ($69.99, www.dlo.com)
- **DLO TransPod** FM transmitter/car charger ($99.99, www.dlo.com)
- **Gomadic Dash Car/Auto Mount** iPod mount ($34.95, www.gomadic.com)
- **Gomadic Vent Car/Auto Mount** iPod mount ($34.95, www.gomadic.com)
- **Gomadic Windshield Car/Auto Mount** iPod mount ($34.95, www.gomadic.com)
- **Griffin DirectDeck** cassette adapter ($14.99, www.griffintechnology.com)
- **Griffin iSqueez** cupholder cradle ($9.99, www.griffintechnology.)
- **Griffin iTrip** FM transmitter ($49.99, www.griffintechnology.com)
- **Griffin iTrip Auto** FM transmitter/car charger ($69.99, www.griffintechnology.com)
- **Griffin RoadTrip** FM transmitter/car charger/mount ($89.99, www.griffintechnology.com), shown in Figure 22.30

FIGURE 22.30
Griffin RoadTrip all-in-one transmitter/charger/mount.

- **Griffin SmartDeck** cassette adapter ($29.99, www.griffintechnology.com)
- **Griffin TuneFlex** car charger/docking cradle ($49.99, www.griffintechnology.com)

- **iRock 410FM** FM transmitter
  ($19.99, www.myirock.com)

- **iRock 440FM** FM transmitter
  ($24.99, www.myirock.com)

- **iRock Car Cassette Adapter**
  ($3.99, www.myirock.com)

- **Kensington Digital FM
  Transmitter/Auto Charger**
  ($79.99, www.kensington.com)

- **Kensington Pico** FM transmitter
  ($49.99, www.kensington.com)

> **AUTHOR'S
> PICKS** For combination kits,
> I like the Griffin
> RoadTrip that combines an FM
> transmitter, power adapter/
> charger, and iPod mount/holder
> into a single compact unit. Also
> good is the Belkin TuneBase FM
> and the DLO TransDock and
> TransPod, all of which perform
> the same combo functions.

- **Kensington RDS** FM transmitter/car charger ($79.99,
  www.kensington.com)

- **Macally Cassette Tape Car Adapter** ($14.99, www.macally.com)

- **Macally BTCUP** FM transmitter/car charger/cupholder mount with
  Bluetooth hands-free operation ($119, www.macally.com)

- **Macally FMCup** FM transmitter/car charger/cupholder mount
  ($59.99, www.macally.com)

- **Macally FMTF** FM transmitter/car charger ($49.99,
  www.macally.com)

- **Macally IceFM** FM transmitter/car charger ($29.99,
  www.macally.com)

- **Maxell CD-330 Cassette Adapter** ($13.99, www.maxell-usa.com)

- **Maxell P-4A Digital FM Transmitter** ($39.99, www.maxell-usa.com)

- **Monster iCarPlay Wireless 200** FM transmitter ($99.95,
  www.monstercable.com)

- **Monster iCarPlay Wireless Plus** FM transmitter/car charger
  ($79.95, www.monstercable.com)

- **NewerTech TrafficJamz** FM transmitter/car charger
  ($34.95, www.newertech.com)

- **Nyko Universal Car Mount** ($39.99, www.nyko.com)

- **Pro.Fit miMount** car mount
  ($29.95–$39.95, www.pro-fit-intl.com/mimount)

- **ProClip Mounting System** car mount ($26.99–$59.99,
  www.proclipusa.com)

- **SiK imp** car adapter/audio output ($29.95, www.sik.com)

- **Sony DCC-E34CP Car Connecting Pack** cassette adapter/car charger ($29.99, www.sonystyle.com)

> **AUTHOR'S PICKS** As to simple FM transmitters, I recommend either the XtremeMac AirPlay Boost or the venerable Griffin iTrip. Both should do a good job in most areas.

- **Ten Technology flexibleDock** car charger/mount ($49.95, www.tentechnology.com)

- **Ten Technology iRide** glove box organizer/mount ($79, www.tentechnology.com)

- **XtremeMac AirPlay Boost** FM transmitter ($49.95, www.xtrememac.com), shown in Figure 22.31

- **XtremeMac MicroFlex Car** auto charger/flexible dock ($49.95, www.xtrememac.com)

FIGURE 22.31

The XtremeMac Airplay Boost clip-on FM transmitter.

Portable Video Displays

If you have a 5G iPod with video capabilities, you might weary of watching your videos on the iPod's rather small screen. Instead, check out these portable video displays that connect to any 5G iPod and provide a much larger viewing experience—or, in some instances, a smaller but more portable screen embedded in a stylish piece of eyewear. (And that small eye-mounted display looks a lot bigger than you'd think when it's right in front of your eyeballs!)

- **22Moo VG-SD** video eyewear ($285, www.22moo.com.au/vg-sd.htm)
- **ezGear ezVision** video eyewear ($399.98, www.ezgear4u.com/ezvision.html)
- **Icuiti iWear** video eyewear ($249.95, www.icuti.com)
- **i-glasses i-Theater** video eyewear ($249, www.i-glassesstore.com)
- **iLuv i1055** 7-inch portable video display ($199.95, www.i-luv.com), shown in Figure 22.32

FIGURE 22.32
The iLuv i1055 portable video display for iPod use.

- **Memorex iFlip** 8.4-inch portable video display ($199, www.memorexelectronics.com)
- **myvu** video eyewear ($299.95, www.myvu.com), shown in Figure 22.33
- **Sonic Impact Video 55** 7-inch portable video display ($199.95, www.si5.com)

FIGURE 22.33
You can watch iPod videos on the myvu video headset.

FM Radio Tuners

One of the drawbacks of the iPod, *vis à vis* competing portable audio players, is the lack of a built-in FM tuner for radio reception. For those radio fans out there, Apple and Griffin have both come to the rescue, with add-on FM tuners designed to fit most iPod models:

- **Apple iPod Radio Remote** ($49, store.apple.com)
- **Griffin iFM** ($49.99, www.griffintechnology.com)

Audio Recorders

The iPod is not only an audio player, but—with the right accessory—an audio recorder, too. All of these units, except for the TuneStudio, fit onto the iPod's dock connector or earphone jack, for portable recording:

- **Belkin TuneStudio**
  ($179.99, www.belkin.com)
- **Belkin TuneTalk Stereo**
  ($69.99, www.belkin.com)

note Learn more about iPod audio recording and the necessary accessories in Chapter 16,"Using Your iPod to Record Audio and Podcasts."

- **Belkin Voice Recorder for iPod** ($49.99, www.belkin.com)
- **Griffin iTalk Pro** ($49.95, www.griffintechnology.com)
- **XtremeMac MicroMemo** ($59.95, www.xtrememac.com)

Video Recorders

These devices present kind of a brute-force approach to getting video programming onto your iPod. Instead of using software-based file conversion, these devices capture video playback in real time—which means you can capture just about any video programming, including commercial DVDs, and save that programming to digital files for your iPod:

> **note** Learn more about recording and playing video on your iPod in Chapter 11, "Videos."

- **DVD Xpress DX2** ($129.99, www.adstech.com)
- **iRecord** ($199.99, www.irecord.com)
- **iSee 360i** ($185, www.atollc.com)

Karaoke

Put a microphone on your iPod and another use comes to mind—karaoke! These accessories turn your iPod into a portable karaoke machine. Just plug in the device and play back any song of your liking. The accessory isolates and fades the vocal track on the song and adds your voice to the track:

- **CAVS IPS-11G Karaoke Station** ($159.99, www.ipskaraoke.com)
- **DoPi Karaoke** ($59.99, www.dopikaraoke.com)
- **Griffin iKaraoke** ($49.99, www.griffintechnology.com), shown in Figure 22.34

FIGURE 22.34
Sing along with your iPod and the Griffin iKaraoke.

Camera Adapters/Media Readers

Want to transfer photos from your digital camera to your iPod? Then check out these camera adapters/cables and media readers designed just for that purpose:

- **Apple iPod Camera Connector** ($29, www.apple.com/ipod/accessories.html)
- **Belkin Digital Camera Link for iPod** ($79.99, www.belkin.com), shown in Figure 22.36
- **Belkin Media Reader** ($99.99, www.belkin.com)

> **tip** These karaoke accessories are especially fun when you've stored lyrics with your music (as discussed in Chapter 7, "Music"), so you can read the lyrics on your iPod's screen as you use the microphone to sing along. Both the Karaoke Station and DoPi Karaoke come with a selection of karaoke-enabled songs—with more available on the companies' websites.

FIGURE 22.35
Belkin's Digital Camera Link lets you transfer photos from your digital camera to your iPod.

Apparel

Yes, Virginia, there is such a thing as iPod clothing. We're not talking T-shirts with iPod logos. No, these are articles of clothing that have either iPod-sized pouches, internal wiring to connect an iPod to earphones, or wiring that connects a hidden iPod to external controls:

> **note** Learn more about transferring photos to and storing them on your iPod in Chapter 10, "Photos."

- **BeatBuckle** iPod belt buckle ($29.95, www.beatbuckle.com), shown in Figure 22.36

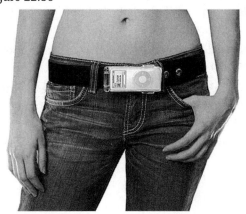

FIGURE 22.36
The BeatBuckle iPod belt buckle.

- **iSoundCap** hats with iPod pouches ($19.95–$29.95, www.isoundcap.com)
- **JanSport** iPod clothing—hooded sweatshirts and jackets wired for iPod control ($50–$200, www.jansport.com), shown in Figure 22.37

FIGURE 22.37

A JanSport jacket with iPod controls on the front.

- **Koyono BlackCoat** clothing—jackets and shirts wired for iPod and earphone control ($25–$275, www.koyono.com)
- **Marware Sportsuit Sensor+**—lets you attach the Nike+ Sport Kit sensor to the tongue of any pair of running shoes ($9.95, www.marware.com)
- **Nike+** running shoes with iPod nano pouch ($100–$130, www.nike.com)
- **Nike+ Featherweight** shorts with iPod pocket and cord management ($35–$50, www.nike.com)
- **Scott eVest SeV** clothing—T-shirts, sweatshirts, pants, shorts, hats, and outerwear with iPod pouches and cord management ($20–$450, www.scottevest.com), shown in Figure 22.38
- **TuneBuckle** iPod nano belt buckle ($59.95, www.tunebuckle.com)

FIGURE 22.38
A Scott eVest jacket, in normal and x-ray view, with integrated iPod and earphone wiring.

Security

One of the big issues with a small, high-priced device like the iPod is theft. It's just too easy for thieves to walk away with it. Hence the introduction of products designed to protect your iPod from theft, typically by locking it to something less totable:

- **BoomerangIt** security ID labels ($9.95, www.shop.avanquest.com)
- **i2 Electronics iLOCKr** security case ($34.95, www.i2electronics.com), shown in Figure 22.39
- **Pod Safe** security lock ($29.95, www.thepodsafe.com)
- **Targus Eyelet Security Lock for iPod** ($19.99, www.targus.com), shown in Figure 22.40
- **Targus Mobile Security Lock for iPod** ($39.99, www.targus.com)

> **AUTHOR'S PICKS** There are fancier solutions, but I'm partial to the simple, tried-and-true Eyelet Security Lock from Targus—it works just like an old-fashioned bicycle lock.

22

FIGURE 22.39

The iLOCKr locking iPod security case.

FIGURE 22.40

From Targus, the small-yet-effective Eyelet Security Lock.

iPod Customization

Want to mod your iPod? Then check out these sites that offer custom iPod cases and the like. (Prices vary by type of customization desired.)

- **ColorWare** (www.colorwarepc.com)
- **iPodMods** (www.ipodmods.com)
- **Skinpod.it** (www.skinpod.it)

Cleaning and Scratch Removal

Want to keep your iPod in tip-top condition? Then check out these cleaning supplies, most designed to remove or buff out scratches and the like:

- **Applesauce iPod Scratch Removal Kit** ($19.95, www.applesaucepolish.com)
- **DLO Care Kit for iPod** ($29.99, www.dlo.com)
- **iCleaner Maintenance Polish** ($19, www.ipodcleaner.com)
- **iCleaner Scratch Remover** ($14.95, www.ipodcleaner.com)
- **iCleaner Ultra Pro Kit** ($35, www.ipodcleaner.com)
- **iDrops** cleaning liquid ($14.95, www.podshop.com)
- **Radtech Ice Creme M** refinishing kit ($25.95, www.radtech.us)

Toys and Oddities

This next batch of iPod accessories defies description. They are, without a doubt, the oddest iPod-related items on the market today!

- **AFT iCarta** iPod speaker dock with toilet paper holder ($99.95, www.atechflash.com), shown in Figure 22.41
- **B2 mi Flower** music-activated electronic flower ($40, www.b2stuf.com), shown in Figure 22.42
- **iAttire** miniature clothing and costumes for iPods ($6.99–$39.99, www.iattire.net), shown in Figure 22.43
- **FUNKit DJ** animated dancing speaker system ($119.99, www.kngamerica.com), shown in Figure 22.44

- **Tiger Electronics i-Cat, i-Dog, and i-Fish** iPod toys ($29.99, www.hasbro.com/tiger/idog), shown in Figure 22.45

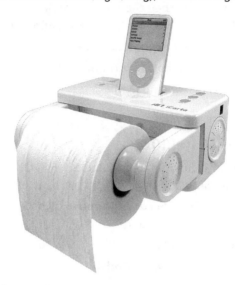

FIGURE 22.41

AFT's unique iCarta—combination iPod speaker and toilet paper dispenser.

FIGURE 22.42

The mi Flower dancing iPod-activated flower thingie.

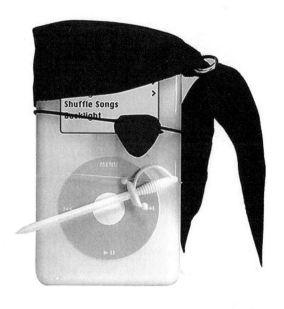

FIGURE 22.43

An iAttire pirate costume for the iPod.

FIGURE 22.44

The FUNKit DJ reacts to iPod music with animation and record scratching.

22

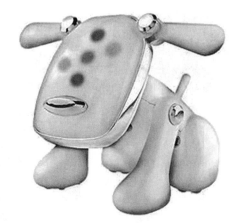

FIGURE 22.45

Connect an iPod to the i-Dog and watch him dance.

Other Accessories

Finally, there are those iPod accessories, most of them quite useful, that simply don't fit in any other categories. Let's take a look:

- **B2 mi Jam Drummer** digital drumsticks ($30, www.b2stuf.com)
- **B2 mi Jam Guitar** digital guitar ($30, www.b2stuf.com), shown in Figure 22.46

FIGURE 22.46

Connect the mi Jam Guitar to your iPod to play along with your music.

- **B2 mi Jam Mixer** DJ scratch disks ($40, www.b2stuf.com)

- **B2 mi Jam Stage Mic** iPod microphone ($20, www.b2stuf.com)

- **Blinkit** LED flashlight ($29.95, www.blinkitnow.com)

- **Griffin iBeams** laser flashlight/pointer ($19.99, www.griffintechnology.com)

- **Griffin radio SHARK 2** AM/FM digital audio recorder ($49.99, www.griffintechnology.com)

- **Nike+iPod Sport Kit** for iPod nano ($29, www.apple.com/ipod/nike)

- **Sima Hitch** USB transfer device ($149.99, www.simaproducts.com)

- **TEN Technology naviPlay** Bluetooth wireless headset kit ($200, www.tentechnology.com)

- **Tekkeon myTalker** Bluetooth telephone headset/adapter ($74.95, www.tekkeon.com/site/products-mytalker.php)

- **Targus Mobile Essentials Kit for iPod**—includes AC adapter, car adapter, battery pack, speakers, headphone splitter, carrying case, and more ($59.99, www.targus.com)

- **Targus SoundUP** high-definition sound enhancer ($39.99, www.targus.com)

> **note** Learn more about the Nike+iPod Sport Kit in Chapter 17, "Using the iPod for Running and Exercise."

> **AUTHOR'S PICKS** The Targus Mobile Essentials Kit makes a good gift for those who travel with their iPod. It includes just about everything you need for using the iPod away from home.

23

Third-Party Software

In the previous chapter, we examined all the various accessories available for the iPod. In this chapter, we present another type of accessory—those third-party software programs that enhance the operation of your iPod and the iTunes software.

Tag Editors

We start with software programs that help you edit the information tags embedded in all your audio files. Use these programs to edit the information for one or a hundred files simultaneously. These programs are necessary when you need to make big changes to the artist, genre, album, or similar information for your music:

note For each program detailed in this chapter, we list the manufacturer's list price and which platforms (Windows or Mac or both) that the program runs on. Note that many paid programs offer a free trial you can use to check out the software at no charge.

- **AudioManage Audio Library** (Windows, $14.95, www.audiomanage.com)

- **AudioShell** (Windows, free, www.softpointer.com/AudioShell.htm)

- **FixTunes** (Windows and Mac, $24.95, www.fixtunes.com), shown in Figure 23.1

- **mp3Tag** (Windows, $24.95, www.maniactools.com/soft/mp3tag/)

- **Tag Clinic** (Windows, $26, www.kevesoft.com)

- **Tag&Rename** (Windows, $29.95, www.softpointer.com/tr.htm)

AUTHOR'S PICKS Most of these tag editors do a good job, but I'm partial to FixTunes, which offers an extremely rich feature set. The Windows version of the program comes with a free Album Browser utility, which lets you decorate your desktop with album covers—kind of a neat bonus.

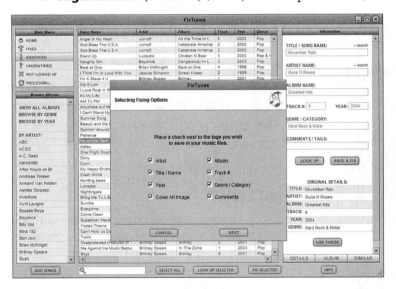

FIGURE 23.1

Edit song information with the FixTunes tag-editing program.

tip Many tag-editing programs also let you edit the album art for your music tracks.

Album Art Importers

Dealing with missing or incorrect album
art is a pain. Although you can manually
locate and import album covers into
iTunes, a variety of third-party utilities
make this chore a whole lot easier. Most of
these programs let you designate one or
more sites to search for artwork, choose the
best image to use, and then automatically
insert the new artwork into iTunes:

- **CoverScout** ($19.95, Mac, www.equinux.com/us/products/coverscout)
- **FixTunes** (Windows and Mac, $24.95, www.fixtunes.com)
- **GimmeSomeTune** (Mac, free, www.eternalstorms.at)
- **iArt** (Windows, $10, www.ipodsoft.com)
- **iAutoArtwork** (Windows, $10, www.jtasoftware.com/iAutoArtwork), shown in Figure 23.2
- **iTunes Album Browser** (Windows, $20, albumbrowser.galleytech.com)
- **iTunes Art Importer** (Windows, free, www.yvg.com/itunesartimporter.shtml)
- **TuneSleeve** (Windows, free, tunesleeve.googlepages.com)

FIGURE 23.2

Import new album art with iAutoArtwork.

Playlist Creators

Playlists are an integral part of the iPod/iTunes experience. You create playlists to match your mood, suit your needs, and serve special occasions. Unfortunately, the iTunes native playlist creation functionality is a tad limited. Turn to one of these third-party solutions to more easily create interesting and focused playlists based on a variety of criteria—from song similarity to tempo:

> **AUTHOR'S PICKS** To be honest, some of these playlist creator programs are a tad confusing to use. Accepting that, Soundflavor DJ lets you select a song from your library, then create a new playlist of songs that sound like that one or are of the same general style or era.

- **Bossa** (Windows, $24, www.mybossa.com)
- **The Filter** (Windows, free, www.thefilter.com)
- **MusicIP Mixer** (Windows and Mac, free, www.musicip.com)
- **Playlist Creator** (Windows, free, www.oddgravity.de)
- **Soundflavor DJ** (Windows, free, www.soundflavor.com), shown in Figure 23.3
- **Tangerine** (Mac, $24.95, www.potionfactory.com)

FIGURE 23.3

Create interesting new playlists with Soundflavor DJ.

Audio File Converters

The iTunes software does an okay job converting WMA and other format files to its native AAC format. But when you want to convert files from AAC to MP3 or WMA, you need a third-party file conversion utility:

AUTHOR'S PICKS Lots of free or low-priced audio file conversion programs are available, but I've found the most reliable to be Easy CD-DA Extractor. It's relatively easy to use and does a good job converting non-DRM files from just about any format to another.

- **Blaze Media Pro** (Windows, $50, www.blazemp.com)

- **dBpoweramp Music Converter** (Windows, $28, www.dbpoweramp.com)

- **Easy CD-DA Extractor** (Windows, $29.95, www.poikosoft.com), shown in Figure 23.4

- **Hijack iT!** (Mac, free, web.mac.com/spkane/iWeb)

- **ImTOO WMA MP3 Converter** (Windows, $19, www.imtoo.com/wma-mp3-converter.html)

- **Xilisoft Audio Converter** (Windows, $23, www.xilisoft.com/audio-converter.html)

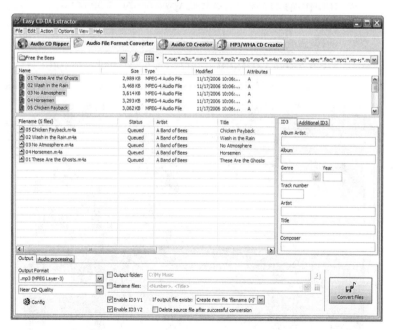

FIGURE 23.4

Convert audio files from one format to another with Easy CD-DA Extractor.

23

DRM Strippers

When you want to remove Apple's FairPlay DRM copy protection from tracks you purchase from the iTunes Store, you use a DRM stripper program. These programs strip the DRM wrapper off the original file, leaving a DRM-free file you can copy, burn, or trade to your heart's content. Most of this software comes from the JHymn Project, an open source forum opposed to DRM:

- **JHymn** (Windows and Mac, www.hymn-project.org/download.php)
- **myFairTunes** (Windows, www.hymn-project.org/download.php)
- **QTFairUse** (Windows, www.hymn-project.org/download.php)

Visualizations

When the iTunes built-in visualizations get too boring, check out these third-party add-on visualizations:

- **Eyephendrine** (Mac, $8, www.giofx.net/GioFX/Eyephedrine.html)
- **iGoom** (Mac, free, www.ios-software.com/?page=projet&quoi=1)
- **Jumping Steve** (Mac, free, www.memention.com/js)
- **SoundSpectrum G-Force and SoftSkies** (Windows and Mac, $20, www.soundspectrum.com), shown in Figure 23.5
- **Steel Skies Gaslight** (Mac, free, www.steelskies.com)
- **Ultragroovalicious iTunes Visualizer** (Mac, $10, www.groovyvis.com)

FIGURE 23.5

SoundSpectrum's SoftSkies iTunes visualization.

Audio Enhancement

Want to improve the sound of your iTunes playback? Then check out these third-party sound enhancement products that use digital signal processing (DSP) technology to make your computer sound like a hi-fi system:

- **SRS iWOW** plug-in (Mac, $19.99, www.srs.com/iwow)
- **Volume Logic** (Windows and Mac, $19.95, www.volumelogic.com)

Lyrics Downloaders

Like your iPod's ability to store and display song lyrics, but don't have the time to enter lyrics manually in iTunes? Then check out these lyrics utilities that search the Web for song lyrics to your iTunes tracks and then automatically import them into iTunes for downloading to your iPod:

- **EvilLyrics** (Windows, free, www.evillabs.sk/evillyrics)
- **Songbook24** (Windows, free, www.songbook24.com)

Other iTunes Music Utilities

There are always a few utilities that don't fit neatly within the major categories. Here are four such programs, all designed to enhance the functionality of the iTunes program:

- **iPod Launcher** automatically launches scripts and applications via AppleScript (Mac, $4.95, www.zapptek.com)
- **MyTV ToGo** lets you play iTunes music through a Windows Media Center PC (Windows, $29.99, www.mytvtogo.com)
- **Pod Player** lets you play music from your iPod through your computer's audio system (Windows, free, www.ipodsoft.com)
- **Tunes Menu** searches the Web for online music stores that have the selected CD for sale (Mac, free, www.mmisoftware.co.uk/pages/tunes)

Audiobook Converters and Managers

If you use your iPod to listen to audiobooks, you'll appreciate these utilities that help you convert audiobook CDs to digital audio files you can easily play on any iPod:

- **Audiobook Builder** (Mac, $9.95, www.splasm.com/audiobookbuilder)

- **MarkAble** (Windows, $15, www.ipodsoft.com), shown in Figure 23.6

- **MarksMan** bookmark creator (Windows, $12, www.ipodsoft.com)

> **AUTHOR'S PICKS** Of these programs, MarkAble does the best job of merging multiple files into a single audiobook file. Use it along with MarksMan to add bookmarks to the long file for easy indexing.

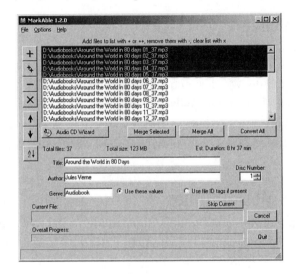

FIGURE 23.6
Convert audiobook CDs to iPod files with MarkAble.

Internet Radio Recorders

Want to listen to Internet radio stations on your iPod? You'll have to record the stations first, which you do with these nifty little programs:

- **Griffin iFill** (Windows and Mac, $19.99, www.griffintechnology.com)

- **Radiotracker** (Windows, $29.95, www.shop.avanquest.com)

- **Replay A/V** (Windows, $49.95, www.replay-video.com), shown in Figure 23.7

FIGURE 23.7

Use Replay A/V to listen to and record Internet radio programming for playback on your iPod.

Video-to-iPod Converters

If you have a 5G video iPod, you're no doubt in search of affordable video programming to watch on your new device. You can, of course, purchase video programming from the iTunes Store, or you can convert existing videos to an iPod-friendly format.

The following programs all convert various format video files to a format you can play on your iPod. Most work in a similar fashion, except for those designed to convert specific types of videos, such as TiVo recordings and downloaded YouTube videos:

- **Cucusoft iPod Movie/Video Converter** (Windows, free, www.cucusoft.com/ipod-movie-video-converter.asp)
- **dvdXsoft iPod Video Converter** (Windows, $29.95, www.dvdxsoft.com)
- **Hawkeye** (Mac, $29.95, www.nitosoft.com/hawkeye.html)
- **InterVideo iVideoToGo Platinum** (Windows, $49.95, www.intervideo.com/InterVideoDVDCopy)
- **iPod Video Converter** (Windows and Mac, $29, www.mp4converter.net)
- **iSquint** (Mac, free, www.isquint.org)
- **iTube** converts YouTube videos (Windows, free, www.benjaminstrahs.com/itube.php)

- **Ivy Video Converter** converts YouTube videos (Windows, $15, www.ipodsoft.com), shown in Figure 23.8

> **AUTHOR'S PICKS** All of these conversion programs work in a similar fashion and have similar performance. For that reason, I like Videora, which has all the same features as the other programs, but can be downloaded for free.

- **M²Convert** (Windows, $29.99, www.m2solutionsinc.com/ipod-converter.htm)

- **Plato Video to iPod Converter** (Windows, $25, www.dvdtompegx.com)

- **PQ iPod Movie Video Converter** (Windows, 29.95, www.pqdvd.com/ipod-video-converter.html)

- **QuickTime 7 Pro** (Windows and Mac, $29.99, www.apple.com/quicktime/pro)

- **TiVo Desktop Plus** converts TiVo recordings (Windows, $24.95, www.tivo.com/desktop)

- **TVHarmony AutoPilot** converts TiVo recordings (Windows, free, www.tvharmony.com)

- **Video to iPod/MP4/PSP/3GP Converter** (Windows, $21.95, www.svssoft.com)

- **Videora iPod Converter** (Windows, free, www.videora.com), shown in Figure 23.9

- **Wondershare Video to iPod Converter** (Windows, $29.95, www.dvd-ripper-copy.com/video-to-iPod.html)

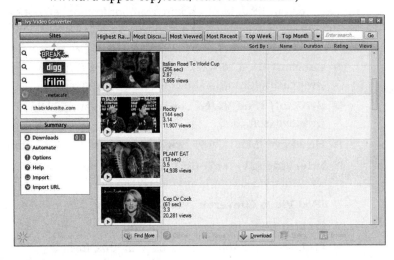

FIGURE 23.8

Ivy Video Converter downloads and converts videos from YouTube and other video file-sharing sites.

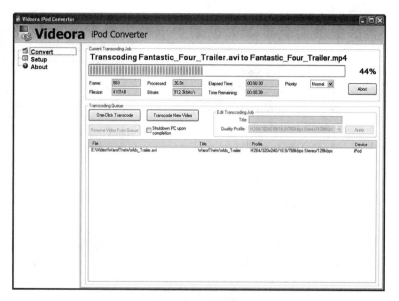

FIGURE 23.9
The freeware Videora iPod Converter converts most video file formats to an iPod-friendly
format.

DVD-to-iPod Converters

Converting a commercial DVD to an iPod-friendly format is slightly more
involved than converting existing video files. (It also takes a lot longer to do.)
When you want to transfer your DVDs to your iPod, check out these DVD-to-
iPod conversion programs:

- **321Soft DVD to iPod PSP Ripper** (Windows, $29.95,
  www.321soft.com)
- **Cucusoft DVD to iPod Converter** (Windows, free,
  www.cucusoft.com/dvd-to-ipod.asp)
- **DVD to iPod Converter** (Windows and Mac, $29,
  www.mp4converter.com)
- **dvdXsoft DVD to iPod Converter** (Windows, $29.95,
  www.dvdxsoft.com)
- **Instant Handbrake** (Mac, free, handbrake.m0k.org)

- **InterVideo DVD Copy Platinum** (Windows, $49.95, www.intervideo.com/ InterVideoDVDCopy)

- **M²Convert** (Windows, $29.99, www.m2solutionsinc.com/ipod-converter.htm)

- **Plato DVD to iPod Converter** (Windows, $29.88, www.dvdtompegx.com)

> **AUTHOR'S PICKS** As with the standard video conversion utilities, most of these DVD rippers have similar features and performance. That said, I tend to like the Wondershare program just a little better than the others, but that might just be a personal preference.

- **PQ DVD to iPod Converter** (Windows, $29.95, www.pqdvd.com/ dvd-to-ipod-converter.html)

- **TransferMyDVD** (Windows, $29.95, www.shop.avanquest.com)

- **Wondershare DVD to iPod Ripper** (Windows, $39.95, www.dvd-ripper-copy.com/dvd-to-iPod.html), shown in Figure 23.10

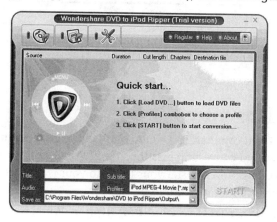

FIGURE 23.10

Use the Wondershare DVD to iPod Ripper to convert your DVDs to iPod-friendly video files.

File Managers

When you want to copy tunes from your iPod back to your computer, you need something other than the iTunes software.

> **note** Learn more about using your iPod to store and transfer files in Chapter 15, "Using Your iPod as a Portable Storage Device."

To that end, check out these file management programs that let you freely copy files of all sorts to and from your iPod and your PC:

- **Anapod Explorer** (Windows and Mac, $20–$30, www.redchairsoftware.com/anapod)

- **Backstage** (Windows and Mac, $9.99, www.widgetfab.com/BackstagePage.html)

- **CopyPod** (Windows, $19.90, www.copypod.net)

- **El iPodo** (Mac, free, www.funkelectric.com/products.html)

- **EphPod** (Windows, free, www.ephpod.com)

- **Floola** (Windows and Mac, free, www.floola.com)

- **iBack** (Windows, $10.99, www.raymondjavaxx.com)

- **iGadget** (Windows, $19.99, www.purpleghost.com), shown in Figure 23.11

- **iLinkPod** (Mac, free, www.ilinkpod.com)

- **iPod Access** (Windows and Mac, $19.99, www.drewfindley.com/findleydesigns/ipodaccess)

- **iPod Music Liberator** (Windows and Mac, $34.99, www.zeleksoftware.com)

- **iPod.iTunes** (Mac, $39, www.crispsofties.com)

- **iPodCopy** (Windows and Mac, $19.99, www.wideanglesoftware.com/ipodcopy)

- **iPodDisk** (Mac, free, ipoddisk.ourbiti.com)

- **iPodRip** (Windows and Mac, $14.95, www.thelittleappfactory.com)

- **Music Rescue** (Windows and Mac, $20, www.kennettnet.co.uk/musicrescue)

- **PodManager** (Mac, $7.95, www.podmanager.com)

- **Podworks** (Mac, $8, www.scifihifi.com)

- **Senuti** (Mac, free, www.fadingred.org/senuti)

- **TransferMyMusic** (Windows, $29.95, www.shop.avanquest.com)

- **Tune Transfer for iPod** (Windows and Mac, $19.99, www.valusoft.com/products/tunetransfer.html)

- **TuneJack** (Windows, $14.99, www.purpleghost.com)

- **TunePlus** (Windows, $19.99, www.encoreusa.com)

- **vPod** (Windows, free, www.vonnieda.org/vPod)

AUTHOR'S PICKS Most of these programs work in a similar fashion, using a type of explorer or file manager to display and manage the files on your iPod. My two favorites are Anapod Explorer and iGadget, both of which let you manage more than just music files.

■ **xPlay** (Windows, $29.95, www.mediafour.com/products/xplay)

■ **YamiPod** (Windows and Mac, free, www.yamipod.com)

FIGURE 23.11

Transfer music and other files from your iPod to your PC with iGadget.

Podcast Creators/Editors

The programs in this next batch aren't necessarily iPod-specific programs. Instead, they're Windows or Mac programs that let you record and edit your own podcasts—which you can then upload to the iTunes Store so that others can play them on their own iPods:

■ **Audacity** (Windows and Mac, free, audacity.sourceforge.net)

■ **ePodcast Creator** (Windows, $89.95, www.industrialaudiosoftware.com/products)

■ **GarageBand** (Mac, $79, www.apple.com/ilife/garageband)

■ **PodProducer** (Windows, free, www.podproducer.net)

■ **Propaganda** (Windows, $49.95, www.makepropandana.com)

■ **WebPod Studio Standard** (Windows, $89.95, www.lionhardt.ca/wps)

note Learn more about creating podcasts for iTunes in Chapter 16, "Using Your iPod to Record Audio and Podcasts."

Email, Contacts, and the Web

Want to view your email or personal contacts on your iPod? Or maybe your favorite web pages? These third-party utilities will let you do just that:

- **iPodulator Pro 2** web page viewer (Windows and Mac, free, www.ipodulatorpro.theplaceforitall.com)
- **k-pod** email management (Windows, free, www.k-deep.com/k-pod.htm)
- **Migo** email and contact management (Windows, $29.99, www.migosoftware.com)

Language Training

Here's something fun and useful. Use these software programs to learn new languages—while you're on the go!

- **coolgorilla language packs**—French, German, Greek, and Spanish (Windows and Mac, free, www.coolgorilla.com)
- **iLingo**—AsiaPack and EuroPack (Windows and Mac, $39.95–$49.95, www.talkingpanda.com)
- **Rambler Audio Phrase Books**—French, German, Italian, Japanese, and Spanish (Windows and Mac, $19.95, www.cyraknow.com), shown in Figure 23.12

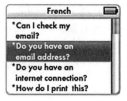

FIGURE 23.12
Learn useful foreign phrases with the Rambler Audio Phrase Books.

Electronic Books, Reference, and Learning

That's right, you can use your iPod as a kind of portable electronic book reader. Just download the appropriate reference or how-to material, dial it up on your iPod's menu, and get ready to read:

- **BiblePlayer**—Hear and read the Bible on your iPod (Windows and Mac, $20, www.bibleplayer.com)

- **coolgorilla Formula 1 Grand Prix Guide**—Instant access to Formula 1 racing facts (Windows and Mac, free, www.coolgorilla.com)

- **coolgorilla iPod World Cup Guide**—Everything you wanted to know about World Cup soccer, on your iPod (Windows and Mac, free, www.coolgorilla.com)

- **iBar**—Cocktail recipes (Windows and Mac, $29.95, www.talkingpanda.com)

- **iPREPpress**—Thousands of downloadable study guides, reference books, and the like for the iPod (Windows and Mac, $3.95–$9.95, www.ipreppress.com)

- **manybooks.net**—Thousands of free downloadable eBooks for the iPod (Windows and Mac, free, www.manybooks.net)

- **Mark Phillips Wine Guides** (Windows and Mac, $34.95 each, www.cyraknow.com)

- **NutriFacts on the GO for iPod**—Nutritional information for fast-food restaurants (Windows and Mac, $9.99, www.bvdtech.com/ngipod), shown in Figure 23.13

- **Pocket Bar & Grill for iPod**—Mixed drink and gourmet food recipes (Windows or Mac, $10, www.enriquequinterodesign.com)

- **Walt Disney World to Go**—Electronic travel guide to Walt Disney World (Windows and Mac, $8, www.eguidestogo.com)

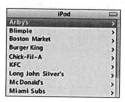

FIGURE 23.13
View fast-food nutritional information with NutriFacts on the Go.

Text-to-Audio Converters

Reading text on the iPod screen can be a trifle tasking, especially for older or blurry-eyed users. Instead, try one of these text-to-audio conversion programs that enables your iPod to read to you:

- **iSpeak It** (Mac, $19.95, www.zapptek.com)
- **MagneticTime MT1** (Windows, $39.99, www.magnetictime.com)

Games

In addition to the iPod games available at the iTunes Store, the following sites offer a variety of text-based games that can be played on any model iPod (except for the shuffle, of course):

- **coolgorilla** movie and rock pop trivia quizzes (Windows and Mac, free, www.coolgorilla.com)
- **iPod Arcade** (Windows and Mac, free, www.ipodarcade.com)
- **Malinche Entertainment** (Windows and Mac, $9.95 each, www.malinche.com/ipodgames.html)

Interface Customization

Want to change the look of your iPod display? If you have the technical wherewithal, these firmware-editor utilities will let you apply new themes, change graphics and fonts, and otherwise make your iPod look like something other than an iPod:

- **iPodWizard** (Windows, free, www.ipodwizard.net)
- **Rockbox** (Windows and Mac, free, www.rockbox.org)

> **note** Learn more about these high-level interface modifications in Chapter 21, "iPod Hacks."

Other Programs

We end this chapter with a handful of iPod-related programs that don't neatly fit into any other category. Here they are, along with brief descriptions:

- **iDirectionz**—Stores driving directions on your iPod (Windows, free, www.verstige.com/iDirectionz/)
- **iPDA**—Transfers calendars, notes, and contacts to the iPod (Mac, $19.95, www.zapptek.com)
- **iPod eBook Maker**—Converts HTML and text files to iPod-readable files (Windows, $9.95, www.ipodebookmaker.com)

- **iPodCALsync**—Synchronizes Google Calendar with your iPod (Windows, free, ipodcalsync.ueuo.com)

note Learn more about installing and using iPodLinux in Chapter 21.

- **iPodLinux**—Installs the Linux operating system on your iPod and lets you use a variety of Linux programs (Windows and Mac, free, www.ipodlinux.org)

- **iPresent It**—Converts PowerPoint presentations to iPod slideshows (Windows and Mac, $17.95, www.zapptek.com)

- **iRocker**—Guitar chords and tuner (Windows or Mac, $29.95, www.talkingpanda.com), shown in Figure 23.14

FIGURE 23.14

Use your iPod to learn guitar chords with iRocker.

- **iWriter**—Creates iPod study tools (Windows or Mac, $29.95, www.talkingpanda.com)

- **MojoPac**—Converts your iPod into a remote Windows PC, using a virtual desktop (Windows, $49.99, www.mojopac.com)

- **PumpOne Trainer**—Personal exercise training with various levels and types of workouts ($19–$124, www.pumpone.com)

caution If you search Google for "iPod software," you're likely to come across a few sites that claim to offer unlimited quantities of iPod software, games, and so on for a $20 or so per-month subscription fee. Beware of these sites; they are, without exception, scams. After you pay up, you'll find a list of links to other sites that offer iPod shareware, freeware, and payware for downloading—links available to you from a normal Google search and nonexclusive to the site you just paid good money to. (And many of these links will be dead links, anyway.)

iPod Troubleshooting

Most people use their iPods day in and day out without experiencing any problems. Others, however, don't have it as easy.

What do you do when your iPod starts acting up? This chapter provides some basic troubleshooting advice for recalcitrant iPods—what to look for and how to fix many common problems.

Understanding Onscreen Icons

The first sign of iPod trouble is often shown onscreen. Your iPod can display a variety of onscreen icons that provide clues to current and pending problems. Table 24.1 details most common such icons.

Table 24.1   iPod Onscreen Icons and Messages

Icon or Screen	Description
	The battery icon displays whenever your iPod is disconnected from your computer—that is, when it's not charging. The icon shows the status of the battery charge. You'll see this "Caution" version of the battery icon when your battery is near empty. Turn off your iPod and connect to your PC to recharge.
	On newer iPods, you might see the Low Battery screen rather than the low battery icon. The cause is the same; your iPod's battery needs to be recharged.
	The recharging icon shows when your iPod is connected to a PC or (via a USB-to-AC adapter) a wall outlet. It's normal.
	The Apple logo normally appears on your iPod's screen when the unit first turns on, or after it's been reset. If the logo does not disappear, you might need to reset the iPod again or restore the unit from within iTunes.
	The "Do Not Disconnect" screen (not an icon) displays when your iPod is connected to your PC for synchronization and file transfer. The screen should disappear when the iPod is done syncing. If not, click the Eject iPod button to manually disconnect the iPod.
	The presence of the folder icon typically indicates that your iPod has some sort of software or firmware problem. For example, you might have your iPod configured for Mac use while trying to use it on a Windows PC. To correct the problem, use the Restore function to reinstall the iPod's firmware.
	The "sad iPod" icon indicates some sort of hard drive problem with your iPod. You can try using the Restore function, although it's possible you may need to replace your iPod's hard disk.
	The disk with magnifying glass icon appears when the iPod is running its built-in hard disk diagnostic program. (See the "Troubleshooting iPod Problems with Diagnostic Mode" section, later in this chapter.) When the diagnostic is done running, you will see one of the following icons that indicate the result of the hard disk scan.
	This is a good icon. It indicates that your iPod's hard disk is in normal working condition.
	This icon indicates that problems were found with your iPod's hard drive, but the problems were corrected. You should run the Restore function from iTunes to put your iPod back in working condition.
	This icon indicates that your iPod's hard disk failed its diagnostic scan. You should reset your iPod to rerun the scan.
	This icon indicates that the diagnostic scan was canceled before it was finished. (You can cancel a scan by holding down the center Select button for three seconds.) The scan resumes the next time the iPod is turned on.

Troubleshooting Common Problems

The good news about most iPod problems is that you're probably not the first person to have that problem. Instead of reinventing the wheel, work through the following sections to deal with these common problems.

Your iPod Freezes

Here is something that happens to most iPod users sooner or later. You're using your iPod and it freezes—that is, you press a Click Wheel button and nothing happens.

This problem can happen for any number of reasons and typically doesn't indicate a serious problem. You do, however, need to unfreeze your iPod so that you can continue using it.

To restart or reset a frozen iPod, you have to press and hold a combination of buttons for about 10 seconds. What buttons you press depends on which iPod you have. See Table 24.2 for detailed instructions.

24

Table 24.2   Restarting a Frozen iPod

iPod Model	Press these Buttons
iPod 1G, 2G, 3G	Menu + Play/Pause
iPod 4G, 5G	Menu + Select (center button)
iPod mini	Menu + Select (center button)
iPod nano	Menu + Select (center button)

Resetting an iPod shuffle is slightly easier. Just turn the shuffle off then back on; this should do the job.

Your iPod Won't Turn On

Second only to the frozen iPod problem is the dead iPod problem. Fortunately, the probable solutions for this problem are easy to isolate.

The most common cause of a seemingly dead iPod is an unwittingly applied Hold button. That's right, if you slide the Hold button on the top of the iPod to the Hold position, all the buttons on the front of the iPod are locked. And if your iPod is turned off at the time, you can't turn it on.

tip Before you reset your iPod, make sure the Hold button is turned off by moving it to the Hold position and back again.

Move the Hold button into the off position to regain control of the Click Wheel and turn on your iPod.

If it's not the Hold button causing your iPod not to turn on, it's probably the battery. You can check this by connecting your iPod to your computer. This sends power from the computer to the iPod, bypassing the iPod's internal battery. If your iPod works on computer power but not on battery, you either need to recharge your battery or (if it refuses to hold a charge) replace it.

Finally, your iPod might not be dead, but just frozen. Follow the instructions in the previous section to reset your iPod and hopefully get it running normally again.

Your Computer Doesn't Recognize Your iPod

Another common problem comes when you connect your iPod to your computer but then your PC doesn't recognize that your iPod is connected—the iTunes software doesn't launch automatically, or when started doesn't show your iPod in the Source pane.

When your iPod doesn't appear in iTunes, the first thing to do is to is check the cable and make sure it's properly connected. (Loose connections cause most problems, believe it or not.) If you have an extra iPod cable, try using it, just in case the original cable has gone bad.

Next, close and then relaunch iTunes. If your iPod still doesn't appear within iTunes, try restarting your PC (with your iPod connected). If that doesn't work, try restarting your iPod, as previously described (press Menu + Select).

Next, try forcing your iPod into disk mode. You do this by connecting your iPod to your PC, doing a Menu + Select reset, and then when you see the Apple logo, pressing and holding the Previous and Next buttons on your iPod.

If your iPod is configured for disk mode, it should appear in My Computer, Windows Explorer, or on the Mac OS X desktop. If it still doesn't appear in iTunes, however, you might need to reinstall the latest version of the iTunes software (go to www.apple.com/ipod/download).

A continuing connection problem could be caused by a flaky USB port on your PC. Try connecting your iPod to a different USB port.

It's also possible that your iPod doesn't like being connected to an external USB hub. Disconnect your iPod from the hub and instead connect it directly to a USB port on your PC.

Another cause of this problem comes from the way iPods are formatted. An iPod can be formatted for either Windows or Mac use. If your iPod is formatted for a Mac, it won't be recognized by a Windows computer. (Windows-formatted iPods are compatible with both Macs and Windows PCs, however.) You can reformat a Mac-format iPod for Windows by connecting it to your PC and running the Restore function from iTunes.

If none of these solutions work, your iPod probably has some sort of hardware problem. You'll need to consult a repair center for more advice.

You Can't Disconnect Your iPod from Your PC

Just as some users have trouble connecting their iPods to their PCs, other users have trouble *disconnecting* their iPods. This particular problem arises when you've connected your iPod to sync or recharge, but then can't get rid of the "Do Not Disconnect" screen.

caution Disconnecting your iPod before the "Do Not Disconnect" screen disappears could damage the files or firmware on your iPod.

In normal conditions, the "Do Not Disconnect" screen should disappear when the last file is synced from your PC to your iPod. At that point, your iPod is doing nothing but recharging, and it should be safe to disconnect it.

However, if your iPod is configured for disk mode (that is, used for portable disk storage), you have to manually force your computer to disconnect your iPod. You do this by clicking the Eject iPod button at the button right of the iPod screen in the iTunes window, as shown in Figure 24.1. After you click this button, wait a few seconds; the "Do Not Disconnect" screen should disappear.

FIGURE 24.1

Click the Eject iPod button in iTunes to disconnect your iPod.

What do you do if the "Do Not Disconnect" screen *doesn't* disappear? First try the Eject iPod button, even if your iPod isn't configured for disk mode; it should work for all iPods, no matter how configured.

note Learn more about the iPod's disk mode in Chapter 15, "Using Your iPod as a Portable Storage Device."

If the Eject iPod button doesn't do the job, try ejecting it from within your computer's operating system. In Windows, open My Computer, right-click the iPod icon, and then select Eject from the pop-up menu. (You can also try clicking the Safely Remove Hardware icon in the Windows system tray, if the icon is present.) On a Mac, click the Finder icon, select the iPod icon on your desktop, and then select File > Eject iPod.

Next, try closing and restarting the iTunes software, and then click the Eject iPod button again. Sometimes it's the software that's hung up, not your iPod.

If worse comes to worst, you can just disconnect your iPod and hope for the best. Chances are your iPod will be frozen at that point, necessitating a Menu + Select restart. If you're lucky, no damage will have been done. If you're not lucky, you might need to restore your iPod's firmware, as described later in this chapter.

Your iPod Skips During Music Playback

Another fairly common problem among iPod users is that of skipping. No, not the users skipping, but their iPods skipping. That is, when you play back music, it skips from the current song to the next song, without you pressing the Forward button. It might skip over all songs or only selected songs.

First, if your iPod skips while you're walking, jogging, or exercising, you might not have a problem at all. Any hard drive iPod (all models except the nano and shuffle) is subject to skipping when jostled; that's because the moving parts in the hard drive get shook out of place. Switching to a Flash memory iPod (such as a nano or a shuffle) might be a better choice for active listeners.

If your iPod only skips one or two particular songs, something might be wrong with the particular audio files. Connect your iPod to your PC, delete those songs from your iPod, and then re-rip or redownload the songs and re-sync them to your iPod. The goal is to replace any damaged files with undamaged versions.

If your iPod skips over more than a few songs, and if the skipping is somewhat random, you might have a problem with your iPod's hard drive. (This obviously isn't a problem with Flash-based iPods, such as the nano and shuffle.) In particular, your iPod's hard drive might be fragmented. To defragment your iPod's hard drive, configure it for disk use and run a disk utility program, such as Norton SystemWorks (Windows, www.symantec.com) or Disk Warrior (Mac, www.alsoft.com/DiskWarrior), treating your iPod as if it were an external drive on your computer. If defragmenting your hard drive in this fashion doesn't help, you might need to erase your iPod's hard drive and run the Restore function, as described later in this chapter.

When defragmenting doesn't work, it's possible that you have more serious hard drive issues with your iPod. Use your iPod's diagnostic mode (discussed later in this chapter) to scan the hard drive for bad sectors and, if possible, repair them.

If using diagnostic mode doesn't solve the problem, you might have an unrepairable hard disk in your iPod. (Listen for clicking or spinning noises from the iPod, even when you're not playing music.) Consult a repair center for advice.

24

Your Music Doesn't Sound Right

If your ears are somewhat picky, you might not be satisfied with the sound coming from the compressed music stored on your iPod. You can do some things to improve the sound quality, however.

First, try a different set of earphones. Apple's factory earbuds are good but not great; a set of better buds or a higher-quality set of headphones will make a noticeable difference in sound quality for most listeners.

Second, make sure you haven't applied an inappropriate equalization setting. Flat EQ is just fine for most listeners, but the iPod includes a lot of different types of equalization, some of which flat out sound bad. Go to Settings > EQ to make changes.

Finally, if you're listening to music you've ripped from CD or downloaded from sites other than the iTunes Store, the files might be ripped at too low a bit rate. The higher the bit rate, the better the sound, so try ripping your tracks again at a higher rate. (Of course, if you downloaded low-bit-rate files, you can't do much about that except suffer through.)

Some Songs Don't Play Back

If a particular song won't play on your iPod, or in the iTunes software, chances are it's because the song is in the wrong file

note Learn how to change the bit rate in Chapter 7, "Music."

format. Remember, the Microsoft WMA format is incompatible with iTunes and the iPod, so any WMA-format tracks you have won't play on your iPod. You'll need to convert those WMA-format tracks to either AAC or MP3 format to play them. (In fact, WMA-format songs won't even be transferred to your iPod, so you'll need to convert before you sync.)

> **note** Learn how to authorize computers for iTunes playback in Chapter 6, "Using the iTunes Store."

It's also possible that you've downloaded tracks from the iTunes Store to one computer, but then transferred them to another computer that hasn't yet been authorized. You'll need to authorize each computer you use to play your purchased music.

iTunes Doesn't Display Album Artwork

When you use the iTunes software to rip tracks from a CD, you rely on iTunes to download the proper artwork for each track/album. If iTunes isn't downloading any artwork, that's probably because it's not properly configured. Select Edit > Preferences, then the General tab, and then check the Automatically Download Missing Album Artwork option. You also need to have signed up for an iTunes Store account to download this artwork from the iTunes Store.

Of course, sometimes iTunes can't find artwork for an album or downloads the wrong artwork. In these instances, you'll want to manually add artwork to iTunes; see Chapter 7 for instructions. Chapter 23, "iPod Software," also details some third-party programs that will greatly assist your efforts to find missing album artwork.

iTunes Displays an "iPod Is Linked to Another Library" Message

Here's one that happens in certain situations. You connect your iPod to a computer and iTunes starts up with this message: "iPod is Linked to Another Library." This happens when you connect your iPod to a computer other than your normal computer. iTunes likes to link one iPod to one computer, and gets a little confused when you try to do something other than that.

24

When you see this message, iTunes also offers to replace all the music on this iPod with the music stored on this particular computer. You probably don't want to do this, so click No. To avoid this message in the future, check the option to Manually Manage Songs and Playlists on the iPod's main page in iTunes.

Troubleshooting iPod Problems with Diagnostic Mode

Previously, we discussed some hard disk–based iPod problems. Naturally, only those iPods with internal hard drives can develop this sort of problem, but a real problem it can be. After all, a hard disk is nothing but an assemblage of moving parts, and anything that moves can wear out or break.

Fortunately, Apple has designed its hard drive iPods with a built-in diagnostic mode. When you activate the diagnostic mode, the iPod scans its hard drive, looking for bad sectors and errors. Many such errors can be automatically repaired; even if bad sectors remain, you'll be aware of the cause of any related problems.

To run your iPod's diagnostic mode, start by turning your iPod off and then back on, and then toggle the Hold switch on and off. Now press and hold the Menu + Select buttons (on 1G–3G iPods: Menus + Play/Pause) for 10 seconds, until you see the Apple logo appear onscreen. Immediately when you see the Apple logo, press the Reverse + Select buttons (on 1G–3G iPods: Reverse + Forward + Select). This should elicit an audible"chirp" from the iPod; then the Apple logo should appear *backward* onscreen.

The presence of the backward logo indicates that you're in diagnostic mode. You can now run a variety of diagnostic tests, which you cycle through using the iPod's Reverse and Forward buttons. To exit diagnostic mode, you must restart your iPod.

> **tip** To cancel any test in progress, press the iPod's Menu button.

What diagnostic tests are available? It depends on the model of your iPod. Table 24.3 details the tests available on 5G iPods (including the nano and mini). Table 24.4 details the tests available on older 1G-4G iPods. (Note that the tests are designated by letter on older iPods, not so on newer models.)

> **caution** The hard drive diagnostic test requires a lot of power. It's best to connect your iPod to a PC before running the test, so as not to drain the iPod's internal battery.

Table 24.3   Diagnostic Tests for 5G iPod, nano, and mini

Test	Description
Auto	This automatically runs the following tests, sequentially: ■ Graphic self-test ■ SDRAM quick test ■ Checksum ■ RTC ■ USBtest ■ Keytest ■ Wheeltest ■ Headphonedetect ■ Accessory test ■ ChargeADC ■ Backlight (brightness) ■ Color
Memory	The memory diagnostics include tests for the following components of your iPod's memory: ■ SDRAM ■ IRAM ■ Flash
IO	The input/output diagnostics test your iPod's various inputs and outputs, including the following: ■ Comms—Tests the iPod's communication ports, including the USB port ■ Wheel—Tests the operation of the Click Wheel with two tests: Keytest (buttons) and Wheeltest (scrolling) ■ LCD—Tests the operation of the iPod display with two tests: Backlight and Color (on color iPods) ■ HeadphoneDetect—Tests the operation of the Hold switch and headphone port ■ HardDrive—Tests the operation of the hard drive with four separate tests: HDSpecs (displays hard disk specs), HDScan (scans for fragmentation and bad sectors), HDSMARTData (for professional technicians), and HDRW (tests the ability to read and write data to the hard drive) ■ Audio—Tests your iPod's audio operation with two tests: Playback (ability to play audio) and MIC (ability to record audio)
Power	The power diagnostics test the power system of your iPod via multiple subtests.
Status	This isn't a test per se, but rather displays the status of several key systems, including the following: ■ Sharp (LCD screen) ■ HP (headphones) ■ FWPWR (FireWire connection/charging) ■ USBPWR (USB connection/charging)
SysCfg	Displays your iPod's key information—hardware version, serial numbers, and so on.

Table 24.4   Diagnostic Tests for 1G–4G iPods

Test	Description
A: 5 in 1	Runs the following five tests: ■ LCM ■ SDRAM ■ RTC ■ FLASH/CHECKSUM ■ FIREWIRE/FW ID
B: Reset	Tests the ability of the iPod to be reset
C: Key	Tests the operation of the iPod's keys/buttons
D: Audio	Tests the iPod's audio subsystem
E: Remote	Tests the iPod's remote (if connected)
F: FireWire	Tests the iPod's FireWire port
G: Sleep	Puts the iPod to sleep (reset the iPod to wake it up)
H: A2D	Tests the iPod's power system
I: OTPO CNT	Tests the scroll wheel
J: LCM	Displays test patterns on the iPod screen
K: RTC	Tests the iPod's real-time clock
L: SDRAM	Tests the iPod's SDRAM memory
M: FLASH	Tests the iPod's Flash memory; also displays firmware information
N: OTPO or Wheel A2D	Tests the analog-to-digital input of the iPod's wheel controller
O: HDD SCAN	Scans the hard drive for fragmentation and bad sectors
P: RUN IN	Performs continuous testing of the iPod's chip set

If your iPod passes all these tests, congratulations. If it fails any particular tests, you might have some sort of hardware problem on your hands; consult a repair center for advice.

Restoring Your iPod's Firmware

In some circumstances, the firmware that controls your iPod's basic information might become corrupted. Corrupted firmware can cause all sorts of problems, including freezing, skipping, and overall deadness.

Fortunately, Apple makes it easy to restore your iPod's firmware to its default condition. This is done from within the iTunes software. Just connect your iPod to your computer, select the iPod in the iTunes Source pane, and then click the Restore button, as shown in Figure 24.2.

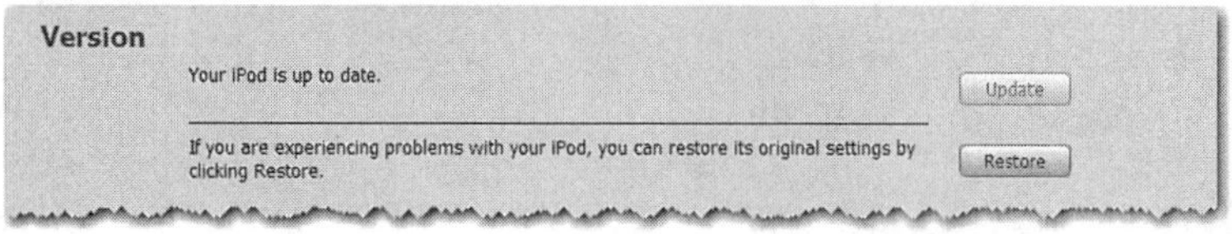

FIGURE 24.2
Click the Restore button to restore your iPod's firmware to its original condition.

When you restore your iPod's firmware, you don't affect any of the iPod's other contents. That is, all your music, video, and other files remain intact on your iPod's hard disk or in its Flash memory. The only thing affected by this operation is the iPod's operating software.

caution Restoring an iPod's firmware *will* erase any firmware-related changes that have been made to the device. For example, iPodLinux, Rockbox, and similar customization utilities work by altering the firmware. Resetting the firmware deletes any changes made by these utilities.

Reformatting Your iPod

An even more drastic fix for severe problems on a hard drive iPod is to reformat the iPod's hard drive. This has the same effect as reformatting the hard drive on a computer system: All data and programs stored on the hard drive are deleted, and you start fresh with a pristine hard drive.

Before you perform this procedure, make sure that the contents of your iPod are duplicated on your computer. In most instances, this is just the case, unless you erased files from your PC after you synced them to your iPod. In this instance, you can use an iPod file management program to copy files from your iPod to your PC for backup.

When you're certain you have the iPod's files on your PC, for later restoration to your reformatted iPod, you can start the formatting process. This process is subtly different on a Windows PC than it is on a Mac.

caution Reformatting an iPod deletes all the files stored on that iPod—music, videos, you name it. There is no undoing this procedure. You'll need to restore your iPod's files by re-syncing your iPod with your computer.

To reformat your iPod's hard drive from a Windows-based computer, start by connecting your iPod to your PC. Open My Computer, right-click the iPod icon, and then select Format. When prompted, select FAT 32 and click the Format button.

To reformat your iPod's hard drive from a Mac running OS X, open the Applications/Utilities folder, open the Disk Utility, select your iPod, and then click the Repair button. When prompted, click the Erase button.

The reformat process leaves your iPod with a completely empty hard disk; not even the iPod's firmware is installed. Which means, of course, that you need to restore the iPod's firmware. You do this from within the iTunes software; select your iPod in the Source pane, and then click the Restore button.

Now it's time to reinstall and reconfigure your iPod, just as you did when it was first new. Follow the onscreen instructions to do this. Finally, you sync your iPod to your PC to transfer all of your library files back to the iPod.

Dealing with a Scratched or Broken Screen

Here's a problem that many users have experienced with certain iPod models, especially the first-generation iPod nanos: easily scratched or broken screens.

When your screen is scratched, try using a scratch repair kit, such as the Applesauce iPod Scratch Removal Kit (www.applesaucepolish.com) or the DLO Care Kit for iPod (www.dlo.com). These kits can remove some smaller and more superficial scratches.

If your iPod has deeper scratches or if the screen itself has cracked or broken, you probably need to replace the screen. If your iPod is relatively new, contact Apple (or where you purchased the iPod) to see whether the repair is covered under warranty. For older models, most iPod repair centers can easily replace the screen.

Dealing with iPod Battery Problems

If you've had your iPod for a few years, you've probably noticed that the iPod's battery doesn't hold as long a charge as it used it. This is a normal consequence of today's lithium-ion battery technology; batteries lose capacity over time.

Of course, you could also notice this problem with a newer iPod. In this instance, it's not so much normal battery aging as it is the sign of a defective battery. And, believe it or not, Apple has distributed a lot of iPods with defective batteries. So if you have a newer iPod with a battery issue, consult your repair center (or Apple itself) for in-warranty replacement.

For older iPods, however, your only solution is to replace the battery.

Unfortunately, the battery is not officially user replaceable, and this can be a costly repair. As explained at www.apple.com/support/ipod/service/battery, Apple will replace your entire out-of-warranty iPod (typically with a similar rebuilt unit) for $59, plus $6.95 shipping/handling. If you go this route, know that you'll get a different iPod back than the one you sent in, which means that you'll lose all the music and videos you had loaded. Make sure your library is backed up to your computer so that you can re-sync it to the replacement iPod you receive.

> **tip** You're not limited to having your battery replaced by Apple. Most iPod repair centers offer similar battery-replacement services. See the list of service centers later in this chapter.

Remember that I said the iPod battery was not *officially* user replaceable? That means you actually can replace your battery yourself, if you don't mind opening the case and mucking about inside. Know, of course, that opening the case in this fashion will void your warranty—but if your iPod was still under warranty, you'd let Apple replace your battery for free, wouldn't you?

If you choose to replace the battery yourself, you can save $30 or more in labor charges. Several companies sell replacement iPod batteries, typically in the $20 to $30 range. That's a bit cheaper than Apple's $59 cost, if you're up to the work.

Know, however, that there's a bit of effort involved to replace an iPod battery. You have to first open the case, which is a little less than intuitive; there are no screws to remove, instead you have to pry open the two halves of the case with some sort of stiff plastic or metal wedge. Next, you have to remove the unit's hard drive, in order to access the battery. Use a small screwdriver to pry the battery out of its holder, then disconnect the battery from the motherboard. Work through all these steps in reverse to install the new battery and piece your iPod back together again.

Where can you buy replacement iPod batteries? Here's a short list:

- iFixit (www.ifixit.com)
- iPod Battery Depot (www.ipodbatterydepot.com)

> **caution** Opening the iPod case to replace the battery voids your iPod's warranty. If your iPod is still under warranty, you should let Apple do the replacement for you.

- ipodjuice.com (www.ipodjuice.com)
- iPodMiniBattery (www.ipodminibattery.com)
- Laptops for Less (www.ipodbattery.com)
- NewerTechnology (www.newertech.com)
- PDASmart (www.pdasmart.com)
- Small Dog Electronics (www.smalldog.com)

Finding Professional Help

If you can't easily troubleshoot an iPod problem on your own, it's time to turn to professional help. Two options are open to you: use Apple's factory repair service or use an independent iPod repair service.

Apple's support services start at the iPod + iTunes Service and Support page (www.apple.com/support/ipod/family), shown in Figure 24.3. Select your iPod model, and then work through the troubleshooting tips and advice on the next page, shown in Figure 24.4. If necessary, use the links in the Repair & Status box to order parts or request a repair. Naturally, if you have Apple do your repairs, you must send your iPod to them.

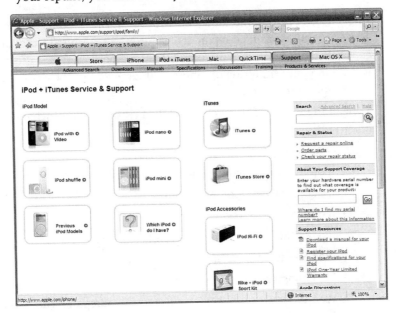

FIGURE 24.3

Apple's main iPod + iTunes Service and Support page.

FIGURE 24.4

Apple's various support options—including links for repair service and ordering parts.

Apple doesn't have a monopoly on out-of-warranty iPod repair, however. There are numerous iPod repair centers around the United States and in other countries, both local and web-based. The web-based services also require you to send in your unit for repair; most do a large volume of service and provide fairly rapid turnaround.

Some of the most popular web-based iPod repair services include the following:

- iKaput.com (www.ikaput.com)
- iPod Mechanic (www.ipodmechanic.com)
- iPodMods (www.ipodmods.com)
- iPodResQ (www.ipodresq.com)
- iPodRestore (ipod.techrestore.com)
- iPod Specialist (www.ipodspecialist.com)
- PDASmart (www.pdasmart.com)
- We Love Macs (www.welovemacs.com/ipodrepair.html)

Appendixes

Additional Resources

Websites

Apple iPod (www.apple.com/ipod)

Apple iTunes (www.apple.com/itunes)

Apple Store (www.store.apple.com)

Hot iPod News (www.hotipodnews.com)

iLounge (www.ilounge.com)

iPod Hacks: The Latest and Greatest News
and Info for Your iPod
(www.ipodhacks.com)

iPod Rumors Archive (ipod.macrumors.com)

iPod Tips & Hints (www.ipodtips.com)

iPod UK (www.ipod.org.uk)

iPodNews.com (www.ipodnews.com)

Playlist: iPod and iTunes Product Guide,
News, Review, How-Tos, and More
(www.playlistmag.com)

Smart iPod Ideas (www.smart-ipod-ideas.com)

Think Secret: Apple Mac Insider News
(www.thinksecret.com)

Blogs, Forums, Message Boards, and Groups

AppleiPod Yahoo! group (tech.groups.yahoo.com/group/AppleiPod)

iPod blog (www.ipodblog.org)

iPod blog (www.ipodosphere.com)

iPod forums at iLounge (forums.ipodlounge.com)

iPod News (ipodnewsblog.blogspot.com)

iPoding (www.ipoding.com)

iPoditude.com (www.ipoditude.com)

iPodWizard.net forums (www.ipodwizard.net)

Playlist: The iPod Blog (www.playlistmag.com/weblogs/ipodblog)

Topix.net iPod forum (www.topix.net/forum/gadgets/ipod)

Books

Absolute Beginner's Guide to iPod and iTunes (Brad Miser, Que, 3rd Edition, 2006)

CNET Do-It-Yourself iPod Projects (Guy Hart-Davis, Osborne/McGraw-Hill, 2006)

Easy iPod and iTunes (Shelly Brisbin, Que, 2006)

iPod & iTunes: The Missing Manual (J. D. Biersdorfer, Pogue Press/O'Reilly, 5th Edition, 2006)

iPod and iTunes for Dummies (Tony Bove and Cheryl Rhodes, Wiley, 4th Edition, 2006)

iPod and iTunes Hacks (Hadley Stern, O'Reilly, 2004)

iPod Fully Loaded: If You've Got It, I Can iPod It (Andy Ihnatko, Wiley, 2006)

The Cult of iPod (Leander Kahney, No Starch Press, 2005)

The iPod and iTunes Pocket Guide (Christopher Breen, Peachpit Press, 2nd Edition, 2006)

The iPod Book: Doing Cool Stuff with the iPod and the iTunes Store (Scott Kelby, Peachpit Press, 3rd Edition, 2006)

The Perfect Thing: How the iPod Shuffles Commerce, Culture, and Coolness (Steven Levy, Simon & Schuster, 2006)

The Rough Guide to iPod, iTunes, and Music Online (Rough Guides, 4th Edition, 2006)

A

Index

Safari®
BOOKS ONLINE
ENABLED

THIS BOOK IS SAFARI ENABLED

INCLUDES FREE 45-DAY ACCESS TO THE ONLINE EDITION

The Safari® Enabled icon on the cover of your favorite technology book means the book is available through Safari Bookshelf. When you buy this book, you get free access to the online edition for 45 days.

Safari Bookshelf is an electronic reference library that lets you easily search thousands of technical books, find code samples, download chapters, and access technical information whenever and wherever you need it.

TO GAIN 45-DAY SAFARI ENABLED ACCESS TO THIS BOOK:

● Go to **http://www.phptr.com/safarienabled**

● Complete the brief registration form

● Enter the coupon code found in the front
of this book on the "Copyright" page

If you have difficulty registering on Safari Bookshelf or accessing the online edition, please e-mail customer-service@safaribooksonline.com.

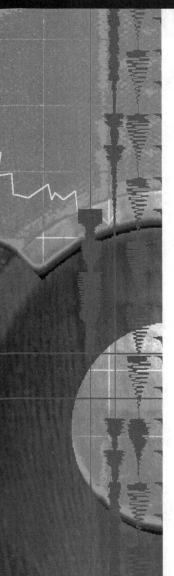